Polyphonic God

Polyphonic God

*Exploring Intercultural Theology,
Churches, Justice*

Edited by
Israel Oluwole Olofinjana
Usha Reifsnider
and
David Wise

© Israel Oluwole Olofinjana, Usha Reifsnider and David Wise 2025

Published in 2025 by SCM Press

Editorial office
3rd Floor, Invicta House,
110 Golden Lane,
London EC1Y 0TG, UK
www.scmpress.co.uk

SCM Press is an imprint of Hymns Ancient & Modern Ltd
(a registered charity)

Hymns Ancient & Modern® is a registered trademark of
Hymns Ancient & Modern Ltd
13A Hellesdon Park Road, Norwich,
Norfolk NR6 5DR, UK

All rights reserved. No part of this publication may be reproduced,
stored in a retrieval system, or transmitted,
in any form or by any means, electronic, mechanical,
photocopying or otherwise, without the prior permission of
the publisher, SCM Press.

The Authors have asserted their right under the Copyright, Designs and
Patents Act 1988 to be identified as the Authors of this Work

British Library Cataloguing in Publication data

A catalogue record for this book is available
from the British Library

ISBN: 978 0 334 06658 3

EU GPSR Authorised Representative
LOGOS EUROPE, 9 rue Nicolas Poussin, 17000, LA ROCHELLE, France
E-mail: Contact@logoseurope.eu

No part of this book may be used or reproduced in any manner for the
purpose of training artificial intelligence technologies or systems.

Typeset by Regent Typesetting

Contents

List of Contributors — vii

Introduction: Intercultural Church Conversations in Britain — 1

Part 1 Intercultural Theology: Foundational Thought and Perspectives

1 Politics of Multiculturalism, Theology of Interculturality: Towards an Intercultural Ecclesiology — 15
 Israel Oluwole Olofinjana

2 The Metaphor of Tapestry: A Theological Framing for Inter-ethnic Congregations — 37
 David Wise

3 You Are Home! The Family Metaphor and Its Impact on Understanding Church and Intercultural Communities in Ephesians — 50
 Oscar Jiménez

Part 2 Intercultural Churches and Practices: Ecclesiology Re-imagined

4 'Re-tuning' Worship: Biblical Principles for a Culturally Diverse Age — 73
 Ian Collinge

5 Intercultural Church as a Direction of Travel: Exploring the Journey of a Korean Diaspora Church (KDC) — 94
 MiJa Wi

6 Feeling Welcome and Accepted: A Case Study of Greenford
   Baptist Church   111
   David Wise

7 Among the Nations, for the Nations: Championing Diversity
   in the Church in Edinburgh   130
   Màiri MacPherson

8 What Even Is My Culture? Exploring Identity in an
   Intercultural Church   147
   Jessie Tang

9 Laying Firm Foundations for a Healthy Intercultural Church 159
   Adam and Karina Martin

10 The New Northern Irish   173
   Nathaniel Jennings

Part 3 Intercultural Justice: Racial Justice and Reconciliation

11 Just Leadership: Developing Radical Empathy to Break
   Systemic Strongholds   191
   Kate Coleman

12 Intercultural Life Together: Racial Justice as Love Lived Out
   in Worship, Fellowship and Mission   215
   Sharon Prentis

13 Intercultural Holiness and Justice: Challenge, Cross,
   Community and Celebration   234
   Mohan Seevaratnam

14 Intercultural Churches as Catalysts for Racial Justice   252
   Dominic De Souza and Catherine De Souza

15 Antiracist Mission in Postcolonial Britain   266
   Usha Reifsnider

Index of Bible References   283
Index of Names and Subjects   289

List of Contributors

Revd Dr Kate Coleman is the founding director of Next Leadership. She has 35 years of leadership experience in the church, charity, voluntary and business sectors, and is a mentor and coach to leaders from diverse sectors, backgrounds and communities.

Kate was the first Black woman Baptist minister in the UK and has been recognized as one of the 20 most influential Black Christian women leaders in the country. A popular speaker, lecturer and author, Kate has gained a reputation as a pioneer, visionary and an inspiration to many. She serves as a strategic advisor mentoring, coaching and supporting leaders and organizations nationally and internationally.

Ian Collinge is an intercultural worship trainer and author with WEC International, a doctoral student at the Robert E. Webber Institute of Worship Studies and an associate lecturer in ethnodoxology for 20 years at All Nations Christian College. As a missionary in Asia, Ian combined music research with helping emerging indigenous believers develop their own worship. Returning to England, he witnessed a monocultural church becoming multicultural and intercultural. Ian founded Resonance, WEC's multicultural worship band, and the arts ministry, Arts Release. He is also a board member of the Global Consultation on Arts and Music in Missions.

Revd Dominic De Souza and **Revd Catherine De Souza** are ordained Elim ministers and have been co-leading and ministering together for many years, most recently at City Church in Cardiff. In 2024, they sensed a call to give themselves more fully to serving the wider Church: Dominic now works itinerantly as a Church and Leadership Catalyst, and Catherine is the CEO of Prison Fellowship England and Wales.

Nathaniel Jennings is of Anglo/Caribbean/American heritage, but was born and spent his childhood in Bangladesh. After completing a degree in South Asian History (SOAS), a Postgraduate Certificate in Education

(London Metropolitan University) and a master's in Contextual Missiology (Queen's University, Belfast), he returned to Bangladesh to be involved in social development and welfare work with SIM. Nathaniel is currently OMF UK's Intercultural Ministries Director. His work focuses on encouraging and equipping churches across the UK and Ireland to share Jesus with people of all backgrounds and cultures and to grow as intercultural communities of worship and witness. Nathaniel also oversees the Intercultural Ministries Ireland network.

Dr Oscar Jiménez is a Colombian New Testament scholar (PhD, New Testament, London School of Theology). His doctoral thesis, 'The Metaphors in the Narrative of Ephesians 2.11–22', published by Brill, has influenced master's and doctoral students in the field. Oscar serves as a pastor in a Hispanic church in London and is an associate lecturer at Fundación Universitaria Seminario Bíblico de Colombia. His research focuses on bridging the gap between academia and the church, aiming to make his writings relevant and applicable to the mission of the church. He has authored a variety of books in both Spanish and English, ranging from popular to academic works. Oscar is married to Julieth Serna, and they have two children, Martina and Mathias.

Màiri MacPherson works as Mission Strengthener for Edinburgh City Mission's Nations ministry. After receiving an undergraduate degree in Modern European Languages from the University of Edinburgh, Màiri studied for an MTh in Missiology at Edinburgh Theological Seminary. She is a PhD candidate in Systematic Theology at University of Edinburgh, where her thesis focuses on human language in the thought of Johan Herman Bavinck. Màiri is an external lecturer at the Faith Mission Bible College in Edinburgh, teaching a course on Christian mission. She is a member of the EAUK Council and the EA Evangelism Advisory Group.

Revd Adam Martin and **Karina Martin** are passionate to see a generation of healthy intercultural churches emerge across Europe. They learnt about building intercultural church by moving into the centre of Derby and planting International Community Church (ICC) in 2003. They also launched Upbeat Communities, a charity serving refugees across Derbyshire.

In 2011, they joined ICC with their mother church 'Reach' with a vision to see the whole church reflect the diversity of the city. During that time Karina co-founded Welcome Churches, now serving over

1,300 churches working with refugees. In 2019, Adam began to develop a UK network for intercultural churches. Through training events, conferences and online huddle groups, the Intercultural Churches UK team is equipping church and ministry leaders across a wide variety of denominations.

Revd Dr Israel Oluwole Olofinjana is the director of the One People Commission of the Evangelical Alliance and founding Director of Centre for Missionaries from the Majority World. He is an African Public Theologian looking at the mission of African Christians in the European context. He is an Honorary Research Fellow at the Queen's Foundation for Ecumenical Theological Education in Birmingham and is on the Advisory Group on Race and Theology of the Society for the Study of Theology (SST). He is on the Christian Aid Working Group of Black Majority Church leaders, exploring the intersection of climate justice and racial justice and a member of Tearfund's Theology Committee. Israel lectures at Christ Theological College, and is a visiting lecturer at All Nations Christian College and London School of Theology.

Revd Dr Canon Sharon Prentis is an ordained Anglican priest. Sharon is a member of the Church of England's Racial Justice Unit (RJU) team and its deputy director. Following a key strategic objective, their role is instrumental in supporting the work of equity, diversity, and belonging in the Anglican Church. With over 20 years of experience in various education, community work, and health settings, including roles in local authorities and charities such as the Salvation Army, Sharon brings a wealth of experience to her current role. Prior to her work at the RJU, she served as the Dean of Ministry at St Mellitus Theological College and worked as a priest, advocating passionately for social justice and diverse leadership.

Dr Usha Reifsnider is a second-generation migrant, first-generation British-Gujarati Christ-follower, wife and mother. Since 1988, she has served in cross-cultural mission mostly with refugees and migrants, including ten years in the Middle East. Usha's PhD is located in the intersections of cultural anthropology, theology and missiology. Usha is an international cultural consultant, researcher and speaker, with a focus on migration and gospel engagement. She serves as regional co-director of Lausanne Europe, is a senior faculty member of Christ Theological College, and is director at the Centre for Missionaries from the Majority World. Usha's published works include *Unmuted: Speaking to be heard*.

Revd Dr Mohan Seevaratnam is ethnically Sri Lankan Tamil and grew up in London. He is bi-vocational, working as Assistant Minister at St Peter's Harrow and also as GP Lead at the medical centre attached to the church. He has a BA in Biblical and Cross-Cultural Studies (All Nations) and spent eight years in Sri Lanka, serving in healthcare mission and Bible teaching. He also has an MA in Contemporary Ecclesiology (King's, London) and is now doing a DMin (Asbury) in Church Planting in Post-Christendom Europe. He has helped plant an intercultural church called Mosaic, and is currently a trustee and on the national leadership team of Intercultural Churches.

Jessie Tang is an ethnomusicologist who has an interest in intercultural church and worship, second-generation immigrants and global missions. Jessie leads the UK network of intercultural worship ministry Songs2Serve and is on the strategic team of Intercultural Churches, both of which work across Europe. She is the Intercultural Ministry Director for the Diocese of Leicester, in the Church of England. Jessie also hosts a podcast called ACross Culture – exploring culture, identity and the Christian faith.

Revd Dr MiJa Wi is a lecturer in New Testament studies and Global Mission and the director of Bridging Worlds: The Centre for Asian Christianities at Nazarene Theological College, Manchester, UK. Her research focuses on themes of wealth and poverty in the Gospels, Asian hermeneutics, diaspora, and intercultural church dynamics. Alongside her academic career, she has co-pastored Manchester YeDam Church – originally a Korean congregation, now embracing intercultural growth – with her husband, Eun Ho Kim, for eight years, and recently planted a new church in Warwick.

Revd Dr David Wise is a Baptist minister. He served for 32 years at Greenford Baptist Church in West London, during which time it transitioned from being a white British congregation to a genuinely inter-ethnic one. Subsequently his DTh researched, mainly through the eyes of the congregation, how this transition took place. For seven years, David was a tutor on an MA in missional leadership followed by five years as the programme leader for an MA in spiritual formation. He now works as a mentor/coach for Christian leaders who are either working inter-ethnically or cross-culturally, speaks at conferences and writes for publication.

Introduction: Intercultural Church Conversations in Britain

REVD DR ISRAEL OLUWOLE OLOFINJANA, DR USHA REIFNSIDER AND REVD DR DAVID WISE

One of the current developments in British Christianity and some other European countries is the emergence of the intercultural approach to church. By 'intercultural church', we mean a church methodology that centres authentic integration and mutual learning instead of a multicultural approach that leans towards assimilation, which measures all other cultures through one dominant culture.

Israel Oluwole Olofinjana is an African who is involved in the intercultural conversation through an intercultural ministry called the One People Commission, which he leads at the Evangelical Alliance. He has observed that intercultural language within the British church landscape started emerging around the death of George Floyd in 2020. We could therefore argue that the death of George Floyd became the catalyst for an intercultural church model in Britain. His death raised many critical and crucial questions around our ecclesiology and missiology because it appeared that for a long time, we have developed traumatic ecclesiologies through a multicultural approach of church that others the existence of people of colour and sometimes dehumanizes them through assimilation to become British Christians. In essence, instead of our various multicultural churches helping people in their discipleship walk towards the image of God, what appears to have happened in reality is that we have discipled people to journey towards a British image. This is one of the reasons why multicultural churches are not the solution to address racism in our churches, because these have become complicit in fostering the process of racializing people of colour. *Polyphonic God* therefore brings a corrective in articulating that, because God is the God of the nations; God is not a tribal, national, regional or colonial God.

Israel Oluwole Olofinjana, Usha Reifnsider, David Wise

As described in Acts 2, the international audience that witnessed the spectacle of *glossolalia* experienced by Jesus' followers were shocked not because Babel was reversed or redeemed, but rather that God did not speak to them in the Hebrew language. God, who was conceived of as speaking in Hebrew, is now speaking in multiple languages. In essence, the revelation of God here is that God is polyphonic. Flowing from this rich understanding, *Polyphonic God* seeks to advocate for diverse voices in theology, church and how we engage justice concerns. The book centres an intercultural approach of church through intercultural theology, case studies of intercultural practices and intercultural justice that can confront racism and otherness of people of colour in our churches.

Apart from the death of George Floyd being a catalyst for intercultural conversation, we also believe it has been followed by a move of the spirit. This is because we have observed that God appears to have raised different agents of interculturality in different regions, denominations and organizations in Britain. Not everyone has caught this prophetic vision yet of an intercultural ecclesiology, but what we are seeing is God's Spirit moving and raising catalysts in different denominations, networks and streams all over the country and using them to pioneer and lead the way. This is beginning to happen within the Elim Pentecostal church with some key leaders engaging in conversations on how to address racial injustice through creating inclusive communities that could be described as templates of an intercultural church. The Elim church also now have a racial justice group seeking to develop more thinking on racial justice within the denomination. Similar conversations are happening within the New Frontiers network of churches, Baptist Unions and networks, and the Anglican community (Olofinjana, 2024). For example, the Anglican Communion in March 2024 organized a national conference on intercultural churches. This conference took place in Leicester and was organized by the Revd Dr Tim Wambunya, who is the Bishop of Wolverhampton and chair of the steering group of Anglican Network of Intercultural Churches (ANIC).

The conference in Leicester was significant for various reasons. First, it was successful in terms of the diversity and number of people attending. There were about 120 people representing different cultures, ethnicities, classes and ages in attendance. Another important aspect of this particular conference was that this initiative was part of the strategy of ANIC, meaning it was more than a conference but rather a movement working towards raising the profile of intercultural approach of church within the Church of England. Another significant aspect of this conference

Introduction

was the creation of a learning community to map out best practices in intercultural mission, develop intercultural mission toolkits and disseminate the resources to intercultural mission practitioners. This was the second Anglican conference on intercultural churches, and, at the time of writing, plans are underway for the third conference.

Conversations on intercultural churches are not limited to church denominations, but are also emerging within unity movements and mission organizations. In Leeds in January 2024, Rev Osoba Otaigbe, who works for the Bible Society and is seconded to the Gather Movement, organized an intercultural church conference with the theme of Intercultural Church and City Transformation. There were different pre-conference gatherings in different cities across the UK such as London, Birmingham, Leeds and Derby to identify crucial issues that unity movements in cities were grappling with. The feedback from the various city gatherings shaped some of the conversations at the conference. The conference was a success with around 150 leaders, practitioners from different denominations and ethnicities in attendance. The conference was also significant because of the collaborative aspect of the work in partnership with key national organizations such as the Evangelical Alliance, Churches Together in England and Share Jesus International to mention a few. Lastly, the conference highlighted in its report some shared learnings that are crucial in the ongoing resourcing of intercultural church and city transformation (Intercultural Church and City Transformation Report, 2024). The second conference of this nature took place at All Nations Centre in London on 31 January and 1 February 2025.

It has been particularly exciting to see these developments and how different people are championing the cause of an intercultural church in their organizations, denominations and church networks. The picture that is beginning to emerge at the moment is that these different agents of interculturality are now connecting through relationships and networking and mapping out what is going on nationally and regionally. An example of this mapping and networking is the setting up of a leadership consultation called Intercultural Leadership Forum, which brings together the majority of the catalysts of interculturality in Britain. All three editors and some of the contributors in this book are part of the forum. This forum has representations from the Church of England, Salvation Army, Elim Pentecostal, Assemblies of God, Baptists and many more. We are observing similar patterns in other European countries, including Switzerland, Norway, Germany, Netherlands and Sweden. Diaspora Christian leaders and indigenous European Christian leaders are coming together to see how they can collaborate better for the sake of God's kingdom purposes.

Purpose and Perspectives of the Book

But as these conversations develop, what are the theological resources that will nurture and sustain this movement? Another way of framing this question is: what theological resources need to be created to capture some of the emerging trends and currents? We are beginning to see more people reflect and write about what is happening, and an example is Martyn Snow's book, *An Intercultural Church for a Multicultural World* (Snow, 2024). This volume therefore seeks to contribute towards the ongoing debate on intercultural ecclesiology and missiology in Britain. The following serves as the purpose of this book:

- To document and capture recent thinking, practice and scholarship on congregational case studies promoting an intercultural approach of church in Britain.
- To encourage, facilitate and establish an intercultural approach of church in Britain.
- To map out key intercultural practices that can enable the growth of intercultural churches and engagement.
- To develop an intercultural ecclesiology and missiology that could shape ministerial, theological and spiritual formation.

The book has 15 chapters reflecting different perspectives in the UK. These perspectives are:

- **Intercultural:** We have contributors from a wide range of backgrounds, including African, African Caribbean, South Asian, Chinese, South Korean, Columbian and white British/European perspectives. It is also worth noting that there are contributions from Northern Ireland, Scotland, Wales and England, therefore giving a fuller picture of the state of intercultural church across the United Kingdom.
- **Interdenominational:** We have different denominations, streams, networks and mission organizations represented in the contributions. These include Pentecostals, Baptists, Church of England, Charismatics and Independents.
- **Intergenerational:** The book has intergenerational perspectives with contributions from first- and second-generation diaspora. *Polyphonic*

Introduction

God also has contributions from young and old British writers, as well as emerging leaders, thereby connecting conversations on intercultural and intergenerational dynamics.
- **Interdisciplinary:** The book encompasses the use of different disciplines and fields of study, including biblical studies, missiology, public theology, practical theology, diaspora studies, world Christianity, contextual theology, church history and the social sciences. Different research methodologies have also been used, including auto-ethnographical, case studies, theological reflection, field studies and congregational studies.

Part and Chapter Divisions and Contributions

The themes and the chapters are divided into three parts covering Intercultural Theology, Intercultural Churches and Practices, and Intercultural Justice.

Part 1 – Intercultural Theology: Foundational Thought and Perspectives

Part 1 deals with intercultural theology, looking at the foundational theologies that shape intercultural practices. It gives the theological and missiological rationale for the development of intercultural churches – in essence, the theological framework that undergirds intercultural engagement and practices.

Chapter 1 – Politics of Multiculturalism, Theology of Interculturality: Towards an Intercultural Ecclesiology

The UK can be described as a postmodern, secular, multicultural, multi-ethnic society, and within this context have emerged multicultural churches. But what are the debates at the heart of multicultural Britain and how do they influence multicultural churches? If the political narrative is that multiculturalism has failed, or needs managing, and that migration needs to be controlled because it has not led to a unified British society with British identity and values, have multicultural churches by default failed, or do we need to journey towards something radically different? This chapter contends that intercultural churches are significant in multicultural Britain to create a countercultural narrative. In essence, the church must create radical inclusive spaces and contexts that transcend multicultural churches. Multicultural churches are the starting point, but we want to journey towards intercultural churches. This chapter gives a descriptive analysis of different approaches to multicultural churches and the need for the UK church to journey towards intercultural churches.

Chapter 2 – The Metaphor of Tapestry: A Theological Framing for Inter-ethnic congregations

This chapter explores the significance of the use of the metaphor of tapestry for the congregation at Greenford Baptist Church as it transitioned from an almost entirely white British congregation to an inter-ethnic one. The biblical roots and the theological framing are traced. The impact of the tapestry metaphor in the development of the inter-ethnic church community is explored through extracts from interviews with five long-serving staff members and leaders who have been on the transition journey with the church. Some of the work of Willie James Jennings in *After Whiteness* is built on. It is suggested that a wider adoption of this metaphor could help other congregations on an inter-ethnic journey.

Chapter 3 – You Are Home! The Family Metaphor and Its Impact on Understanding Church and Intercultural Communities in Ephesians

Paul uses the experience of being incorporated into a family to help his readers understand the church in the letter to the Ephesians. This chapter analyses how the thesis 'In love, king Jesus has incorporated believers into the Father's household as beloved children' shapes believers' identity, relationships, ethics and church life. Using conceptual metaphor theory, this chapter explores how understanding the church as a family breaks down barriers between Jews and Gentiles, answers the question, 'Who is the people of God?', and becomes the foundation upon which an intercultural family 'in Christ' can stand.

Part 2 – Intercultural Churches and Practices: Ecclesiology Re-imagined

Part 2 focuses on case studies and congregational studies of intercultural churches and ministries from different perspectives and regions in the UK. It also explores key practices that can foster the development of intercultural churches and ministries. It considers themes and practices such as worship, identity, unity, diversity and city transformation

Introduction

Chapter 4 – 'Re-tuning' Worship: Biblical Principles for a Culturally Diverse Age

In this chapter, ethnodoxologist and intercultural worship practitioner Ian Collinge sets out some outlines for an interdisciplinary theology of intercultural worship. He shows that today's church has a unique opportunity to discover that such worship paves the way for personal and communal transformational encounters with God, engagement with the Scriptures and enhanced ways to do theology in action. Churches can contextualize worship, 're-tuning' it, like a stringed instrument, for cultural diversity. He introduces the 'constants' and 'variables' of worship, illustrating these with practical examples of how leaders can tap into the cultural strengths of their fellow worshippers.

Chapter 5 – Intercultural Church as a Direction of Travel: Exploring the Journey of a Korean Diaspora Church (KDC)

Diverse diaspora churches in the UK breathe new life into post-Christian Western society, meeting the needs of believers on the move in new contexts. However, their growth has not significantly impacted broader British society and presents internal challenges for future diaspora generations. This essay navigates the future of UK diaspora churches, focusing on a Korean church's journey toward becoming an intercultural community. It first evaluates the benefits, limitations and challenges faced by UK diaspora churches. Using a Korean diaspora church as a case study, it then explores how these churches can overcome limitations and challenges, particularly those related to in-group-focused ministries. The Korean church in question seeks to serve the Korean community, collaborate with local British churches, and reshape its congregation beyond typical diaspora norms. This chapter considers whether the intercultural odyssey of the Korean diaspora church might offer insights for the future trajectory of UK diaspora churches.

Chapter 6 – Feeling Welcome and Accepted: A Case Study of Greenford Baptist Church

This chapter draws on doctoral research to present a case study of migrants and third-culture kids at Greenford Baptist Church (GBC) in West London. Through their words, several aspects are explored: the use of first language in sung worship; the experience of movement/dance during congregational worship; using patterns of prayer, including first language, from 'back home' as a normal part of church life; Sunday morning meetings being restructured in order to create opportunity for inter-ethnic engagement; food, sharing food prepared by people from different ethnic contexts and the significance of that, both for those who prepared and those who consumed it. The final section reflects on the experience of Third-Culture Kids (TCK) who were a part of GBC. TCK are people born in the UK to parents who were born and grew up in a different country. Those at GBC who were interviewed were adults, and it was their opinion that their experience of growing up as a part of GBC gave them advantages over their peers who had not had a similar experience. The themes that emerged from their focus group and interviews are presented.

Chapter 7 – Among the Nations, for the Nations: Championing Diversity in the Church in Edinburgh

Headlines over recent years have presumed the decline of Christianity as a whole in Scotland, claiming that there is a 'religious retreat' and that the church is 'running out of disciples'. Yet in many of these arguments, there is no acknowledgment of Christian communities created, revived or bolstered by the presence of believers from other countries. God is gathering people from all nations into Scotland; the church in Scotland is becoming richer in ethnic, linguistic and cultural diversity. Edinburgh City Mission has recognized this growing diversity, along with the sad realities of racism, exclusion and isolation that exist in Scotland. Their Nations ministry has a vision to champion diversity and build unity in the wider church through creating meaningful and mutual engagement between local and global Christian communities in Edinburgh, reflecting the heavenly vision of Revelation 7.9. This chapter will examine Edinburgh City Mission's Nations ministry, its context in the city, its theological foundations, and its vision to stimulate mission in over 70 global Christian communities and encourage intercultural engagement in the wider Edinburgh church. As Edinburgh City Mission strives to be 'in our city *for* our city', Nations seeks to be 'among the nations, for the nations'.

Chapter 8 – What Even Is My Culture? Exploring Identity in an Intercultural Church

Written from the perspective of a bi-cultural second-generation immigrant involved in intercultural church and worship for the last eight years, this chapter explores the tensions and opportunities of identity exploration in an intercultural church. This chapter argues that the intercultural church is a 'third space', where the cultures in the church shape the shared culture of the church – a dynamic and ever-developing space. While this paints a beautifully messy picture, the identity challenges of a rootless, British-born Chinese remain, as many may wrestle with wondering how to authentically bring their culture to the table when they are caught between worlds and not perceived to be fully inhabiting any of them.

Chapter 9 – Laying Firm Foundations for a Healthy Intercultural Church

This chapter draws from 20 years of experience developing an intercultural expression of church in Derby, East Midlands, and from the wider experience the authors have gained through developing two national networks: Welcome Churches UK and Intercultural Churches UK. Using the metaphor of clearing the ground and laying foundations, this chapter outlines the 'roots and rocks' of thinking and practice that need to be challenged, before going on to consider the key biblical foundations that need to be in place for an intercultural church to become established. Illustrating these from the authors' own mistakes and discoveries, the chapter demonstrates the importance of fostering a culture of welcome, growing in relational unity, honouring our cultural diversity, working towards a distribution of power in leadership and a commitment to the Great Commission. Finally, this sets the story within the wider picture of how the authors have seen the Spirit of God at work at a national level, stirring leaders to embrace the challenging call to intercultural church ministry and to connect across denominations and cultural backgrounds to learn together and support one another.

Chapter 10 – The New Northern Irish! Intercultural Developments in Northern Ireland

This chapter starts by setting out the unique context and culture of Northern Ireland. This includes its 'troubled' history that has led to its contested identity and politics. The chapter unpacks how this history has led to large-scale migration from NI and relatively little migration into NI until recent times. How this has shaped the culture of churches in NI, and particularly their posture toward 'outsiders', is also considered. The chapter then focuses on the more recent, post-Good Friday history of NI, and particularly how the relative peace and prosperity has led to the arrival of the 'New Northern Irish' from around the world in significant numbers. A significant part of the chapter gives voice to the experiences of these 'New Northern Irish', particularly relating to their contributions to Christian worship and witness in NI.

Part 3 – Intercultural Justice: Racial Justice and Reconciliation

Part 3 considers the racial justice dimension of intercultural theology and practices, looking at examples that go beyond just the Black and white dichotomy. It offers different perspectives on racial justice.

Chapter 11 – Just Leadership: Developing Radical Empathy to Break Systemic Strongholds

In an increasingly globalized world, mass migration and rapid demographic shifts demonstrate that rising cultural diversity is an inevitable global phenomenon. The cultural composition of Western churches today also reflects this reality as the centre of gravity of global Christianity has shifted with the dramatic rise of Christianity in the Two-Thirds World. This diversification is evident not only within our cities, but also across the whole UK: from diaspora church plants to the increasing cultural diversity of local churches and their communities. This also presents new challenges and opportunities for a leadership that is just and justice centred. Through historical and scriptural examples, this chapter demonstrates that God's plan for diversity and unity is evident from the beginning, and that intercultural church approaches ultimately provide a context within which racial and cultural power imbalances can be challenged and transformed in our discipleship to Christ.

Chapter 12 – Intercultural Life Together: Racial Justice as Love Lived Out in Worship, Fellowship and Mission

As Christians, we are called to live out this justice in our neighbourhoods, illustrating it within our diverse church communities. Our discipleship should involve the practice of justice, reflecting our commitment to the teachings of Christ and living it out with one another – especially when that other has a significantly different experience of life from our own. Understanding the church's role in justice is a crucial part of church life and practice together. This chapter explores the theme of justice as a key element in the biblical narrative of the kingdom, emphasizing the call for Christians to exemplify justice in their interactions with their neigh-

Introduction

bours and within the diverse church community. Historical and current missional examples drawn from work with traditionally excluded and minoritized cultures are used. Ultimately, the author suggests that enacting justice in diverse contexts requires cross-cultural humility and, equally important, love.

Chapter 13 – Intercultural Holiness and Justice: Challenge, Cross, Community and Celebration

As God's holy people, we are called to be set apart from the world. What does it mean in a world, where Jesus said 'nation (*ethnos*) shall rise against nation', to live and walk in intercultural holiness? With regards to our own culture, we are both to recognize it as God's gift but also to die to it as part of dying to self. With regards to our view of other cultures, we must learn to see them through Christ's eyes. This chapter unpacks how, to walk in intercultural holiness, we need to embrace four things: the challenge, the cross-centred solution, the celebration and the community.

Chapter 14 – Intercultural Churches as Catalysts for Racial Justice

This chapter explores the role of intercultural churches as catalysts for promoting racial justice within the church and community. The chapter looks at how churches can effectively address racial injustice within their midst and beyond – examining the principles, challenges, and transformative potential inherent within the intercultural church model. Drawing on theological and sociological insights, we address issues such as racial and ethnic disparities in leadership, cultural insensitivity, and the marginalization in decision-making of minority voices – encouraging readers to reflect on their own attitudes and behaviours too. We draw on real-life examples from the Elim Pentecostal Church/City Church Cardiff to outline practical strategies that churches can employ.

Chapter 15 – Antiracist Mission in Postcolonial Britain

Racial justice in mission seems obvious to the point of embarrassment. On the one hand, we can quote Scriptures of equality and justice. Regardless of the fact that the majority of the world's Christians are not white, nor living in the West, the dominant voices whether echoing in the mega cities of Asia, Africa or Latin America are from the West. This chapter gives the listener the choice to believe us and engage with us on the issues of racial injustice in ministry. But it will risk putting the shame and guilt and fragility of the dominant to one side while we contemplate a future that holds the past carefully in a way to influence a better future.

Bibliography

'Intercultural Church and City Transformation Report', Bible Society, 2024.

Jennings, W. J., 2020, *After Whiteness: An Education in Belonging*, Grand Rapids, MI: Wm. B. Eerdmans Publishing Co.

Olofinjana, Israel, 2024, 'Spiritual Renewal in Britain: Intercultural Pentecostal Theology', *Eucharisma* 1, Spring, pp.72–8, https://eucharisma.co.uk/spiritual-renewal-in-britain/ (accessed 7.2.25).

Snow, Martyn, 2024, *An Intercultural Church for a Multicultural World: Reflections on Gift Exchange*, London: Church House Publishing.

PART I

Intercultural Theology: Foundational Thought and Perspectives

I

Politics of Multiculturalism, Theology of Interculturality: Towards an Intercultural Ecclesiology

ISRAEL OLUWOLE OLOFINJANA

Introduction

The substance of this chapter was delivered as a keynote address at an Intercultural Church Conference (ICC) held at Life Church in Manchester in 2023. The key question at the heart of the conference was: why are intercultural churches significant in twenty-first-century Britain? But perhaps more importantly, a research question I want to explore in this chapter is: what are the differences between a multicultural church and an intercultural church?

To begin exploring this question, I will start by examining multicultural Britain, that is, the development of multicultural and multi-ethnic Britain as the context for the emergence of multicultural churches. I will then propose five descriptive approaches to multicultural churches and the necessity to journey from multicultural towards intercultural churches. Lastly, I will argue, giving four rationales, why intercultural churches are important, and end by outlining five important intercultural practices.

Key Literature and Current Developments on Intercultural Churches

In understanding current developments on intercultural churches in the British context, it is important to start this chapter with a brief exploration of some key literature and the use of the terms of 'multicultural' and 'intercultural'. The existing literature in Britain on intercultural churches focuses largely on developing multicultural churches. There are a few exceptions that explore the need for an intercultural approach of church through intercultural preaching (Reddie, Abel-Boanerges and Searle, 2021), intercultural worship (Resonance Band, 2011) and intercultural church (Aldous, Dunmore and Seevaratnam, 2020). In addition, the *Oxford Journal for Intercultural Mission* (2023) produces articles and essays on intercultural mission, albeit with a focus on the Church of England.

Multicultural

From my initial observation, not many books have been published looking at multicultural churches in Britain. However, this has changed gradually so that today we have some published books. Perhaps one of the first of these, written by a Canadian but nevertheless influencing a lot of thinking in the British context, is Bruce Milne's *Dynamic Diversity* (2006); this describes a multicultural church through the lens of a theological anthropology of a new humanity church. Influenced by American authors such as David A. Anderson's *Multicultural Ministry* (2004) and Michael O. Emerson's *People of the Dream* (2006) was Owen Hylton's *Crossing the Divide* (2009). This was because there were more published works in the American context than the British context. Owen's work explores the need for the UK church to move from welcoming ethnic and cultural diversity to embracing it in our churches. My own work, *Turning the Tables on Mission* (2013), an edited volume, brought together practitioners who were leading multicultural churches and ministries to tell their own stories. One of the unique aspects of this book is that all the contributors are drawn from the Majority World background. Andrew Hardy and Dan Yarnell's *Forming Multicultural Partnerships* (2015) gave us a different angle to the conversation by looking at the need for developing multicultural church plants and partnerships.

From 2016 onwards, there was an increase in the publications on multicultural churches. That year alone, there were two significant publications. One was Malcolm Patten's *Leading a Multicultural Church* (2016), which focuses on helping church leaders to develop theories and strategies in leading a multicultural church. This work was based on Patten's doctoral research at Spurgeon's College. The second was Osoba Otaigbe's work, *Building Cultural Intelligence in Church and Ministry* (2016), which introduces a corporate and business language of cultural intelligence (CQ) into the conversation as a way for the church to develop multicultural churches and ministries, and engage wider society in mission. Building on this corporate and business language, Hirpo Kumbi's work, *The Culturally Intelligent Leader* (2017), considers a cultural intelligent leadership able to lead a multicultural, multi-ethnic church. John Root's works, *Worship in a Multi-ethnic Society* (2018) and *Building Multi-Racial Churches* (2020), explored the challenges involved in multi-ethnic worship in local churches and the need to address racial injustices if we are to build a multiracial church. The key word here is multiracial.

Harvey Kwiyani's *Multicultural Kingdom* (2020) uses the language of mosaic to develop a multicultural kingdom theology that should shape our ecclesial practices and mission. This significant work articulates the need for a multicultural missiology. A significant study to highlight is that of David Wise, one of the editors of this volume. His doctoral thesis uses the language of tapestry to describe Greenford Baptist Church as a multi-ethnic church using an auto-ethnographic research method (Wise, 2022). Wise's contributions in chapters 2 and 6 shed more light. A recent book is Martyn Snow's *Intercultural Church for a Multicultural World* (2024), which describes interculturality as a gift exchange. This book, written from an Anglican perspective, explores the question of how we can be gift to one another.

Intercultural

There seems to be a shift in language from around 2020 from the use of 'multicultural' to 'intercultural'. While the language of 'intercultural' has been in mission studies circles, the usage has been to describe overseas mission and mission training. In this usage, the word 'intercultural' replaces 'cross-cultural'. 'Intercultural' has also been used to describe the nature of world Christianity as expressed in the Majority World (Cartledge and Cheetham, 2011). The current usage in the British context is in reference to the need to develop an inclusive ecclesiology for churches and organizations. This usage is emerging in three ways: new roles, network initiatives and conferences. First, we now have church and mission organizations intentionally creating new roles using the language of 'intercultural' to describe those jobs. Take these two examples as illustrations: the Salvation Army has an Intercultural Mission Enabler, and Global Connections now have an Intercultural Engagement Co-ordinator.

Second, we have new initiatives emerging with an intercultural vision. An example is Intercultural Ministries Ireland, whose vision is to create Christ-centred communities and intercultural worship across the island of Ireland. Lastly, there is an increase in the number of national conferences looking at the theme of intercultural church. One example is the two Anglican intercultural church conferences that took place in 2023 and 2024. The second conference had several learning points, but for the purposes of this chapter, one of them was establishing ideas and best practices for intercultural worshipping communities. This recommendation is very important, but when talking about best practices in regards to intercultural churches and by extension mission, what do we mean by intercultural churches and are they any different from multicultural churches, or are the words 'multicultural', 'multi-ethnic', 'multiracial', 'cross-cultural' and 'intercultural' all interchangeable?

Defining 'intercultural'

Possibly one of the first people to clarify the difference between multicultural and intercultural churches in the British context is Kate Coleman, whose contributions are in Chapter 11, although Tayo Arikawe (2013) and others made a distinction between multicultural churches and multi-ethnic churches.

> We are becoming increasingly multi-ethnic, but we are still far from being multicultural. By this I mean that we have people groups from different countries, but the diverse cultures of these people are not reflected in the mode of running the church. We have remained a white middle-class church in almost everything we do. Most of our sermons would appeal more to Westerners in the style of delivery, but all the same have been a huge blessing to all of us. We don't have a diversity of cultures in our eldership, but this may not necessarily be the fault of the church as they have to work within certain limits of the people from other cultures who are available. As a church that sends out missionaries to Africa and Asia, we do not have any Africans or Asians on our missions committee. My point is that a church can be multi-ethnic but not necessarily multicultural, unless all of these issues and their implications have been thought through. (Arikawe, 2013, pp. 140–1)

While this is a discussion that has evolved, Arikawe raised some crucial points, which will be investigated throughout this chapter. One is that representation of different cultures does not necessarily translate into integration of those cultures. Another concerns the power dynamics in a multicultural church in terms of whose culture is being used as the benchmark. Referring back to Kate Coleman, she described three important approaches in her new book *Metamorph: Transforming your Life and Leadership* (2024). These are cross-cultural, multicultural/multi-ethnic and intercultural approaches.

> In cross-cultural churches, one culture is often considered 'the norm' and all other cultures are compared or contrasted to this dominant culture, which is viewed as superior (the others are treated as inferior and often 'exist' in survival mode). In multicultural churches, several cultural or ethnic groups live alongside one another, but each cultural group does not necessarily have meaningful interactions with each other. They tend to focus on representation with less powerful groups in survival mode. 'Inter' conveys the idea of sharing, reciprocity, and equality. In these churches, there is robust contact between cultures and a deep understanding and respect for all cultures. Intercultural communication focuses on the mutual exchange of ideas and cultural norms and the development of deep relationships. In an intercultural church, no one is left unchanged because everyone learns from one another and grows together. (Coleman, 2024, pp. 132, 237)

While Arikawe made a distinction between multi-ethnic and multicultural, Coleman grouped them together but made an important distinction between cross-cultural, multicultural and intercultural. Building on Coleman's helpful analysis, I will be proposing a five-way approach to multicultural and intercultural churches and also utilizing her clarification of multicultural and intercultural churches. For the purposes of this chapter, my own definition of multicultural churches is churches that have different nationalities, cultures, generations, ethnicities and classes represented, coexisting and working most of the time towards a British way of doing church. In essence, representation, tolerance, coexistence and assimilation to the British way of doing church are the essential ingredients in these types of churches. I shall expand further on this in my five-way description of multicultural and intercultural approaches to church.

Intercultural churches are churches that have embraced God's vision and gift of ethnic and cultural diversity, and therefore intentionally create spaces and contexts where different cultures, nationalities, ethnicities, generations and classes integrate mutually and meaningfully to create something new for the purposes of God's kingdom. The key elements here are intentionality, integration and mutual inconvenience, to use Michael Jagessar's (2015) description of intercultural engagement and God's kingdom. But why is it important to make these distinctions between multicultural and intercultural churches, and why are intercultural churches important for Britain?

Multiculturalism, Migrants and Britishness

This section is adapted from one of my previous published papers (Olofinjana, 2022). I want to consider the genesis of multicultural and multi-ethnic Britain in order to understand the emergence of multicultural churches. There is a general assumption, both in public and political discourse, that Britain became multicultural with the arrival of Caribbean immigrants in the 1940s. In some right-wing political discourse, this is perpetuated by the myth that pure white Britishness needs to be preserved in the face of immigration. The place we know today as Britain has its foundations in mixed cultures; cultural diversity is therefore nothing new. While little is known about the first people who inhabited these islands, we do know that the Celts arrived on these shores around the first millennium BC (*Roots of the Future*, 1997). The people spoke Celtic languages, which are still used today in parts of Wales, Scotland and Ireland. They had a sophisticated culture and economy, and merged with the original population.

History of multicultural Britain

In the first century AD, Celtic Britain, south of Hadrian's Wall, was ruled by the Roman Empire. The Roman invasions and subsequent conquest began with Julius Caesar's visit around 55 BC. The Romans (who were themselves multicultural and multi-ethnic) ruled Britannia for around 400 years, after which its Empire declined. In the fifth century AD, new Germanic tribes from northern Europe invaded Britain. These warring tribes were the Angles, Saxons, Jutes and Frisians, coming from what is known today as northern Germany, southern Denmark and the northern part of the Netherlands. The Venerable Bede, in his *Ecclesiastical History of the English People* (Bede, 2008, pp. 26–7), wrote that the Angles, Saxons and Jutes were invited by the British people to come and fight the Romans on their behalf, but they ended up conquering Britain itself. Their conquest of Britain led to a synthesis of culture and language known as Anglo-Saxon.

In the eighth and ninth century AD, fresh invasions and migrants came from Scandinavia, particularly Vikings from Norway and Denmark.

The introduction of the Norse cultures led to further mixing of cultures in Britain. In AD 1066, another invasion occurred, this time by the Normans. This invasion was led by the popular William, Duke of Normandy (part of France today), also known as William the Conqueror. The Norman culture, language and customs were introduced and had a significant influence on the population.

One of the things William the Conqueror did during his British reign was to encourage large Jewish settlements in Britain. He allowed Jews from France to settle, offering them royal protection, and leading to such an influx of Jews that by the thirteenth century there were Jewish populations in 27 cities including London. Other European migrants to Britain during the Medieval period included Germans and Italians. Some of these were merchants or visitors. The Reformation era, launched by Martin Luther, Ulrich Zwingli, John Calvin and others, led to religious wars in Europe. These religious wars resulted in thousands of highly skilled Protestant refugees fleeing to Britain for protection. Not everyone welcomed these refugees, with some lamenting 'Tottenham is turned Flemish' and referring to Bermondsey as 'Petty Burgundy' (Frow, 1997).

The eighteenth century witnessed the rise of the Black population in Britain. This was due to the evil and inhumane trade known as the transatlantic slave trade, which had begun in the fifteenth century. This trade was well established by the eighteenth century and resulted in a population of about 15,000 Africans who were scattered in the major port cities of Britain by the year 1700 (Killingray and Edwards, 2007, pp. 17–21).

The twentieth century saw skilled German workers coming to settle in Britain. By 1914, the German population in Britain had risen to about 40,000, to be joined later by Russian and Polish workers fleeing mass unemployment after the Great Depression of 1929. Finally, the post-war years saw Caribbean people coming to Britain in response to invitations to come and rebuild the country after the devastation of the Second World War. Workers were also recruited from India, Pakistan and Bangladesh. The independence of some African countries from colonial rule also witnessed a great number of African diplomats and students coming to settle in Britain from the 1960s. Ghana became independent in 1957, followed by Nigeria and several other African countries in 1960.

This quick survey of history demonstrates that what we know today as Britain has always been multicultural since its origins, and it can be further argued that, with the arrival of the Windrush generation (Caribbean migrants) in the 1940s–60s, as well as other workers from South

Asian countries and African migrants, Britain became multi-ethnic, adding to the layers of its multiculturalism. But how has this multicultural, multi-ethnic Britain been viewed in political discourse, and, in particular, how has it affected what it means to be British?

Politics of multiculturalism

Modern multicultural Britain, that is, since around the 1940s, has given rise to two main political discourses. The first belongs to those on the right wing of British politics, whose contention is that cultural diversity is a threat to national identity and security. They have argued that an over-tolerance of multiculturalism has allowed immigrants to segregate rather than integrate. They therefore call for assimilation, i.e. the absorption and conformity of all other cultures into British culture, identity and values. Extreme versions of this ideology would be the National Front and the British National Party (BNP). The National Front was formed in 1967 with one of its chief aims being to prevent people migrating to Britain, especially people of colour. They embraced an ideology of nationalism that was rooted in the pseudo-science of 'racial purity'. The BNP was founded in 1982, and though less aggressive and overt in their policies, they continued the campaign to protect white Britishness.

The second political discourse is that of the liberals and those on the centre-left who advocate for cultural diversity. The kind of multiculturalism they have historically fought for can be summed up in the former Home Secretary Roy Jenkins' famous 1966 definition of integration as 'equal opportunity accompanied by cultural diversity in an atmosphere of mutual tolerance' (Kundnani, 2007, p. 27). They have consciously fought against assimilation in favour of such a model of integration.

However, this type of 'integration' is changing, giving way to a new integration paradigm that, while still campaigning for equal opportunities, in fact has assimilation as its objective. Among the reasons for this change were the events of 11 September 2001 in New York, the later 7 July 2005 bombings in London by home-grown perpetrators, and the racialized disturbances that took place in Oldham, Burnley, Bradford and Leeds in 2001. In addition, the brutal murder of Lee Rigby on the afternoon of 22 May 2013 in Woolwich by two Black Islamist extremist British men has also highlighted this notion, forcing questions of integration, race and religion back to the fore of public debate.

From around that period, liberals and those on the centre-left have advocated community cohesion as a form of integration. Community cohesion is defined as the government's attempt to bring togetherness into a given community through funding local projects that will bond people of different ethnicities, religions and cultures. Therefore, those on the right now have allies from those on the left and centre-left who all agree that multiculturalism must be 'managed'.

One extension of this approach is the argument that managed migration is needed at our borders to crack down on illegal immigration and combat terrorism. This is leading to measures such as the increased use of surveillance technologies, immigration caps, visa restrictions, deportations, detentions and mistreatment of people seeking asylum. The Windrush scandal of 2017 is a prime example, which saw many of the African Caribbean community deported or not allowed re-entry into the country. The rhetoric of fighting terrorism comes under the guise of the 'war on terror', and this has led to the mistreatment and stigmatization of immigrants coming from Islamic countries and cultures. The language of 'illegal' or 'bogus' immigrants generally seems to apply only to non-white immigrants – white Australians, South Africans and New Zealanders being exempt – although eastern European migrants such as Polish, Romanians and Bulgarians are also being stereotyped. The British cry is that immigrants are not integrating; therefore, the multicultural agenda has failed. However, the question is, why are immigrants not mixing?

Using immigrants as scapegoats for the failure of multiculturalism or accusing them of not integrating is just one side of the story; the other side is to recognize and deal with the issues of institutional, cultural and personal racism that still exist in British society today. Britain likes to think of itself as 'postracial': that it has wrestled with racism and expunged it. However, events such as the recent race riots, the Windrush scandal and the disproportional impact of the pandemic on people of colour point to the fact that racism still exists in our society. Perhaps most revealing was the leaked Home Office report titled *The Historic Roots of the Windrush Scandal*, which states that the British immigration system and law between 1950 and 1981 were designed to control Coloured migration (Gentleman, 2022).

Politics of Britishness

In a contested multicultural, multi-ethnic society, what does it mean to be British, or in particular English? As hinted at, those on the extreme right such as the National Front and BNP were fighting for a national ideology of preserving white Britishness. Those on the left such as New

Labour from 2001 after the riots in the North of England campaigned for a national story of Britishness and its values in their efforts to tackle terrorism and reduce immigration. This Britishness, as mentioned before, was couched in the language of integration around promoting certain sets of values. The Conservative–Lib Dem coalition government of 2010 appeared to continue in Labour's footsteps, pronouncing an end to state multiculturalism. This was evident in comments made by the then Secretary of State for Communities and Local Government, Eric Pickles, who pledged to end the era of multiculturalism, arguing that Britain needed community cohesion around British values and identity (Walford, 2012). If state multiculturalism has failed, can we pronounce an end to multicultural churches as well, or do we need to rethink how we engage as a church? I will come back to this question.

A further quest in defining what it means to be British is perhaps revealed in the Brexit vote of 2016. While it cannot be argued that everyone who voted to leave the European Union is against immigration – it is more complex and nuanced than that – the Brexit vote nevertheless revealed dissatisfaction and a struggle with what it means to be British in a European economic system. Another British wrestling with national identity and the tightening of borders was the passing of the Nationality and Borders Act 2022, with the aim of targeting illegal migration and homegrown terrorism. But migration to these shores and how it has constantly defined what it means to be British is an integral part of the country's history, as demonstrated above; one can therefore argue that Britishness has been shaped by multiculturalism rather than monoculturalism.

In summary, the National Front and BNP wanted to preserve white Britishness, while the Labour and Conservative parties are also promoting the preservation of a British national identity based around a commitment to so-called British values. In order to have a British national identity into which migrants can be integrated, it is considered necessary to have a national story based on British history and values of tolerance, fairness, respect, rule of law, democracy and individual liberty. If the political discourse on assimilation disguised by the language of integration is centred on a British national identity and story, and this has in turn influenced public perceptions and understanding of Britishness and Englishness, how have these understandings influenced multicultural churches and why do we need intercultural churches?

Descriptive Analysis of Approaches to Multicultural and Intercultural Churches

Britain as a multicultural, multi-ethnic society has given rise to the birth of multicultural churches. While we still have congregations that could be described as monocultural – that is, churches with one majority culture – from observation, it is fair to say that the UK church has embraced multicultural churches, with several multicultural churches across the UK. What are the different approaches to multicultural churches, and how have the politics of Britishness influenced them? In addition, if state multiculturalism as indicated above has been perceived as a failed project, do we need to end multicultural churches and rethink how we do church?

In addressing some of these questions, I am proposing different approaches of multicultural churches that have emerged and the necessity to journey towards an intercultural church.

Segregational inclusivity

This context describes a multicultural church with different cultures, ethnicities, ages or class represented and coexisting, but with no meaningful interaction (Coleman, 2022) or mutual inconveniencing (Jagessar, 2015). The different groups attend church together, but each keeps to their own groups with little or no interaction with other groups. Another way this happens is when a particular people group emerge or grow within a congregation to the extent that they want their own service in their own language but still want to remain part of the mother church. Therefore, you have the main service taking place in English in the morning, while in the afternoon or later in the day, there is another service in another language. Another context in which segregational inclusivity plays out is through sharing of church buildings, community centres or schools, where two or more churches use the building without engaging each other.

Performative or functional inclusivity

This is a multicultural church where ethnic diversity becomes window dressing through flags of different nations, a fancy website with pictures of people from different cultures, or any other visible imagery to demonstrate that the church is multicultural. While the display of flags, the beautiful website and so on are a good way of celebrating different cultures in our churches, the problem sometimes is that this visible imagery does not in reality reflect the internal processes of the church. It is therefore possible for a church to have flags of different nations displayed, but the people represented by those flags do not have a voice in how the church operates or participate in the life of the church.

On other occasions, performative inclusivity happens when issues around ethnic and cultural diversity are an afterthought and not central to or embedded in the visions and values of the church. Therefore, a multicultural church can have a mission committee planning an event who suddenly realize after all speakers are confirmed that they are all white. It is an afterthought because inclusivity or integration have not become part of the framework of the church.

Selective inclusivity

This is an approach of multicultural churches where one person of colour is taken to represent all people of colour. For example, the presence of a Ghanian person on a leadership team means they can speak for all Africans, Asians and Latin Americans. By default, this person becomes the expert on all things relating to ethnic and cultural diversity. This could also happen when someone from Hong Kong is expected to understand and know everything about China. Another way selective inclusivity functions in a multicultural church or context could be in the limitations of the church's theological framework. This could create blind spots such as having African men on the leadership team and not African women, because of the church's theological position on complementarianism.

Accidental inclusivity

This is a model of multicultural church where the church or organization suddenly experiences an influx of ethnic and cultural diversity. In this context, a church suddenly becomes multicultural because people of colour or Eastern Europeans have started attending the church having migrated to the church's vicinity. In essence, the church is not really prepared for this, but circumstances and migratory patterns have brought people to the church. This often creates tension, as sometimes the congregation and, in particular, the leadership are not really sure how to respond. Another context in which accidental inclusivity occurs is when another church nearby – for example, a Latin American or Caribbean church – closes or two different churches merge because of low numbers or resources. This situation suddenly makes another church multicultural as new people started attending. This accidental inclusivity forces the church to act or continue business as usual.

Radical inclusivity

The four approaches discussed describe the various models of how multicultural churches operate. One thing common to all these approaches is assimilation into the culture of the church. Church culture is shaped by the theology of the church, the denomination, the traditions, the dominant group of the church and an underlying British way of doing church expressed through language, worship, liturgy and preaching. Language matters because many multicultural churches still use English as the dominant language in all aspects of their services. The styles and the content of our worship are deeply influenced by Anglo-American contemporary Christian worship, while liturgy is shaped by the English language and rooted in various British church traditions. Preaching is measured, as Arikawe (2013) commented, through the style of delivery, often a cerebral, rationalistic expository sermon or talk.

Radical inclusivity, on the other hand, is a model of church that starts with integration as an overarching framework. This begins with a conviction and conversion into God's intercultural purposes as revealed in Scripture through creation, incarnation, the Cross, the Great Commission, Pentecost and re-creation. It is aligning our will with God's redemptive work so that we are confronted with our own prejudices and biases. This, in turn, prepares us to be ready to leave our comfort zones, stepping out into new spaces, unfamiliar territories and other cultures. This can be expressed in a local church when we seek to develop an intercultural church that embraces God's vision and gift of diversity, thereby intentionally creating contexts where different cultures, nationalities, ethnicities, classes and generations integrate mutually and meaningfully for the sake of God's kingdom purposes. The goal of a multicultural church is assimilation and that of an intercultural church is integration; we therefore start with a multicultural church but journey towards an intercultural church.

An important question to ask at this stage is why is an intercultural approach to church significant in the UK?

Why Are Intercultural Churches Important?

Sociological rationale

Britain being a multicultural and multi-ethnic society necessitates that the church seeks to reflect the demographic make-up of Britain. The 2021 census data reveals that white British ethnicity in England and Wales has decreased from 86.0% in 2011 to 81.7%, while other non-white ethnicity has increased from 14% in 2011 to 18.3% (Census, 2021). This increase in non-white ethnicity brings a challenge to the UK church and its public theology, which has little to say when it comes to the issues around racial justice. If the UK church is going to speak collectively into racial justice concerns and reach multicultural, multi-ethnic Britain with the gospel, it will require an intercultural missionary movement. To create such a movement, we need the formation and growth of intercultural churches across the UK that can lament, agitate and advocate together on racial justice concerns. Part of that racial justice advocacy will require intercultural churches that can create a different narrative on the need to recognize the humanity of economic migrants, refugees and asylum seekers and express a multiculturalism that has not failed. This mission is crucial for the prophetic witness of the UK church in this season.

Anthropological rationale

God created one human race in his image, but that humanity is expressed with different skin pigmentations, physical features and geography and is shaped by different histories. This is God's anthropology, which reflects who he is as three distinct persons in the Father, the Son and the Holy Spirit but remaining one in essence. This why the heavenly liturgy sung in John's apocalyptic vision (Rev. 5.9–10) does not blur the distinctions of the tribes, the languages, the peoples and the nations, meaning God is not colour blind! God is not colour blind because he created people of colour in the first place (Olofinjana, 2021, p. 103). Therefore, are churches reflecting God's anthropology? Part of the problem in multicultural approaches to church is that sometimes they operate on a theological paradigm that does not want to see colour because it is assumed that, by not seeing colour, everyone is being treated equally. While sometimes people have good intentions for not wanting to see colour, it is important to affirm that God created humanity with some of those distinctive features for a reason. A church that does not see colour can easily assimilate people towards a British and sometimes an English way of doing church. If our churches are going to reflect God's anthropology of a humanity rooted in the Trinity yet maintaining each distinctiveness of the human family, we have to journey towards an intercultural church that integrates each distinctive element of humanity while staying rooted in the triune God. This is the incredible vision that the UK church should be working towards.

Ecclesiological rationale

The work of the Cross was set to correct what went wrong with God's anthropology because disintegration, de-creation and fragmentation had set in because of sin. Therefore, the church is meant to be the incarnation of the Cross creating a new humanity. This is where the language of Milne (2006) is very useful in capturing the new humanity church. The work of the Cross is the foundation of the church, meaning that Jesus' death on the Cross was never about redeeming one nationality or people group; Jesus died for humanity in its diverse expressions. The implication is that our ecclesiology should embody God's humanity, expressing that in each locality with its distinctive context.

Missiological rationale

The gospel is about loving God and loving our neighbour. Therefore, the gospel is about reconciliation between God and humanity, and between polarized and divided humanity. This has implications for intercultural mission. Paul talks about Christ's work on the Cross breaking down the barriers between Jews and Gentiles (Eph. 2.11–22). Paul goes on to expound on how Christ's work on the Cross reconciles us back to God and also pulls down the walls of hostility that divide humanity. In the biblical period and patristic period, these walls of division existed among different communities such as Jews and Gentiles, Jews and Samaritans, Romans and Barbarians, Greeks and non-Greeks, men and women, slaves and masters and so on. The New Testament church therefore had a twofold mission of reconciling humanity back to God and reconciling divided humanity with itself.

In today's multicultural, multi-ethnic Britain with different ethnic communities coexisting alongside each other, an intercultural church with a mission to bridge the divide is essential. How can our churches bring a message of reconciliation between the Black community and the police? How can our churches speak into issues of reparative justice that can bring restoration rather than punitive or retributive justice? How can our churches engage in advocacy work that helps to change perceptions on refugees and asylum seekers? An intercultural church that is shaped by the authenticity of the gospel can begin to engage some of these concerns in our society.

Important Intercultural Practices

Having explored the genesis of multicultural, multi-ethnic Britain, and the various models of multicultural churches, and the significance of developing intercultural churches, what are the key practices that can enable the growth of intercultural churches? I mentioned earlier that establishing best intercultural practices was one of the recommendations from the second Anglican intercultural conference. In this final section, I want to offer my own intercultural practices as a contribution towards the ongoing conversations, and will therefore highlight five key practices.

Power and language

For an intercultural church to emerge, the power dynamics in terms of who are the gatekeepers, the dominant culture and theology are all crucial. Arikawe (2013) noted this when he observed that we are still using one culture as a benchmark in our churches. Power can be in the form of the culture of the church, that is, this is 'the way we do things around here'. It can be the leadership of the church or the theology being drawn from one stream. If we are to develop and grow intercultural churches, we have to constantly interrogate the power dynamics and ask difficult questions, such as who are the gatekeepers and are they willing to share power?

This is a difficult conversation to have in any church because it is uncomfortable, but our discipleship was never meant to be rooted in comfort; therefore, having some discomfort in the church is essential for a discipleship model shaped by suffering and sacrifice (Olofinjana, 2021). One of the dominant ways power manifests in our churches in Britain is through language. I have had people complaining in churches because of not understanding other people's accent. The truth is, we all have an accent, even God had an accent in Jesus who spoke in the Aramaic tongue. If Jesus were to visit our churches today, we might not be able to hear him properly, because he would speak English with an

Aramaic accent! If language is one way in which power is expressed, is it possible to begin to interject another language into some of our services? Can we disrupt our services by having someone read the Bible in a different language, while having the English translation alongside for others to follow?

There are some churches in the UK who have managed to engage in intercultural worship by using different languages and styles in their worship. Many churches might not be able to engage in intercultural worship with different languages because that requires certain skills, but we can start small, either by someone praying in another language or by sharing a blessing in another language.

Intercultural leadership

For any intercultural church to develop, grow and be sustained, it will require a visionary intercultural leadership who can embed this in the church's structure. An example in Scripture is the Antioch church (Acts 11), which had a visionary intercultural leadership in the persons of Barnabas and Paul. Barnabas, who had a dual identity as a Levite-Hebrew born in a Greek city and culture, intentionally sought out Paul for the new church plant in Antioch because Antioch was not in a Jewish settlement. Paul had a tripartite identity as a Jew born in Tarsus, a Greek city, who also had Roman citizenship. Both Barnabas and Paul understood Greek and other cultures and therefore helped to develop the new church plant in Antioch, which had people from North Africa and other regions.

Anderson Moyo commented, 'The Antioch church is a good model of a multi-ethnic church with a distinct identity in its establishment, leadership and ethnic mix' (2017, p. 67). An intercultural leadership will centre integration as an overarching principle as this is essential to create something distinct in that locality. An intercultural leadership will also drive the vision of an intercultural church and sustain it when it is difficult to continue. Leading a multicultural church is challenging, and therefore leading an intercultural church is *very* challenging. An intercultural leadership also enables an intercultural church to flourish through visible representation, modelling something evident for the church community to see. This fosters an atmosphere of integration rather than assimilation because the core of the church is shaped by integration.

Unmuting marginal voices and perspectives

Muted Group Theory was a communication theory used by anthropologists Edwin Ardener and Shirley Ardener to look at how marginalized groups are muted and excluded (Ardener, 2005). This was later applied to feminist theory to look at how women's perspectives had to conform to the male perspective in order to be accepted. The research of Usha Reifsnider, one of the other editors of this book, formulates the use of Muted Group Theory as a way to comprehend and articulate the long-term ideological shift that results from Christian conversion of Hindus in diaspora. The convert's expression is confined within a Western culture that mutes Majority World cultural experiences based upon a hierarchical system of dominance and subordination (Reifsnider, 2022a; 2022b). Muted Group Theory recognizes that there are dominant groups that have a dominant voice, thereby leading to the muteness of others.

Applying this theory to the development of intercultural churches will necessitate asking the question: who is muted in our churches because of their disability, class, age, nationality and so on? Whose voices do we need to unmute in our churches so that we can benefit from a wider perspective, and which dominant voices do we need to mute to allow that to happen? In other instances, it might just be the need to turn up the volume on certain voices and reduce the volume on other voices that are too loud.

Encouraging polyphonic voices

Following on from the process of unmuting muted voices in our churches will be the need to develop a polyphonic environment where different symbolic sounds can create a symphony.

One of the pillars in world Christianity is recognizing that mission is no longer flowing from one direction but can now be done from anywhere to everywhere. This is adequately termed 'polycentric missiology' (Yeh, 2016), recognizing the rise of and need for multiple centres of mission activity.

A further extension of polycentric thinking in mission studies is the idea of polyphonic voices: allowing a church or mission organization to intentionally create a space and atmosphere where different voices and perspectives can be heard. It is important to stress that the development of polyphonic voices in our churches cannot and should never be done in isolation but always in conjunction with unmuting muted voices. This is because if we have not attempted the hard work of unmuting marginal voices before entering the use of polyphonic voices, there is the danger of reverting to giving spaces to dominant groups and voices. Polyphonic voices can be very powerful after certain voices have been unmuted. The ideal is journeying towards having everyone in our church sharing and using their authentic voice and perspectives to build the church.

Intercultural justice

While it might be possible to develop a multicultural church without engaging in racial justice concerns, it is essential in growing an intercultural church to tackle racial justice concerns as part of the framework. This is because if intercultural churches are meant to tell a different narrative on multiculturalism, as argued before, they will have to lament, agitate and advocate on racial justice concerns that affect their members. Intercultural churches cannot ignore the concerns of their members who are asylum seekers, refugees and economic migrants.

Take, for example, a church that has a large number of African Caribbean and African members. It will be important for such a church to engage – if only for discussion and pastoral care – around issues that concern the Black community, such as criminal justice system, policing, education, mental health and health care. But one of the major challenges we face in the UK church is the danger of reducing racial justice concerns to a Black-and-white issue. While the Black experience is the most obvious because of the history of slavery and colonization, it is important to address racial injustices within other communities such as south Asians, Chinese and Latin Americans. What are the justice issues that need addressing with the arrival of Hong Kong migrants who are now part of our churches? What justice concerns need highlighting within the wider Chinese communities in the UK? What are the ongoing legacies of conquest, colonization and imperialism that Latin Americans suffered at the hands of Europeans that need tackling today?

To widen the parameters of racial justice, I have developed intercultural justice as a broader theological framework that can address racial justice concerns within other marginalized communities. Intercultural justice, therefore, is an attempt to situate the discourse on race and racial justice within the theological disciplines and framework of intercultural theology and world Christianity instead of limiting it to sociology and political philosophy. It is a broader lens of conceptualizing racial justice concerns within other marginalized cultures and ethnicities, rather than limiting its scope to the binary template of Black and white. It must be noted that intercultural justice is not a substitute for racial justice but rather a healthy addition that helps engage justice concerns from other oppressed communities that are not Black. It must also be noted and clarified that, because of its history, the Black experience still gives us a visible template to help develop thinking and activism within other communities.

Concluding Reflections

The chapter has explored the development of multicultural, multi-ethnic Britain in order to understand the emergence of multicultural churches. One of its conclusions is that Britain did not become multicultural because of the Windrush migrants, but that through successive migrations over a long period of its history became multicultural and multi-ethnic.

Politically, multiculturalism has become problematic – hence the narrative to control migration and manage multiculturalism. The chapter has therefore argued that in this contested space, we need an intercultural church that challenges society on multiculturalism and migration. I have proposed a five-way descriptive analysis of multicultural and intercultural churches to help understand the different approaches. This also helped to clarify the distinctions betweeen them, as well as the need for multicultural churches to journey towards becoming intercultural. This chapter has also highlighted the significance of intercultural churches, outlining four key rationales. Lastly, the chapter considered how we can develop intercultural churches, by looking at five key practices.

Bibliography

Aldous, Ben, Dunmore, Idina and Seevaratnam, Mohan, 2020, *Intercultural Church: Shared Learning from New Communities*, Oxford: Grove Books.

Anderson, A. David, 2004, *Multicultural Ministry: Finding your Church's Unique Rhythm*, Grand Rapids, MI: Zondervan.

Ardener, Shirley, 2005, 'Ardener's "Muted Groups": The genesis of an idea and its praxis', *Women and Language*, 28, No. 2, pp. 50–4, 72.

Arikawe, Tayo, 2013, 'Multi-ethnic or Multicultural Churches in Bristol?', in Olofinjana, Israel, ed., *Turning the Tables on Mission: Stories of Christians from the Global South in the UK*, Watford: Instant Apostle, pp. 133–47.

Bede, 2008, *The Ecclesiastical History of the English People*, Bertram Colgrave, Judith McClure and Roger Collins (trans.), Oxford: Oxford University Press.

Cartledge, Mark and Cheetham, David, eds, 2011, *Intercultural Theology: Approaches and Themes*, London: SCM Press.
Census, 2021, Office for National Statistics, https://www.ons.gov.uk/peoplepopulationandcommunity/culturalidentity/religion/bulletins/religionenglandandwales/census2021 (accessed 18.2.25).
Coleman, Kate, 2024, *Metamorph: Transforming Your Life and Leadership*, Birmingham: 100 Movements Publishing.
Emerson, Michael, 2006, *People of the Dream: Multiracial Congregations in the United States*, Princeton: Princeton University Press.
Frow, Mayerlene, 1997, *Roots of the Future: Ethnic Diversity in the Making of Britain*, London: Commission for Racial Equality.
Gentleman, Amelia, 2022, 'Windrush Scandal caused by "30 years of racist immigration laws"', 29 May, the *Guardian*, https://www.theguardian.com/uk-news/2022/may/29/windrush-scandal-caused-by-30-years-of-racist-immigration-laws-report (accessed 18.2.25).
Hardy, Andrew and Yarnell, Dan, eds, 2015, *Forming Multicultural Partnerships: Church Planting in a Divided Society*, Watford: Instant Apostle.
Hylton, Owen, 2009, *Crossing the Divide: A Call to Embrace Diversity*, Nottingham: Inter-Varsity Press.
Jagessar, Michael, 2015, *Ethnicity: The Inclusive Church Resource*, London: Darton, Longman & Todd.
Killingray, David and Edwards, Joel, 2007, *Black Voices: The Shaping of Our Christian Experience*, Nottingham: Inter-Varsity Press.
Kumbi, Hirpo, 2017, *The Culturally Intelligent Leader: Developing Multi-ethnic Communities in a Multicultural Age*, Watford: Instant Apostle.
Kundnani, Arun, 2007, 'Integrationism: The Politics of Anti-Muslim Racism', *Race and Class: A Journal of Racism, Empire and Globalisation*, Volume 48, No. 4, pp. 24–44, Institute of Race Relations, London.
Kwiyani, Harvey C., 2020, *Multicultural Kingdom: Ethnic Diversity, Mission and the Church*, London: SCM Press.
Milne, Bruce, 2006. *Dynamic Diversity: The New Humanity Church for Today and Tomorrow*, Nottingham: Inter-Varsity Press.
Moyo, Anderson, 2017, 'Church Planting considerations for African Reverse Missionaries in Britain in the Postmodern Era', in *African Voices: Towards African British Theologies*, Cumbria, UK: Langham Global Library.
Olofinjana, Israel, 2021, *Discipleship, Suffering and Racial Justice: Mission in a Pandemic World*, Oxford: Regnum Books.
Olofinjana, Israel, 2022, *The Legacy of Daniels Ekarte: Implications for the Urban and Public Mission of African Churches in the UK*, William Temple Foundation Temple Tract.
Olofinjana, Israel, ed., 2013, *Turning the Tables on Mission: Stories of Christians from the Global South in the UK*, Watford: Instant Apostle.
Otaigbe, Osoba, 2016, *Building Cultural Intelligence in Church and Ministry*, Milton Keynes: AuthorHouse UK.
Oxford Journal for Intercultural Mission, 2023, produced by St Paul's, Slough – the designated intercultural mission-resourcing hub in the Diocese of Oxford, available at: https://www.oxford.anglican.org/ojim-issue-one-spring-2023.php (accessed 18.2.25).

Patten, Malcolm, 2016, *Leading a Multicultural Church*, London: SPCK.

Reddie, Anthony, Abel-Boanerges, Seidel, Searle, Pam, eds, 2021, *Intercultural Preaching: Congregational Resources*, Oxford: Regents Park College.

Reifsnider, Usha, 2022a, 'Reclaiming British Gujarati Culture after Conversion to Evangelical Christianity', PhD thesis, University of Middlesex.

Reifsnider, Usha, 2022b, Series of Lectures on Theological Implications of Muted Group Theory, organised by Oxford Centre for Mission Studies (OCMS).

Resonance Band, 2011, Arts Release Ministry of WEC, available at: https://artsrelease.org/en/music-worship/playlists (accessed 18.2.25).

Root, John, 2018, *Worship in a Multi-ethnic Society*, Cambridge: Grove Books Limited.

Root, John, 2020, *Building Multi-Racial Churches*, London: Latimer Trust.

Snow, Martyn, 2024, *An Intercultural Church for a Multicultural World: Reflections on Gift Exchange*, London: Church House Publishing.

Walford, Charles, 2012, '"We need community cohesion": Ministers' pledge to end era of multiculturalism by appealing to "sense of British identity"', *The Daily Mail*, available at: https://www.dailymail.co.uk/news/article-2104049/Eric-Pickles-signals-end-multiculturalism-says-Tories-stand-majority.html?ITO=google_news_rss_feed (accessed 18.2.25).

Wise, David, 2022, 'Developing a genuinely multi-ethnic local church congregation: an auto-ethnographic investigation into Greenford Baptist Church 1987–2014', PhD thesis, University of Roehampton, available at: https://pure.roehampton.ac.uk/portal/en/studentTheses/developing-a-genuinely-multi-ethnic-local-church-congregation (accessed 18.2.25)

Yeh, Allen, 2016, *Polycentric Missiology: Twenty-first Century Mission from Everyone to Everywhere*, Downers Grove, IL: InterVarsity Press.

2

The Metaphor of Tapestry: A Theological Framing for Inter-ethnic Congregations

DAVID WISE

Introduction

From October 1987 until January 2019, I was a pastor at Greenford Baptist Church (GBC) in West London. During this time, the church transitioned from being a white British congregation to one with people from approximately 45 nationalities regularly attending. Every aspect of congregational life reflected the cultures from the different ethnicities that made up the congregation. GBC was considered to be a good example of an inter-ethnic church. In the autumn of 2017, I commenced doctoral research exploring how this transition took place. My research included focus groups and interviews with 47 research participants who were still, or had previously been, members of GBC. My aim was to see if there were any principles that I could uncover that might assist other church congregations wishing to take the journey towards inter-ethnicity.

In the concluding chapter of my thesis (Wise, 2022), I explore several interlocking components that seem to have enabled the transition that took place. I grouped these under four headings. The first is thinking that enabled transition. Under this heading is the tackling of racial prejudice and in particular the role of the tapestry metaphor. The second is attitudes that enabled transition; this surfaces in the practices of hospitality and vulnerability. The third is structures that enabled transition; here the key components are the Sunday morning meetings especially 'Connection Time' (this was a 25-minute segment in the middle of the two-and-a-half hour Sunday morning meeting that enabled and encouraged people to connect with each other), as well as the numerous social events with food and conversation. Finally, leadership that encouraged thinking, attitudes and structures that enabled transition. How some of these worked in practice is explored in Chapter 6.

In this chapter I will explore the theological thinking that lay behind the tapestry metaphor and its theological and practical significance. I have chosen to focus solely on the theology surrounding the tapestry metaphor that was uniquely used at GBC, but I believe has potential for use in other church contexts. In my thesis (Wise, 2022), there is extensive theological reflection on other aspects of inter-ethnic theology and on ecclesiology as it had developed at GBC. There is also engagement with a wide range of other academic theological material that seeks to address the issues of racism and the development of inter-ethnic church.

Tapestry as a Metaphor for Church

For around 25 of the 32 years I was at GBC, we used the metaphor of tapestry as a way of understanding the church. The metaphor was used during Sunday sermons and small-group discussions, but most significantly, it was a lens used by the GBC leaders as they looked at current and potential developments within the congregation.

The power of metaphor

There is extensive academic literature about metaphors. Here I want to draw on only two authors to illustrate the power that a metaphor can have to shape the way that people think and therefore behave. Craig Ott writing in the journal *Missiology* explores how biblical metaphors can aid intercultural communication of the gospel. He comments that 'metaphor is a powerful communication tool that not only illustrates truth, but can touch emotions and can shape cognitive functions' (Ott, 2014, p. 358). He points out that metaphor 'can communicate a whole complex set of meanings, relationships, dynamics and emotions' (2014, p. 360).

Raymond Gibbs, in a paper delivered at the 5th International Cognitive Linguistics Conference, asserts that 20 years of research had shown that 'metaphor is not merely a figure of speech, but is a specific mental mapping that influences a good deal of how people think, reason, and imagine in everyday life' (Gibbs, 1999, p. 145). As will become clear below, at GBC it seems from the research that the metaphor of tapestry had a profound effect on the way that the church developed and on how individuals behaved, not only within the church community but also in the other parts of their lives.

The biblical roots of the tapestry metaphor

It was my reading of Colossians 2.2, rendered in the Message Version as 'I want you to be woven into a tapestry of love', that led to my adoption of the tapestry metaphor as an image to guide the development of GBC. The underlying Greek verb rendered 'woven' is συμβιβάζώ. The standard Ancient Greek–English lexicon, Liddell and Scott, describes συμβιβάζώ as 'causal of συμβάινώ, *bring together*: Pass., *to be put together, to be knit together, framed*' (Liddell and Scott, 1968). New Testament commentators take a variety of positions on the interpretation of this verb. A detailed examination of the various options is not undertaken here, as I simply want to note that this rendering is how I understood and used this verse and that this use is supported by mainstream biblical commentators. Peter O'Brien in his Word Biblical Commentary states that 'the majority view ... takes the verb συμβιβάζω in the sense of "unite", "knit together", a meaning equally well known from ancient times' (O'Brien, 1982, p. 93).

At GBC, Colossians 2.2 was read in conjunction with Ephesians 2.10: 'we are God's workmanship' (all Bible quotations in this chapter are from the NIV unless otherwise stated). The underlying Greek noun here is ποίημα. Commentators note that ποίημα refers to a work of art or a masterpiece made by an artisan (Bruce, 1961, p. 52; Barth, 1974, p. 226; Hoehner, 2002, pp. 346–7; Thielman, 2010, p. 145; Fowl, 2012, p. 79). O'Brien made a further point:

> The term rendered *workmanship* which often appears in the LXX to denote creation as God's work, has the same nuance of the physical creation in its only other New Testament occurrence (Rom. 1.29). But here in Ephesians 2.10, which stresses what believers are because of God, the cluster of creation terms, including this word and *created*, along with *good works*, is applied directly to the *new creation*. (O'Brien, 1999, p. 178)

The significance of this meaning is that Romans 1.19–20 states that God can be 'clearly seen' through creation. This revealing of God takes place not only via the natural world but also via the church, God's new creation. GBC believed that as God wove the tapestry of GBC, God was revealed through the emerging image to those inside and outside of the church community.

Ephesians 3.10 states that 'His [God's] intent was that now, through the church, the manifold wisdom of God should be made known.'

O'Brien pointed out in his commentary that 'manifold' (πολυποίκιλο) 'was poetic in origin, referring to an intricately embroidered pattern of "many-coloured cloaks" or the manifold hues of a "garland of flowers"' (O'Brien, 1999, p. 245). 'Many-coloured cloaks' is reminiscent of the tapestry metaphor. David Byrd commented in his doctoral thesis:

> 'The manifold wisdom of God' in a real sense is the multiethnic [*sic*] wisdom of God. Further, this wisdom is 'made known through the church'. God intends for the church to display this incredible variety and diversity of peoples as one new body in Christ and the triumph of His wisdom. (Byrd, 2013, p. 94)

The most significant colours in a tapestry are not usually the ones that there are most of, which are often the background colours. The most significant colours are those that mark out detail. There may be only a few threads of a particular colour, but they can make a substantial contribution to the overall image. In the body metaphor for the church, found in 1 Corinthians 12, it is noted that parts that are 'weaker' or are hidden have been given 'greater honour' by God. This meant that at GBC we worked to ensure that, as far as possible, aspects of every ethnicity represented in the congregation were visible in the life of the church.

At GBC, the theological interpretation of the tapestry metaphor was framed by Revelation 7.9–12, in which the image of heaven is one with people 'from every nation, tribe, people and language' standing and worshipping God together. We believe that there is something eternal about people's ethnicity and language, that in the future, people from every single ethnic group would be worshipping God together and that in the meantime, people can anticipate, live out and reveal aspects of heaven in their corporate worship (Wise, 2004; 2009; 2018; 2021, p. 97).

Racism

Willie James Jennings in his book, *The Christian Imagination. The Theology and the Origins of Race* (2010), traces the origins of racism back to medieval Christian theology. Jennings developed the concept of 'the diseased social imagination', which he sees as a legacy from this period (2010, p. 6). By 'diseased social imagination', Jennings is referring to the way that whiteness is consciously and unconsciously imagined and taken as the norm, the standard against which everything else is assessed. Jennings also sees a key role for contemporary Christian theology in addressing 'the diseased social imagination'. It is my view that the tapestry metaphor developed at GBC was a way of imagining church that to some extent displaced the 'diseased' way of imagining it.

This is not the place for a detailed summary and critique of Jennings' argument. However, I do here want to briefly outline two events that Jennings sees as key in the development of the 'diseased social imagination'. The first of these is the arrival of 235 African slaves in Lagos, Portugal on 8 August 1444. Jennings draws on a detailed account of their sale written by an eyewitness, the Royal Chronicler Zurara. The account is theological; there is prayer, there is the payment of a tithe to the church, and there is the expectation that these slaves become 'good and true Christians'.

Jennings comments:

> Something more urgent and more life altering is taking place in the Christian world, namely, the auctioning of bodies without regard to any form of human connection ... This auction will draw ritual power from Christianity itself while mangling the narratives it evokes, establishing a distorted pattern of displacement. Christianity will assimilate this pattern of displacement. Not just slave bodies, but displaced slave bodies, will come to represent a natural state. From this position they will be relocated into Christian identity. The backdrop of their existence will be, from this moment forward, the market. (Jennings, 2010, p. 22)

Zurara also described the slaves being valued according to their skin colour. Those who are almost white were viewed positively; those who are Black were viewed as 'deformed' (Jennings, 2010, p. 23). Jennings comments:

> Herein lies the deepest theological problem. Zurara brings into view the crossing of a threshold into a distorting vision of creation. This distorting vision of creation will lodge itself deeply in Christian thought, damaging doctrinal trajectories. (Jennings, 2010, p. 25)

From this distorting trajectory, Jennings argues that 'whiteness emerges' as 'an organizing concept' that is used to reshape colonial life and lands. Also from this trajectory, the partnership was born between commercial exploitation and the mission to bring those considered 'lost' inside the Catholic Church so that they would be 'converted' and receive salvation (Jennings, 2010, pp. 25–7). 'From the beginning of the colonialist moment, being white placed one at the centre of the symbolic and real reordering of space. In a real sense, whiteness comes into being as a form of landscape with all its facilitating realities' (Jennings, 2010, p. 59).

The second event is the arrival from Spain of a Jesuit, Jose de Acosta Porres in Lima, Peru, in 1572. After arriving in Peru, Acosta came to view the natives as stupid, ignorant and lacking intellectual ability. Jennings comments that this is:

> far more than problems of adjustment to the New World. He draws theology and theological tradition into an evaluative form from which it cannot escape. What comes into effect is a new form of ecclesial habitus in which the performance of theology – in teaching, preaching, writing, and other ministry – becomes the articulation of processes of colonialist evaluation. These processes of evaluation carry within them what Acosta perceives as the soteriological and social distance between himself and his student barbarians. (Jennings, 2010, p. 105)

Jennings describes other developments in Acosta's thinking as 'the ground upon which the ideologies of white supremacy will grow' (2010, p. 109). He further asserts:

> What will grow out of this horrid colonial arrangement is a form of imperialism far more flexible, subtle, and virulent than could be explained by appeals to cultural difference or ethnic chauvinism. This imperialist form drew life from Christianity's lifeblood, from its missionary mandate and its mission reflexes. (Jennings, 2010, p. 112)

Jennings' contention is that these events came to shape the way that white people in the Western world view people whom they perceive as other than white.

Willie Jennings' later book *After Whiteness* (2020) 'reflects on the distortions wrought by whiteness' (back cover). Although the context for this book is the theological academy in the USA, the conceptualization he develops seems to be a helpful way of reflecting on the transition that took place at GBC, and the theological implications of the tapestry metaphor. Jennings notes that the distortion he observed in the American theological academy is a 'microcosm' of problems in Western education and as a result in Western society as a whole (2020, p. 7). Jennings draws on the understanding he developed in *The Christian Imagination* to assert that the goal of Western Education/Society is to promote 'white self-sufficient masculinity' (2020, p. 8). In contrast, Jennings claims God's goal is the creation of 'the crowd, that is the gathering of hurting and hungry people who need God ... people who would not under normal circumstances ever want to be near each other' (2020, p. 13).

The central part of *After Whiteness* gives numerous examples and illustrations from Jennings' lived experience of how 'the tragedy of distorted institutional practice ... steals from people what God gives to every creature ... the desire to build together' (2020, p. 99). In the final two chapters of *After Whiteness*, Jennings sought to develop an alternative way forward for the theological academy in particular and for Western education in general. What is significant here are the parallels between Jennings' suggestive concepts and the use of the tapestry metaphor at GBC.

Jennings writes of a 'diseased centeredness ... sickened by whiteness' growing from 'the pedagogical imperialism of the Euro-colonialists' that shaped education, language, ideas and 'rituals of evaluation' (2020, pp. 140–1). He describes the 'consistent refusal ... to place oneself in the journey of others ... where I am willingly changed ... by non-white peoples' and thereby 'to release oneself to the crowd' (2020, p. 141). It is striking, from the findings of the research at GBC, that people did allow themselves to be changed and enriched by their encounters with people from different ethnicities. Jennings further comments that 'in the long histories of Western colonial education, rarely if ever have people or peoples been allowed to name and voice ... disagreements separate from the refereeing positioning of whiteness' (2020, p. 142). Again, the research shows evidence that within GBC the ability to disagree without whiteness being the reference point was developed.

Writing of friendship Jennings comments: 'Friendship is a real thing where people open their living to one another, allowing the paths of life to crisscross ... making possible a reality of intimacy, communication, reciprocity and mutuality that builds from a deepening sense of connection' (2020, p. 147). Jennings further observes that 'we inhabit a social world constricted through whiteness that has left us with limited options for imagining how we might be with each other' (2020, p. 151).

However, it seems to be easier to critique whiteness and the way that it distorts relationships and communities, than to envisage what a healthy multi-ethnic community might be like. The research shows that the research participants at GBC had developed friendships that allowed 'the paths of life to crisscross'. From these friendships a community was built where whiteness as an organizing conviction had been decentred.

At GBC, a viable and stable genuinely multi-ethnic church congregation seems to have been formed. Although practical and structural changes were clearly important, the prominent role of the tapestry metaphor in the life of the church seems to have been a crucial element in enabling this process. It is significant that the tapestry metaphor envisages engagement that moves beyond just Black and white. The ethnic landscape in Greenford was far more complex than a binary construct of Black and white with Asians, Chinese, Eastern Europeans, Latin Americans and Middle Easterners also among the church members. The tapestry metaphor, with a diverse range of colours, is a visualization of the inclusion of people from any ethnic group.

In Colossians 3, as part of a challenge to the readers to live holy lives by putting off lying, immorality, filthy language etc. and instead putting on compassion, gentleness, forgiveness etc., the writer makes the statement, 'Here there is no ... barbarian, Scythian, slave or free, but Christ is all, and is in all' (Col. 3.5–14). James Dunn observes that 'the thought is clearly that Christ makes irrelevant ethnic, cultural and social distinctions ... in the church' (Dunn, 1996, p. 223). Dunn points out that the term 'barbarian' 'carried a derogatory significance' referring to someone who only spoke an 'unintelligible language'. 'Scythians' were 'synonymous with crudity, excess and ferocity ... Josephus ... refers to Scythians as "... little different from wild beasts"' (Dunn, 1996, pp. 225–6). It is not difficult to find in our contemporary world parallels in the way people from one ethnic group are viewed by people from another. The point in Colossians is not that in Christ all distinctions vanish – people still reflect their own ethnicity; the point is that in Christ all are equal, all equally made in God's image.

I am a practical theologian, and so it is important for me to look at how this theological approach worked in practice. As a part of my research into the transition at GBC, I conducted a pilot research project into the significance of the tapestry metaphor at GBC. I conducted five interviews with people who had been, or still were, a part of GBC's leadership.

The Impact within GBC of the Tapestry Metaphor

From the analysis of the interviews, five themes emerged that illustrate the significance of the tapestry metaphor at GBC. The names used below are pseudonyms that reflect the interviewee's self-described ethnicity and gender.

Subconscious identity

The five research participants each believed that the tapestry metaphor had entered GBC's shared subconscious identity. Kunle said: 'It [the tapestry metaphor] has become, if you like, the DNA of the church because everything is woven together and conscious effort is made to live that out in the way that we do things, the way we relate to each other and ... the way we live our lives as well.'

Brian commented: 'Something I heard someone said in a conversation yesterday made me think that is the tapestry metaphor coming up, even though they may not say that or realize it for themselves ... that is whatever their core understanding is.'

Alvita related that people 'have kind of in a sense grown accustom [sic] to it being in a sense a natural part of what the church is about. Then they have kind of just grabbed hold of it ... welcoming people of all cultures'.

The perspective of Alvita, Brian and Kunle, based on their lived experience as leaders at GBC, was that the tapestry metaphor was both at a conscious and a subconscious level shaping the congregational life, behaviour and self-identity at GBC.

Experiencing difference in unity

Dianne commented: 'In order to appreciate a tapestry, you need the different colours. You need the different shades and tones, so therefore in a congregation there needs to be appreciation of the differences there are, rather than trying to make everybody the same.'

Kunle observed: 'The tapestry is where every ethnic and cultural group is woven together and they enrich each other to make life, if you like, better in terms of the way that we worship God.' Brian, commenting on worship within a recent Sunday service, said: 'I don't think you would get that unless the tapestry metaphor was at the core of the church and there was that understanding of our uniqueness within togetherness.' Alvita commented: 'It is all about the different mix so to speak. People from different backgrounds coming together, being in one place, being as family ... all his [God's] people of different nations, colours, class, being together'.

Each of the research participants talked about how, in their lived experience, the tapestry metaphor helped enable difference to be experienced in a context of unity. This feature is one of the distinctives of the tapestry metaphor that differences are maintained, even celebrated, rather than there being an attempt to produce a blend.

Being 'woven together' leading to personal change

Kunle said: 'The strength of each group comes out when we are all together ... we are able to be a better people than if we just look at our individual cultural or ethnic group ... to actually see people as equals, rather than one group being inferior to the other.'

Brian commented: 'It means this brother or sister from another ethnicity or people-group is able to be my close friend, even though we might have a difference of opinion or a different viewpoint, we can still at our core talk about it, reconcile and walk forward together, recognizing our differences and even celebrating them.'

For both Kunle and Brian, one aspect of the impact of the tapestry metaphor was a change in the way they viewed people from other ethnicities. They came to appreciate that difference was something they could celebrate and that could be a source to enrich their own lives. Brian further commented that a single person from another ethnicity 'can bring a difference without having to think I'm only one person over here from one ethnic group. They realize they have something to play out in this'. The single thread of a different colour can make a significant contribution to the emerging picture.

Dianne saw the tapestry metaphor as a tool to help combat racism:

> It is that awareness that racism was around ... and seen as this is not who we should be. This is not what the Gospel says ... If the congregation could be self-aware, it is that recognition of that's not how it should be and therefore once that's identified, having the strength and the tools to say no, what needs to change.

With the tapestry metaphor, there is no 'us' and 'them'; rather all are 'us', woven together as part of the same picture with all of the ethnic differences being incorporated.

Embodying the gospel

Brian said: 'First and foremost, the Gospel is about reconciliation ... we, especially here in west London in our multi-cultural, multi-ethnic, diverse town are embodying reconciliation between people groups ... that shows into the community outside.'

Dianne commented that for her the tapestry metaphor applied to all of life not just church: 'For me, particularly living in London, being aware of the different nationalities and ethnicities that I live and work with, because I think the metaphor is a good one and a valuable one – I don't think it just applies to church. It can apply to every area of life.'

For Alvita the tapestry metaphor 'kind of reflects what God wants us to do or what he wants us to be ... that is just a representation of what it will be like in heaven'.

The living out of the tapestry metaphor meant, in the view of the research participants, that the gospel was embodied within GBC in ways that otherwise might not have been the case. In particular the embodiment of reconciliation, which Brian describes as 'at the heart of the gospel', was seen by the local community in the way that people from many different ethnicities within GBC shared life together. At GBC, guided by the tapestry metaphor, a community of people united in their Christian faith yet maintaining their ethnic identity and diversity was visible, which GBC believed revealed something of God.

The cost of living the metaphor

Several of the research participants commented that the changes that had taken place within GBC during its transition had been difficult for some to cope with and that some people had withdrawn from the congregation.

The Wider Significance of the Tapestry Metaphor

As we have seen, five research participants, all of whom were drawn from the leadership of GBC, believed that the tapestry metaphor had a significant role in shaping the development of the GBC congregation. The tapestry metaphor was a concept that people could easily grasp. The research participants believed that the metaphor had become an aspect of GBC's self-identity that helped shape the experiencing of unity within a context of diversity, that it helped facilitate personal change, and that it helped embody reconciliation. The research participants' responses pointed to the acceptance and celebration of ethnic difference in the context of an experience of unity that became a hallmark of GBC and was rooted in living out the tapestry metaphor of church.

In *The Christian Imagination*, Jennings introduced the concept of a 'diseased social imagination' after relating an account of a visit by two white evangelists to his home in Grand Rapids, Michigan, and an account of the response by some Dutch Reformed professors to his first sermon in the chapel of Calvin College where he was a student

(Jennings, 2010, pp. 1–6). Rooted in Jennings' lived experience is an awareness that something is 'missing'. That something is a sustained 'ability to see the profound connections' between 'very different people' (Jennings, 2010, p. 7).

Romans 12.2 says, 'Do not conform any longer to the pattern of this world, but be transformed by the renewing of your mind.' 'Diseased social imagination' needs transforming for the potential joining between different people to take place. I began my research with a desire to understand what had taken place at GBC that enabled the creation of a genuinely inter-ethnic church congregation. Early in my research, I discovered the significance of the role of the tapestry metaphor. However, it was not until I engaged with Jennings' writing that I saw that potentially the tapestry metaphor was of crucial significance in that it displaced the 'diseased social imagination'. Jennings poses the question in his commentary on Acts: 'Could you imagine a new way of seeing and being yourself, a way that weaves together the ways of many people?' (2017, p. 156). The findings of my research imply that at GBC, a new imagination, in the form of the tapestry metaphor, took root that, to some degree, overwrote the 'diseased social imagination' articulated by Jennings. There seems to have been transformation by the renewal of the mind.

Conclusion

What developed at GBC seems to be an embodiment of a theological conviction that all human beings are of equal value. In Chapter 6 in this book, I explore aspects of this including the use of first language, prayer and worship (including dance) that drew on styles and customs from 'back home', the restructuring of Sunday morning meetings, food, artwork and flags, and the experience of Third-Culture Kids, all of which helped people to feel fully accepted and welcome.

It is my view that the use of the tapestry metaphor was a crucial component that helped enable these developments. It is a metaphor that is simple to grasp but profound in its implications. I believe that using this metaphor in other church congregations could help with their own journey towards becoming inter-ethnic.

Bibliography

Barth, M., 1974, *Ephesians 1–3: Introduction, Translation, and Commentary*, New York: Doubleday.
Byrd, D. M., 2013, 'The Multiethnic, Multicongregational Church: Developing a Model for Urban Church Revitalization', PhD thesis, Mid-America Baptist Theological Seminary.
Bruce, F. F., 1961, *The Epistle to the Ephesians*, Basingstoke: Pickering Paperbacks.
Dunn, J. D. G., 1996, *The Epistles to the Colossians and to Philemon*, Carlisle: Paternoster Press, and Grand Rapids, MI: William B. Eerdmans Publishing Company.
Fowl, S. E., 2012, *Ephesians: A Commentary*, Louisville, KY: John Knox Press.
Gibbs, R. W., 1999, 'Taking metaphor out of our heads and putting it into the cultural world', in Gibbs, R. W. and Steen, G. J., eds, *Metaphor in Cognitive Linguistics: Selected papers from the 5th International Cognitive Linguistics Conference, Amsterdam, 1997*, Philadelphia: John Benjamins Publishing Company, pp.145–66.
Hoehner, H. W., 2002, *Ephesians: An Exegetical Commentary*, Grand Rapids, MI: Baker Academic.
Jennings, W. J., 2010, *The Christian Imagination: Theology and the Origins of Race*, New Haven, CT: Yale University Press.
Jennings, W. J., 2017, *Acts: A Theological Commentary on the Bible*, Louisville, KY: Westminster/John Knox Press.
Jennings, W. J., 2020, *After Whiteness: An Education in Belonging*, Grand Rapids, MI: Wm. B. Eerdmans Publishing Co.
Liddell, H. G. and Scott, R., 1968, *A Greek–English Lexicon* (9th edn), London: Oxford University Press.
O'Brien, P. T., 1982, *Colossians, Philemon: Word Biblical Commentary, Volume 44*, Waco, TX: Word Books.
O'Brien, P. T., 1999, *The Letter to the Ephesians*, Cambridge, UK: William B. Eerdmans.
Ott, C., 2014, 'The power of biblical metaphors for the contextualized communication of the gospel', *Missiology: An International Review*, 42, No. 4, pp. 357–74.
Thielman, F., 2010, *Ephesians*, Grand Rapids, MI: Baker Academic.
Wise, D., 2004, 'A Taste of Heaven?', *Ministry Today*, 31, available at: https://www.ministrytoday.org.uk/magazine/issues/31/187 (accessed 19.2.2025).
Wise, D., 2009, Greenford Baptist Church in 'Worship: A Taste of Heaven?', *The South African Baptist Journal of Theology*, 18, pp. 225–8.
Wise, D., 2018, 'Greenford Baptist Church, London', in *Baptists Together*, Spring, pp 17–18.
Wise, D., 2021, 'Understanding Intercultural Congregations', in Reddie, A. G., Boanerges, S. A. and Searle, P., eds, *Intercultural Preaching*, Oxford: Centre for Baptist Studies in Oxford, pp. 84–98.
Wise, D., 2022, 'Developing a genuinely multi-ethnic local church congregation: an auto-ethnographic investigation into Greenford Baptist Church 1987–2014', PhD thesis, University of Roehampton, available at: https://pure.roehampton.ac.uk/portal/en/studentTheses/developing-a-genuinely-multi-ethnic-local-church-congregation (accessed 18.2.25)

3

You Are Home! The Family Metaphor and Its Impact on Understanding Church and Intercultural Communities in Ephesians

OSCAR JIMÉNEZ

Introduction

The Epistle to the Ephesians paints a vivid portrait of the church in all its cosmic significance (see Bruce, 1971, pp. 5–16; Dodd, 1929, pp. 1224–5). In Ephesians, perhaps more than in any other New Testament writing, the church is elevated to its highest conception – not merely as a human institution, but as the very body of Christ – the fullness of him who fills all in all (Eph. 1.23). This exalted ecclesiology answers the question, 'Who is the people of God?'

It is important to clarify, at the outset of this chapter, that I am writing from the perspective that Paul wrote Ephesians as a circular letter to churches throughout Asia Minor, including Ephesus, around AD 60–1 (Moo, 2021; Cohick, 2020; Arnold, 2010). Drawing from three elements within the text, it is reasonable to conclude that the majority of the recipients of Ephesians seem to be Gentiles, most likely living in Asia Minor.

First, Paul addresses the Gentiles directly throughout the letter (Eph. 2.11; 3.1, 6, 8; 4.17). As Dahl (2000, p. 441) correctly notices, the writer focuses primarily on the Gentiles' status and lifestyles, which the author describes in somewhat negative terms (Eph. 2.1–3, 11–12; 4.17–19; 5.3–13). Second, the author deliberately emphasizes the differences between Gentiles ('you') and Jews ('us'). Intriguingly, the writer never alludes to the Jews directly, but deploys pronouns and the phrase, 'those who are close' (Eph. 2.13). This might imply that while Paul talks *about* the Jews, he talks *to* the Gentiles; they were the first recipients of this letter. As Rosen-Zvi and Ophir (2015, p. 16) write, 'the Gentiles become [the addressees] of an entire theological formation'.

Third, the letter defines the members of God's people as a broader community: Ἐκκλησία appears nine times in Ephesians (Eph. 1.20; 3.10, 20; 5.23, 24, 25, 27, 29, 32), and it is never used to refer to a particular community, but rather to refer to a universal community. Since this is the case, answering the question, 'Who are God's people?' becomes even more poignant.

Scholars have long grappled with the richness and complexity of Ephesians, proposing various interpretations of its genre, purpose and central themes. For instance, German scholarship has primarily focused on the importance of the church as the main subject of Ephesians (see Merklein, 1973; Gnilka, 2002; Burger, 1975; Fischer, 1973) while Anglo approaches have been more concerned with identifying unifying motifs (see Arnold, 1989; Smith, 2011; Gombis, 2004). It makes sense that German scholarship has focused on the importance of the church. As Morgan (2023, p. 116) wrote recently, 'the ἐκκλησία, the church, is not a footnote to Pauline theology; it is at the very heart of that theology.' However, the term ἐκκλησία – assembly or gathering – is one of the many terms Paul uses to describe the church's nature and internal dynamics.

This chapter is structured in two parts. Part 1 provides the exegetical foundations, examining the literary features of the letter to the Ephesians in its historical context. Part 2 explores the implications of this analysis for contemporary Christian theology, ecclesiology, and practices, with a particular focus on intercultural communities today.

Part 1: Exegetical Foundations: The Concept of the Family in Ephesians

In this study, I argue that the answer to the question 'Who is the people of God?' and the understanding of Paul's vision of the church as an intercultural community lies in Ephesians' central thesis: *In love, king Jesus has incorporated believers into the Father's household as beloved children* (this is my understanding of Paul's central theme). By employing conceptual metaphor theory, I will explore how the experience of being incorporated into God's family shapes the understanding of church and intercultural communities. This methodology will allow us to move beyond a mere literary analysis, to grasp the reality Paul might be trying to convey in Ephesians.

As we will learn, the family is not just a rhetorical device or 'fictive kinship' in Ephesians, but rather a Spirit-created reality that redefines identity, reshapes relationships and revolutionizes the understanding of church life. Seeing church through this lens breaks down barriers between Jews and Gentiles, creating a new, intercultural family 'in Christ'. Or said differently, understanding church as a family prescribes the nature of relationships within the church, fostering mutual love, respect and unity amidst diversity.

Analysis of Ephesians' Central Thesis

In love

The often-ignored concept of love is a fundamental thread woven throughout the Epistle to the Ephesians. In the letter's opening chapter, Paul declares that 'In love he predestined us for adoption to sonship through Jesus Christ' (Eph. 1.4–5, NIV throughout). According to Paul, love is the motivating force behind God's plan. This statement is not merely rhetorical; it sets the stage for the entire epistle, presenting divine love as the wellspring from which all subsequent acts and affirmations flow. The apostle further emphasizes this by praying for the Ephesians to have the Spirit of wisdom and revelation, so that they may know God better (Eph. 1.17). While love is not explicitly mentioned in this prayer (Eph. 1.17–23), the desire for deeper knowledge of God implicitly includes understanding his love, as will become clear in the epistle's second prayer in Chapter 3.

Chapter 2 builds upon this foundation by illustrating the transformative effect of God's love. Paul contrasts believers' former state as 'children of wrath' with their new status as objects of God's love (Eph. 2.3–4). This juxtaposition serves to highlight the radical nature of believers' transformation, which is attributed explicitly to God's love: 'But because of his great love for us, God, who is rich in mercy, made us alive with Christ' (Eph. 2.4–5).

The theme of love reaches a crescendo in Chapter 3, where Paul prays that Christ may dwell in believers' hearts through faith, and that they may be 'rooted and established in love' (Eph. 3.17). The apostle reiterates the importance of comprehending 'how wide and long and high and deep is the love of Christ' (Eph. 3.18–19), suggesting that understanding Christ's love is crucial for spiritual maturity and for experiencing the fullness of God. This chapter presents love not merely as an attribute of God or a characteristic of believers, but as the very essence of the Christian life and the key to spiritual growth.

In Chapter 4, Paul urges believers to 'speak the truth in love' as part of growing into maturity in Christ (Eph. 4.15). The instructions to put off the old self and put on the new self, created to be like God in 'true righteousness and holiness' (Eph. 4.22–24), imply a life characterized by love. This is made explicit in the command to 'be kind and compassionate to one another, forgiving each other, just as in Christ God forgave you' (Eph. 4.32). These are the practical expressions of love in the Christian community.

Chapter 5 opens with an explicit exhortation that encapsulates the letter's emphasis on love: 'Follow God's example, therefore, as dearly loved children and walk in the way of love' (Eph. 5.1–2). This exhortation directly connects believers' status as God's children with the imperative to love, echoing the adoption theme introduced in Chapter 1. In the rest of the chapter, Paul presents Christ's sacrificial love as the model for Christian behaviour, particularly in the context of marriage. The instruction for husbands to 'love your wives, just as Christ loved the church' (Eph. 5.25) not only provides practical guidance, but also reinforces the parallel between Christ's love for the church and the love that should characterize Christian families.

Chapter 6 completes the thematic arc – the letter concludes with a blessing of love from God the Father (Eph. 6.23) – forming an *inclusio* with the opening of the letter. In a nutshell, throughout Ephesians, love is presented as the foundation of God's salvific plan (Chapter 1), the transformative power that gives new life to believers (Chapter 2), the essence of Christ's relationship with the church (Chapter 3), the guiding principle for Christian conduct (Chapter 4), and the model for human relationships, particularly within the family (Chapter 5). This pervasive emphasis on love demonstrates that the incorporation of believers into God's family 'in love' is indeed central to the letter's message and structure.

King Jesus

In the letter to the Ephesians, Paul portrays Jesus as the expected king. The repeated use of the phrase 'in Christ' emphasizes both the believers' location under Christ's reign as well as their participation in his kingdom (see Campbell, 2012; Morgan, 2019). The use of 'in Christ' (ἐν Χριστῷ = in the Messiah = king Jesus) and its variants occur over 30 times (see Hewitt, 2020). This phrase suggests a distinctly locative sense that extends to living under the lordship and protection of Christ (see Morgan, 2020).

In Chapter 1, Paul states that God 'blessed us in Christ with every spiritual blessing' (Eph. 1.3), suggesting that to be 'in Christ' is to be within the sphere of his royal influence and benevolence. The author goes on to say that God's purpose is 'to bring unity to all things in heaven and on earth under Christ' (Eph. 1.10). This language of unification under Christ further reinforces the image of his kingship. What is more, in Ephesians 1.20–21, Paul describes Christ in royal terms, beginning with the opening blessing where God is described as having 'seated him at his right hand in the heavenly realms, far above all rule and authority, power and dominion' (Eph. 1.20–21). This language evokes the imagery of enthronement, placing Christ in a position of supreme authority. Paul then concludes his prayer saying that God 'placed all things under his feet and appointed him to be head over everything for the church' (Eph. 1.22). In brief, this chapter portrays Christ as the cosmic ruler.

Chapter 2 develops this theme when the transformation of believers is described in terms of a change of location and allegiance: 'And God raised us up with Christ and seated us with him in the heavenly realms in Christ Jesus' (Eph. 2.6). The spatial metaphor places believers in the throne room with Christ, underlining their incorporation into his kingdom (being children = being co-heirs = ruling along with Christ). Later in the chapter, Paul uses the 'in Christ' language to describe the unification of Jews and Gentiles into one new humanity. This unity is achieved 'in Christ Jesus' (Eph. 2.13) and 'in him' (Eph. 2.21–22), portraying Christ as the royal figure who brings peace and reconciliation to formerly hostile groups (see Jiménez, 2022, pp. 84–123). This portrayal fits well with ancient concepts of kingship, where a ruler's primary role was to maintain peace and unity within the realm.

In Chapters 3 and 4, the phrase 'in Christ' is used in connection with the revelation of the 'mystery' of God's plan (Eph. 3.4, 11) and the unity of the faith (Eph. 4.13). Therefore, to be 'in Christ' is to be privy to the king's plans and to participate in the unified life of his kingdom. And the ethical exhortations in Chapters 4—6 can be understood as instructions for proper conduct within Christ's realm. The letter concludes with a call to 'be strong in the Lord and in his mighty power' (Eph. 6.10), followed by the armour of God. This military imagery, when considering the royal Christology developed throughout the letter, evokes the picture of believers as soldiers in Christ's army, protected by his power and fighting under his banner.

In conclusion, to be 'in Christ' means to be incorporated into his kingdom, to live under his lordship, to enjoy his protection and blessings, and to participate in his temporal and eternal purposes.

Beloved children

From the outset of the letter, Paul establishes the believers' status as beloved children. In Chapter 1, he writes that God predestined believers for adoption to sonship through Jesus Christ (Eph. 1.5). This adoption is rooted in love: 'In love he predestined us' (Eph. 1.4–5). The language of predestination and adoption emphasizes both the sovereignty of God (kingship) and the intimate relationship believers now have with Him (kinship).

This theme develops further in Chapter 2, where Paul contrasts the believers' former state as 'children of wrath' (Eph. 2.3) with their new reality as objects of God's great love (Eph. 2.4). This transformation is not merely a label change but a fundamental shift in their relationship with God and with each other. Again, Paul describes this change using both royal and familial imagery. As a powerful king, God rescues believers from their captivity to sin and death: 'But because of his great love for us, God, who is rich in mercy, made us alive with Christ even when we were dead in transgressions' (Eph. 2.4–5). Yet this same act of power also brings them into an intimate family relationship: 'Consequently, you are no longer foreigners and strangers, but fellow citizens with God's people and also members of his household' (Eph. 2.19). Their new status as beloved children grants them unprecedented access to the Father: 'For through him we both have access to the Father by one Spirit' (Eph. 2.18).

In Chapter 3, Paul presents Christ's love as a vast, multi-dimensional space, inviting believers 'to grasp how wide and long and high and deep is the love of Christ' (Eph. 3.18). This spatial metaphor portrays Christ's love as the all-encompassing reality in which believers exist. Paul then elaborates on this concept by describing Christ's love as a soil and a foundation: 'being rooted and established in love' (Eph. 3.17). So just as plants draw sustenance from the soil and buildings stability from their foundation, God's people as a community are to be grounded in Christ's love, deriving their spiritual nourishment and firmness from it.

Moving to Chapter 5, Paul further develops what it means to live as beloved children. He presents love as a path, exhorting believers to 'walk in the way of love, just as Christ loved us' (Eph. 5.2). The dynamic shifts the focus from being rooted in love to actively moving along the path of love, with Christ, the beloved Son, as the guide and exemplar for God's adopted children. Paul then characterizes this path by describing Christ's love as 'a fragrant offering and sacrifice to God' (Eph. 5.2). This olfactory experience illuminates how God's beloved children should live

– in sacrificial love that pleases their Father. Just as a fragrant aroma pervades its surroundings, the sacrificial love of Christ should permeate the lives of God's children as they journey along this path.

Paul weaves together space, soil, building, path and fragrant sacrifice – all connected to Christ – to help us understand what it means to be 'beloved children'. Christ is both the environment in which they exist and the way of life they are called to pursue. Being beloved children involves not only receiving love, but also being thoroughly transformed by God's beloved Son's love, which is expressed in every aspect of life through a sacrificial living that pleases God. In this way, God's beloved children grow to reflect the character of their divine family, embodying the love that defines their new identity in Christ.

The concept of 'beloved children' shapes the believers' understanding of salvation (adoption), their relationship with God (intimacy with the Father), their ethical behaviour (imitating God), and their relationships with each other (family bonds transcending cultural divisions). God's people are those who are loved by the Father-King, and from the wellspring of this love, are empowered to love others and live as a unified family in a divided world.

In his excellent work, *Self-designations and Group Identity in the New Testament*, Trebilco (2014, p. 16) explains that 'the most common word used as a term of address … in the New Testament is ἀδελφοί – brothers and sisters'. In the same vein, and building on Trebilco's work, Darko (2016, p. 333) argues against scholars who see 'Ephesians [departing] from the Pauline notion of "fictive siblings" to construct the social identity of its readers along the lines of the patriarchal mores of its time'. He then concludes that 'Ephesians … adopts fictive kinship lexemes to construct the identity of the church as the multi-ethnic household of God in which mutual interdependence and concord are imperative' (Darko, 2016, p. 345).

Although I agree with Darko's conclusion, I struggle with the terminology of 'fictive siblings/kinship' for two reasons: first, 'fictive' coveys the idea of something being false or unreal; and second, because it ignores the metaphorical nature of this language, which leads authors to speak about the implications for church life as a paraphrase rather than a lens.

Family and Conceptual Metaphor Theory

Lakoff and Johnson (2003, p. 5) defined a metaphor as 'understanding and experiencing one … thing in terms of another'. Later, Dancygier and Sweetser (2014, p. 14) defined a metaphor as a 'unidirectional mapping projecting conceptual material' from one frame (the Source) on to another frame (the Target). What is key, as Jindo (2013, p. 2.8) summarizes, is how a metaphor provides two types of knowledge: 'propositional' – 'descriptive knowledge about beings, conditions, or events (*what* people think, feel, or believe)' and 'perspectival' – the viewpoint from which the reader unconsciously ends up seeing the scenario the metaphor describes '(*how* people think, feel, or believe)'. Returning to the biblical text, Paul taps into the audience's experience, living in a cultural world where people were incorporated into a royal family, via adoption (the Source) to speak about the audience's relationship with God and with their fellow believers (the Target). And this should not be surprising. As Talbert (2007, p. 16) suggests: 'One must recognize that the audience functions not only as the cause of the composition of Ephesians but also the catalyst for the selection of its language, style, arguments, and *topoi*.'

This dual function of metaphors – conveying both propositional and perspectival knowledge – effectively casts Paul's use of the church as a family in Ephesians as a kind of participatory drama. Just as a drama does not merely describe events but invites the audience into a new reality, Paul's metaphorical language does not simply inform his readers about the church; it transforms their very understanding of reality and their place within it. The household becomes a stage upon which the cosmic drama of redemption unfolds, with believers cast not as mere spectators, but as active participants in God's household. This dramatic quality of the metaphor explains its power to reshape identities, redefine relationships and revolutionize the readers' world-view. As we study Paul's use of the family metaphor in Ephesians, we are not just uncovering static theological concepts, but tracing the contours of a divine drama that continues to unfold in the life of the church today.

Jeffers (1999, p. 238) explains that 'the most significant feature of the Roman household (*familia*) was that its power was concentrated in the hands of the male head, the *paterfamilias*'. As Saller (1994, p. 75) and White (2016, p. 172) discuss, *familia* basically refers to all the persons who are under the power (*potestas*) of the *paterfamilias* either by nature (i.e. descent) or by law (i.e. adoption or ownership).

The household was so central to life in the first century that it became a metaphor – THE ROMAN EMPIRE IS A HOUSEHOLD – that explained and structured people's perception of the nation: the nation was a household, and the emperor was the *pater* of the Empire. According to Cicero:

> The first bond of union is that between husband and wife; the next, that between parents and children; then we find one home *[domus]* with everything in common; and this is the foundation *[principium]* of the city and, as it were, the seedbed *[seminarium]* of the state. (Cicero, *De officiis* 1.54; see further in Lacey, 1987, pp. 121–44)

So the logic of the argument is the following: (1) Paul employs the experiential frame of household as a conceptual source to illuminate the more abstract realm of spiritual relationships; (2) this use of one experiential frame to speak about another experiential frame is what is described as metaphorical language; (3) in this metaphorical mapping, some attributes, relational dynamics and experiential knowledge from the experience or witness of someone's incorporation into a royal household, via adoption, are systematically projected onto the frame of believers' relationship with God; (4) as the recipients engage with this metaphor, they are invited to think about and experience their relationship with God through the lens of household membership.

In Ephesians, the household provides an overarching umbrella under which other themes can exist. The language of unity is one example. The unity Ephesians describes is not abstract or disembodied, but rather the natural result of incorporation into a single family. The theme of reconciliation in Ephesians is intrinsically linked to the idea of being brought into God's family. The reconciliation between God and humanity, and between different human groups, is portrayed as the process of inclusion into the divine household. Ephesians 2.16 speaks of Christ reconciling 'both of them to God through the cross', with the result being incorporation into 'one body'. This reconciliation is not an end in and of itself but how formerly estranged individuals and groups are brought into the family of God.

For instance, Turner very insightfully argues that Ephesians should be read along with Colossians and Philemon, because all three hold 'reconciliation' as a central theme. According to him, Ephesians highlights human reconciliation; Colossians underlines cosmic reconciliation; and Philemon illustrates what the process of reconciliation looks like in a specific case in church life (Turner, 2006, pp. 37–47). Although Turner's observation is accurate and helpful, he overlooks the centrality of familial language in Philemon.

Paul's epistle to Philemon opens with greetings to 'Philemon our dear friend and fellow worker' and 'the church that meets in your home' (Philemon 1–2), immediately establishing a familial context. Then, Paul refers to himself as a 'Father' to Onesimus, whom he has 'begotten' in his chains (v. 10). This kinship language sets the stage for Paul's central appeal: Philemon should receive Onesimus back 'no longer as a slave, but better than a slave, as a dear brother' (v. 16). The reconciliation Paul seeks is thus framed not in terms of social or legal status, but in terms of family relations. Paul even offers to pay Onesimus' debts, acting as a kinsman-redeemer would in a family context (vv. 18–19). The letter concludes with further familial language, as Paul expresses confidence in Philemon's obedience as a brother (v. 21) and sends greetings from others, whom he names as kinfolk (vv. 23–24). Thus, in Philemon, we see how the concept of incorporation into God's family serves as both the context for and the goal of reconciliation, providing a powerful model for addressing relational breaches in the church.

Conclusion of Part 1

My exegetical analysis has stressed the pervasive way in which Paul understands the church as a family in Ephesians. We have seen how the thesis *'In love, king Jesus has incorporated believers into the Father's household as beloved children'* shapes the entire letter's theology and rhetoric.

By employing conceptual metaphor theory, we have moved beyond viewing this family language as merely 'fictive kinship' to understanding it as a powerful lens through which the early Christians were invited to perceive their new reality in Christ.

As we transition to Part 2, we will explore how this rich understanding of the church as God's family informs and transforms various aspects of Christian theology and practice, while paying particular attention to its implications for intercultural communities and church unity.

Part 2: Implications for Understanding Church and Intercultural Communities

Having established the centrality of the family metaphor in Ephesians and its profound significance in the context of first-century Asia Minor, we now turn to explore its implications for contemporary Christian life and practice. The thesis *'In love, king Jesus has incorporated believers into the Father's household as beloved children'* offers a powerful lens through which to reimagine our understanding of church, both locally and universally. This shift in perspective is not merely theoretical but has far-reaching practical implications.

In the following sections, we will examine how this divine incorporation transforms our approach to church life, theology and intercultural relationships. We will contrast two paradigms: the church as a business, which often unconsciously shapes our current practices, and the church as a family, which aligns more closely with Paul's vision in Ephesians. This comparison will illuminate how our underlying metaphors profoundly influence our attitudes, actions and aspirations as a community of faith.

Church as a Business

'... we need to talk about our numbers,' were some of the initial statements Pastor Andres mentioned when he addressed his leadership team. 'Ever since the lockdown, attendance has been a real struggle, and giving is down 15% from last year. We are not meeting our growth goals.'

Elder Eduardo chimed in, 'Maybe we should consider a new programme to attract young families? First Baptist down the street seems to be thriving with their children's ministry.'

'Good thinking,' Pastor Carlos nodded. 'We definitely need to make sure we are meeting the needs of our community. What about our worship style? Maybe we need to update it to be more engaging for newcomers?'

Another person in the room leaned forward, 'I have been looking at some church growth seminars we could attend. A couple of churches saw their attendance increase by about 20% after implementing what they learned.'

Imagine that you also sat in this meeting, you probably could not help but notice how their approach to ministry mirrored secular business strategies. The church leaders see themselves as executives running a religious organization: They talk about 'running' programmes or ministries. The focus on numbers, comparing themselves to other churches, appealing to newcomers, and growth techniques all reflect an underlying assumption: church success can be measured and achieved like business success.

But it is not just church leaders who are shaped by this mentality. Congregants often unconsciously adopt the role of customers, 'shopping' for the best religious experience – worship in one place, preaching in another, prayer groups somewhere else. Some treat spiritual experiences as products to be consumed. This mentality is especially palpable when people make comments about the service, almost always in connection to the worship or the sermon. And most of the time, they are introduced with phrases like, 'I really enjoyed worship this morning,' or, 'I did not feel the sermon was great this morning.' These types of comments are made from the perspective of a consumer; if you feel like a customer, you will evaluate your church involvement based on what you are 'getting out of it', much like consumers reviewing a product or service. That is why we also hear comments like, 'I'm not being fed at this church,' or, 'The children's programme at the other church seems to be much better.'

Seeing church through the lens of a business, prayer becomes transactional, seen mainly as a way to 'get results'. Consciously or unconsciously, believers might approach prayer like a business negotiation, focusing on what they can get from God rather than deepening their connection with him. Prayer warriors are sometimes viewed as a kind of spiritual sales team, tasked with closing deals with the divine. This perspective has led to workshops, seminars and literature aimed at training people to be 'effective' in prayer, much like sales training programmes. Such initiatives reinforce the business model, treating prayer as a skill to be honed for optimal results rather than a relational practice.

This transactional view of prayer aligns closely with the prosperity gospel in many corners of the church. The prosperity gospel operates from this business model, treating faith as an investment that should yield tangible, material return. It reduces the complex, relational nature of faith to a simple input–output equation, where the right prayers or actions are expected to produce specific, desired results from God.

Discipleship is reduced to a series of programmes or classes to complete, rather than a lifelong journey of transformation. Much like an assembly line, the focus is to move people effectively through a standardized process of spiritual development. New believers are treated as raw materials to be shaped into a finished product through a predetermined sequence of classes or experiences. The unique, personal nature of each individual's growth in Christ is overshadowed by the desire for a uniform, scalable approach (see Rossow, 2020, pp. 244–5). This assembly-line mentality in discipleship leads to several problems. It can create a false sense of spiritual maturity based on programme completion rather than genuine heart transformation. The standardized approach may discourage exploration and questioning, as these do not fit neatly into the prescribed process.

Church as a Family

Let us now contrast the business model just discussed by reimagining the church as a family, with God as the loving Father and believers as brothers and sisters. This shift in perspective is not just a nice idea, but it fundamentally reorients how we understand the church's identity and purpose. To illustrate this shift, imagine a different kind of church meeting:

'Let us share how we have seen God at work in our lives this week,' Pastor Mario began. The leadership team, gathered in a circle, leaned in attentively. One by one they shared stories of struggles and joys, of small victories and ongoing challenges.

Elder Juan spoke up, 'I've been praying for my neighbour, and yesterday he asked me about my faith. I wasn't sure what to say, but I invited him over for dinner next week.'

'That's beautiful, Juan,' Pastor Mario smiled. 'Let's all keep your neighbour in our prayers. Anyone want to share ideas on how we can support Juan in this?' The room buzzed with suggestions and encouragement.

In Ephesians, Paul paints a vivid picture of this family dynamic. He reminds us that we were once 'foreigners and strangers' but have now been brought near by the blood of Christ (Eph. 2.13). We are 'no longer foreigners and strangers' but fellow citizens with God's people and also members of God's household (Eph. 2.19). In this family model, Jesus is not a product to be marketed or a brand to represent. Instead, he is our brother (Eph. 1.5–6). Through him, we have been adopted into God's family, receiving the full rights of sons and daughters. This adoption fundamentally changes how we relate to God and to each other.

This family perspective reshapes our understanding of salvation itself. In Ephesians, Paul presents salvation not as a mere legal transaction or change of status, but as incorporation into God's family. This family-oriented soteriology has profound implications. First, it emphasizes the relational aspect of salvation. The goal is not just forgiveness of sins but a restored relationship with God as Father and with fellow believers as brothers and sisters. This relational focus transforms our understanding of the Christian life from a set of beliefs or practices to a lived experience of familial belonging.

Second, it provides assurance of salvation. The language of predestination and adoption (Eph. 1.4–5) grounds believers' confidence not in their own efforts but in the Father's choice and love. This assurance stands in stark contrast to the performance-based mentality often fostered by the business model of church, where one's standing might feel dependent on measurable contributions or achievements.

In the business model, salvation can unintentionally be reduced to a transaction: a 'deal' closed between God and the individual. This can lead to a contractual view of faith, where blessings are expected in return for good behaviour or contributions. The family model, however, reminds us that our relationship with God is based on his unconditional love and adoption, not on our performance or what we can offer him.

Prayer, in this context, becomes intimate communication within a loving relationship. It is not about trying to get God to do what we want, but about aligning our hearts with his will. As Paul prays in Ephesians 3.14–19, we come before our Father, asking him to strengthen us with power through his Spirit, that Christ may dwell in our hearts through faith, and that we may grasp how wide and long and high and deep is the love of Christ.

Discipleship takes on a new meaning in this family context. It is not a programme to complete or a series of classes to attend, but a process of 'growing up' in the Father's likeness. And even the one-to-one sessions we might have with people are understood in the context of family relations. Paul talks about this growth in Ephesians 4.15–16, where he describes the body of Christ 'growing and building itself up in love, as each part does its work'. This growth happens in community, with each member contributing to the maturity of the whole.

This approach to discipleship addresses the issue of burn-out prevalent in the business model. Instead of constantly striving to meet performance metrics, both leaders and members find rest and rejuvenation in family relationships. The pressure to produce results is replaced by the joy of growing together.

Church leadership, viewed through this lens, becomes less about management and more about nurture and guidance. Leaders are called to equip God's people for works of service 'so that the body of Christ may be built up until we all reach unity in the faith and in the knowledge of the Son of God and become mature, attaining to the whole measure of the fullness of Christ' (Eph. 4.12–13).

As already mentioned, the proliferation of titles and honorifics in some charismatic contexts (e.g., 'Apostle', 'Prophet', 'Man of God') can – if not careful – establish hierarchical relationships that are at odds with the horizontal, sibling-like relationships emphasized in Ephesians. Instead, understanding the church as a family encourages a flatter structure, where leadership is understood as a facilitation of family growth rather than domination or control.

This family-oriented leadership model naturally counteracts the problematic top-down structures often seen in the business model. Instead of a hierarchical system with a singular 'anointed' leader, the family model promotes shared responsibility and mutual edification (Eph. 4.16).

The goal of this family is not primarily numerical growth or financial success, but to become mature, attaining to the whole measure of the fullness of Christ (Eph. 4.13). This maturity is expressed in how we treat one another – with humility, gentleness, patience and love (Eph. 4.2–3). It is about reflecting the character of our heavenly Father in our relationships with each other and in how we relate to the world.

In this reimagined vision of the church, our approach to the world and to other churches also changes dramatically. We are not looking at people as potential customers to be acquired or members to be counted, but as potential family members to be loved and welcomed. Other churches are no longer seen as competitors in a religious marketplace, but as fellow branches of the same family tree, each playing a vital role in God's grand design.

Along this line, the contemporary challenge of ecclesial consumerism, where individuals float between churches without developing a sense of belonging, stands in stark contrast to Paul's vision of the church as a committed family. This consumer mentality leads to easy disengagement from local church communities and presents a significant obstacle to experiencing the kind of deep, familial relationships Paul envisions. The vision of the church as family, as Paul describes in Ephesians, offers a necessary corrective to this trend, highlighting commitment, perseverance and mutual responsibility over individual preference and convenience.

And yet, seeing the church as a family aligns with the context of Ephesians itself. Paul wrote this letter not to a single congregation, but to a network of churches across Asia Minor. This regional focus reminds us that the family of God extends far beyond our local assembly. Just as Paul addressed multiple churches as one unified body in Christ, we too are called to see ourselves as part of a larger family that transcends our individual congregations. Our mission is neither to 'close the sale' nor to outperform other churches.

However, the relationship between local churches and the universal church requires careful navigation. While Paul's letter to the Ephesians stresses a universal ecclesiology, local congregations must grapple with how to maintain a sense of connection to the broader body of Christ while addressing the immediate needs of their specific context. This tension between the local and the universal continues to shape ecclesial identity and practice (through church networks and mission collaborations further afield).

Additionally, seeing the church through the lens of the family helps us to spot the right enemy. In the religiously charged atmosphere of first-century Asia Minor, where spiritual forces were believed to control various aspects of life, the message of incorporation into God's household offered a profound sense of security. As Arnold (1989, pp. 123–4) notes, pagan gods (i.e. demonic powers) were often seen as unpredictable powers that needed to be appeased or manipulated. However, Ephesians presents a God who, out of love, purposefully chose and predestined believers for adoption into his family (Eph. 1.4–5). This adoption means 'that they have been transferred to the control of another and more powerful *paterfamilias*' (Sumney, 2022, p. 218).

Seeing the church as a family also changes our approach to evangelism and community engagement. Instead of viewing outreach as a marketing campaign, we see it as an opportunity to expand our family circle. We might host community meals, offer support to local families in need, or simply be present and available in our neighbourhoods, always ready to share the love of Christ in practical ways.

This family model fundamentally reshapes how we understand and live out our identity as God's church. It is a shift from performance to relationship, from programmes to people, from metrics of success to spiritual growth. It is a return to the biblical vision of the church as God's household, where all are welcome and all have a place at the table.

Even if people operate within the business model, it is likely that deep inside they still long for the family model. This is because when people do not experience the church as a loving, supportive family – when they instead experience dysfunction, conflict or lack of belonging – the model of the family allows us to explain why we feel hurt.

With all that said, it is important to acknowledge that implementing this model is not without its challenges. Our ingrained business mindset can be hard to eradicate. And we are by no means suggesting that numerical growth is unimportant, or that finances are not part of being a healthy church. The family model is not an excuse for lack of organization or accountability.

While the family model is foundational, it is important to recognize that ministry within God's family still requires intentionality, accountability and hard work. The Bible often uses agricultural metaphors to describe spiritual growth and ministry (1 Cor. 3.6–9), reminding us that while God gives the growth, we are called to plant and water diligently.

Just as in a healthy family, members work together towards common goals, in the church, we collaborate in the work of the gospel. This includes thoughtful planning, responsible stewardship of resources and a commitment to fruitfulness in our mission.

The key is to approach these aspects of ministry as natural expressions of our identity as God's children. This balance allows us to be both relational and purposeful, maintaining our family identity while pursuing the mission God has given us with diligence and care.

When we picture the church as a family, it is important to understand it as both a present reality and an eschatological aspiration. We need to keep in mind that the family model describes what the church is becoming in Christ, even as it struggles with the imperfections of its current state. By holding this tension, we can maintain a balanced view that acknowledges the church's divine calling and human frailty, its present reality and future hope. This recognition fosters patience, grace and perseverance as we work towards embodying the ideal of God's household more fully. As we embrace this model, we may find that the church not only grows in depth and maturity but also becomes a more authentic and attractive expression of God's love to the world around us.

Having explored the implications of viewing the church as a family, let us now consider how this particular lens addresses the challenges and opportunities presented by intercultural church communities.

The Family Model and Intercultural Churches

By viewing the church through the lens of family, we gain a framework for addressing the complexities and challenges of cultural diversity within Christian fellowship.

First and foremost, the concept of adoption into God's family provides a new, shared identity that transcends cultural differences. In Ephesians 1.5, Paul speaks of believers being 'adopted as his sons through Jesus Christ'. In an intercultural church context, members are challenged to see one another first as siblings in Christ, rather than as representatives of different cultural backgrounds. This perspective can help mitigate cultural misunderstandings and conflicts by reminding believers of their fundamental unity in Christ.

The family model also implies mutual responsibility and care that should characterize relationships within intercultural communities. In an intercultural context, this mutual care takes on added significance. It may involve practical support across cultural lines, such as more established members helping newer immigrants navigate unfamiliar systems, or cross-cultural mentoring relationships. This familial love and care, when expressed across cultural boundaries, can be a powerful testimony to the transformative power of the gospel.

Furthermore, the family model helps in the process of conflict resolution in intercultural settings. Intercultural church communities can approach conflicts with the understanding that they are dealing with family members, not outsiders or opponents. This perspective aligns with Paul's exhortation in Ephesians 4.2–3: 'Be completely humble and gentle; be patient, bearing with one another in love. Make every effort to keep the unity of the Spirit through the bond of peace.' When cultural misunderstandings or disagreements arise, the family model encourages believers to approach these issues with grace, seeking understanding and reconciliation rather than division.

The family model also allows us to view cultural diversity as a strength rather than a challenge to be overcome. In a healthy family, each member's unique gifts and perspectives are valued and contribute to the family's overall wellbeing. Similarly, in an intercultural church family, diverse cultural backgrounds can be seen as enriching the community's life and witness. This aligns with Paul's vision in Ephesians 3.10 of the church displaying the 'manifold wisdom of God'. The varied cultural expressions of faith within an intercultural community can provide a richer, more multifaceted reflection of God's character and work in the world.

Finally, viewing intercultural church communities through the family lens offers an alternative to both cultural assimilation and segregation. Assimilation in church contexts often manifests as pressure on minority cultures to conform to the dominant church culture, potentially losing their unique cultural expressions of faith in the process. On the other hand, segregation in churches can occur when different cultural groups coexist but rarely interact meaningfully, perhaps holding separate services or ministry activities based on cultural or linguistic lines. While this preserves cultural distinctiveness, it can hinder true community integration and mutual understanding. The family model, however, provides a middle ground. In a family, members do not lose their individuality but rather find their unique identity affirmed within the context of belonging. The family model encourages a form of unity that does not demand uniformity. It allows for the preservation and celebration of diverse cultural expressions while maintaining a core unity in Christ. In practice, this might involve incorporating diverse cultural elements in worship services, ensuring leadership representation from various cultural backgrounds, and creating intentional spaces for cross-cultural learning.

Conclusion of Part 2

The concept of incorporation into God's household, as presented in Ephesians, is not merely a theological abstraction but a transformative reality that reshapes every aspect of Christian faith and practice. It provides a holistic framework for understanding salvation, church, ethics and mission.

In a world longing for genuine belonging and grappling with divisions, the message of Ephesians offers a compelling vision: in Christ, we are home. We are beloved children in the household of God. This reality, when fully embraced, has the power to transform not only individual lives but also communities, crossing cultural boundaries. It offers a path to reconciliation, a model for unity amidst diversity, and a sense of belonging that transcends cultural boundaries. As the church grapples with the challenges of the twenty-first century, perhaps a renewed appreciation of our identity as God's family can guide us toward more faithful and fruitful expressions of Christian community.

Bibliography

Arnold, C. E., 1989, *Power and Magic: The Concept of Power in Ephesians*, Eugene: Baker Book House.

Arnold, C. E., 2010, *Ephesians*, ZECNT, Grand Rapids, MI: Zondervan.

Bruce, F. F., 1971, 'Some Thoughts on Paul and Paulinism', *Vox Evangelica*, 7, pp. 5–16.

Burger, C., 1975, *Schöpfung und Versöhnung: Studien zum liturgischen Gut im Kolosser- und Epheserbrief*, Neukirchen-Vluyn: Neukirchener Verlag.

Campbell, C. R., 2012, *Paul and Union with Christ: An Exegetical and Theological Study*, Grand Rapids, MI: Zondervan.

Cohick, L. H., 2020, *The Letter to the Ephesians*. NICNT. Grand Rapids, MI: Eerdmans.

Dahl, N. A., 2000, 'Gentiles, Christians, and Israelites in the Epistle to the Ephesians,' in Blomkvist, V., Fornberg, T., and Hellholm, D., eds, *Studies in Ephesians: Introductory Questions, Text- and Edition-Critical Issues, Interpretation of Texts and Themes*, WUNT 131, Tübingen: Mohr Siebeck.

Dancygier, B. and Sweetser, E., 2014, *Figurative Language*, Cambridge: Cambridge University Press.

Darko, D. K., 2016, 'Adopted Siblings in the Household of God: Kinship Lexemes in the Social Identity Construction of Ephesians' in Tucker, B. and Baker, C. A., eds, *T&T Clark Handbook to Social Identity in the New Testament*, London: Bloomsbury T&T Clark, pp. 333–46.

Dodd, C. H., 1929, 'Ephesians', in Eiselen, F.C., Lewis, E., and Downey, D., eds, *The Abingdon Bible Commentary*, New York: Abingdon, pp. 1224–5.

Fischer, K. M., 1973, *Tendenz und Absicht des Epheserbriefes*. Göttingen: Vandenhoeck & Ruprecht.

Gnilka, J., 2002, *Der Epheserbrief*, Freiburg: Herder.

Gombis, T. G., 2004, 'Ephesians 2 as a Narrative of Divine Warfare', *Journal for the Study of the New Testament*, 26, No. 4, pp. 403–18.

Hewitt, J. T., 2020, *Messiah and Scripture: Paul's 'In Christ' Idiom and Its Ancient Jewish Context*, WUNT 2/522, Tübingen: Mohr Siebeck.

Jeffers, J. S., 1999, *The Greco-Roman World of the New Testament Era: Exploring the Background of Early Christianity*, Downers Grove: InterVarsity Press Academic.

Jiménez, O. E., 2022, *Metaphors in the Narrative of Ephesians 2:11–22: Motion towards Maximal Proximity and Higher Status*, Linguistic Biblical Studies 20, Leiden: Brill.

Jindo, J. Y., 2013, 'Metaphor Theory and Biblical Texts,' in McKenzie, S. L., ed., *The Oxford Encyclopedia of Biblical Interpretation*, Oxford: Oxford University Press, pp. 1–10.

Lacey, W. K., 1987, '*Patria Potestas*', in Rawson, B., ed., *The Family in Ancient Rome: New Perspectives*, Ithaca: Cornell University Press.

Lakoff, G. and Johnson, M., 2003, *Metaphors We Live By*, Chicago: University of Chicago Press.

Merklein, H., 1973, *Christus und die Kirche: Die theologische Grundstruktur des Epheserbriefes nach Eph 2,11–18*, Stuttgart: Bibelwerk.

Moo, D. J., 2021, *A Theology of Paul and His Letters*, Grand Rapids, MI: Zondervan.

Morgan, M. J., 2019, *Participating in Christ: Explorations in Paul's Theology and Spirituality*, Grand Rapids, MI: Baker Academic.

Morgan, M. J., 2023, 'Church,' in McKnight, S., Cohick, L. H., and Gupta, N. K., eds, *Dictionary of Paul and His Letters: A Compendium of Contemporary Biblical Scholarship* (2nd edn), Downers Grove: InterVarsity Press, pp. 476–82.

Morgan, T., 2020, *Being 'in Christ' in the Letters of Paul: Saved Through Christ and in His Hands*, WUNT 449, Tübingen: Mohr Siebeck.

Rosen-Zvi, I. and Ophir, A., 2015, 'Paul and the Invention of the Gentiles', *The Jewish Quarterly Review*, 105, pp. 1–41.

Rossow, J., 2020, *Preaching Metaphor: How to Shape Sermons that Shape People*, Next Step Press.

Saller, R. P., 1994, *Patriarchy, Property and Death in the Roman Family*, Cambridge: Cambridge University Press.

Smith, J., 2011, *Christ the Ideal King: Cultural Context, Rhetorical Strategy and the Power of Divine Monarchy in Ephesians*, Tübingen: Mohr Siebeck.

Sumney, J. L., 2022, 'Family and Filial Language in Ephesians', in Black, A., Thomas, C. M., and Thompson, T. W., eds, *Ephesos as a Religious Center under the Principate*, WUNT 488., Tübingen: Mohr-Siebeck, pp. 205–26.

Talbert, C. H., 2007, *Ephesians and Colossians*, Paideia Commentaries, Grand Rapids, MI: Baker Academic.

Trebilco, P., 2014, *Self-designations and Group Identity in the New Testament*, Cambridge: Cambridge University Press.

Turner, M., 2006, 'Human Reconciliation in the New Testament with Special Reference to Philemon, Colossians and Ephesians', *European Journal of Theology*, 16, No. 1, pp. 37–47.

White, L. M., 2016, 'Paul and *Pater Familias*,' in Sampley, J. P., ed., *Paul in the Greco-Roman World: A Handbook*, Vol. 2, London: Bloomsbury T&T Clark, pp. 457–87.

PART 2

Intercultural Churches and Practices: Ecclesiology Re-imagined

4

'Re-tuning' Worship: Biblical Principles for a Culturally Diverse Age

IAN COLLINGE

Introduction

It was Pentecost Sunday in Mosaic South Church, Leeds. The room was decorated with colourful flags of the 15 nations in our congregation. Some people came in clothing from cultures they relate to. After an introduction, an Arabic speaker instructed us how to stretch hands forward as we heard words of praise from Jeremiah 10.6–7 in Arabic; all then declared the same in English. Just then, a hidden group of five *djembe* drummers (from different West African countries and one from Yorkshire) started a beat from the back, processing into the hall, weaving in and around the congregation. Some people danced, following the drummers. The atmosphere was electric! It transported us mentally to West Africa, as well as to the excited hubbub of the Day of Pentecost. On a signal, Dave Fahrer, our guitarist worship leader, repeatedly called, 'There is no one like our God!' – echoed by the congregation – leading into 'Tribes' (Victory Worship, 2019), a song from the Philippines in English, Tagalog and Spanish, then into 'Praise' (Elevation Worship, 2023), based on Psalm 150, with its opening chants (each echoed by the people), 'Let everything', 'that has breath', 'praise the Lord' and eventually into the well-known song 'How Great is Our God' (Tomlin, 2004).

Later, we were guided into a conversation with our neighbours, discussing our 'heart' languages and songs, before one of our leaders, Jonah Ulebor, a Nigerian PhD researcher in racial justice in education, preached on Acts 2, highlighting the multi-ethnic nature of the early church and how to overcome cultural differences. We were led in prayer for India and Nigeria by people from those backgrounds. In response to all this, the modern trinitarian hymn 'King of Kings' (Hillsong, 2019) led us through the gospel story, the Zulu/English South African song, 'Come Holy Spirit | *Uthando*' (Worship Central South Africa, 2018) welcomed the Spirit of Pentecost to 'move among us', and the Zambian-originated 'God is so good' (Makai, c.1970), expressed our praise with increasing delight – in English, Chinese, German and Farsi. The service host invited people to call out 'How Great is Our God!' in languages other than English. It was uplifting to hear many taking the microphone to praise God in their own tongues: Twi, Yoruba, Punjabi, French, Polish, Chinese, Farsi and Greek. There was an excited buzz as we were dismissed with a blessing and led out by the drummers in a processional dance to enjoy fellowship together with snacks from some different cultures.

This service was an occasional event, not what worship always looks like in our church. But it is a sign of what could be. We find that such events become catalysts, gradually changing the way we do things more regularly. They celebrate who we are as a community in vibrant acts of worship to the God who made all nations. Such experiences are becoming more frequent in churches seeking to grow in intercultural life. Culturally diverse worship is not about tokenistic, politically correct representation but about the worship of a genuinely loving community. What, then, are the top theological reasons to adopt it?

General Theological Principles

Like all true worship, intercultural worship is *God-centred*, focused on giving glory to the God of love, justice and power (Ps. 96; Rev. 5.9–10), who calls his people to be a blessing to all nations (Gen. 12.3). Intercultural worship is *Christ-centred*, as we encounter God through Jesus, who was born into human culture (John 1.14) and, by his death, destroyed dividing walls between races (Eph. 2.14). It is *Spirit-empowered*, since Christ poured out his Spirit on his followers, unleashing a countercultural power that resulted in a church for all cultures (Acts 1.8; 2.9–11; Gal. 3.28; Eph. 2.11–22; Col. 3.11). Further, it looks back to the ways God has spoken and acted in the past, but meets God in the present and anticipates the eschatological worship of 'every nation, tribe, people and language' (Rev. 7.9; 21.26). These are foundational reasons for intercultural worship since it reflects the nature of the God who created all nations to worship him (Ps. 86.9) and to do so *together* (Isa. 19.23–25). Importantly, therefore, 'culturally conscious worship' (Black, 2000, p. 1) is not diversity for diversity's sake; it is about reflecting God to the world, embodying the gospel in our time and community and engaging with God in ways that are profoundly transformative.

If the above are theological 'headlines' for intercultural worship, the theme of this chapter is that intercultural worship paves the way for transformational encounters with God that we are unlikely to experience in other ways. In such spaces, our horizons are expanded and cultural blinkers lifted. We discover that no culture, including our own, is sufficient to worship such a great God, as we gasp at the beauty, wisdom and vibrancy of contributions of worshippers from other backgrounds. That's the nature of the body of Christ: we need one another in our difference not our sameness (1 Cor. 12.12–13).

There are usually two questions around intercultural worship: *why?* (the rationale) and *how?* (the practicalities). The aim of this chapter, therefore, is to address both by pointing towards a biblical and practical interdisciplinary theology of intercultural worship. Here I will draw on the disciplines of ethnodoxology ('the interdisciplinary study of how Christians in every culture engage with God and the world through their own artistic expressions', GEN, 2025), ethnomusicology ('the study of music in its social and cultural contexts', SEM, no date), missiology and worship studies. As we do so, we will observe ways to approach the practice of intercultural worship, whether in a local congregation, a small group or large-scale events.

What Is Worship?

> Worship is the act of adoring and praising God, ascribing worth to Father|Son|Spirit as the one who deserves homage, allegiance, and faithful service. From individual to corporate devotion, worship denotes a lifestyle of being in love with God. The global Church exhibits an astounding array of worship patterns, demonstrating the enormity of God's creativity and the diversity of the Body of Christ. (GEN – Global Ethnodoxology Network, 2025)

As this definition helpfully highlights, 'worship' is broad. It is local, global and 'glocal' (Kim, 2013, p. 46). It is individual and corporate. In all these, it is 'a lifestyle of being in love with God'. This chapter intentionally focuses on corporate, 'gathered worship', rather than 'scattered worship' (Cosper, 2013, pp. 76–9). Further definitions of 'worship' abound (Man, 2023, pp. 5–11), but for our purposes, Ron Man's elegant summary is both succinct and pertinent to diverse settings: 'Worship is our response to the glory of God – all that we are responding to all that God is' (p. 59).

Let's note two things. First, the essence of worship is our *response* to God's prior *revelation*. This points to the unchanging nature of God but also the diverse possibilities for *how* we respond. Second, we respond with 'all that we are', including our personal, social and cultural identities. Acknowledging this is vital to help each worshipper connect their experience of worship to who they are in their daily lives, since, as missiologist Andrew Walls says, 'there is only culture-specific humanity' (Walls, 2007, p. 32). These twin aspects underpin any theology of intercultural worship.

Constants and Variables in Worship

Christian worship is remarkable for the plethora of possibilities that exist worldwide for every aspect of worship: meeting place, time, duration, layout, dress, participant involvement, greetings, prayer, readings, sacraments, creeds, presentations, talks, music, movement, visual symbols, food and so on. So how can we determine those components that are biblically and historically universal (constant) and those that are open to flexibility (variable)? Some scholars have provided insights that we will examine (Man, 2023, pp. 404–8; Maynard-Reid, 2000, pp. 41–50).

'Re-tuning': A Musical Analogy

This chapter is titled, 'Re-tuning Worship' because stringed instruments the world over provide a picture of constants and variables (for another helpful analogy, see Man, p. 404). Instruments with strings are constructed out of a solid body and changeable components.

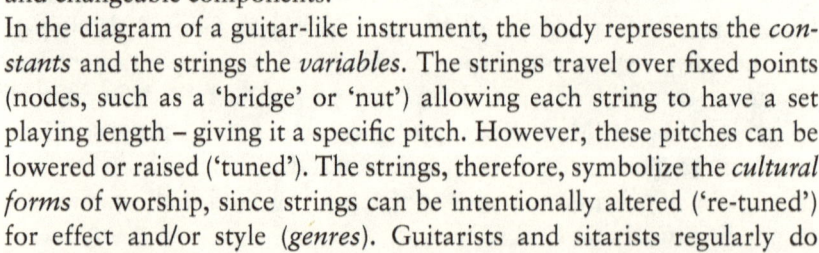

In the diagram of a guitar-like instrument, the body represents the *constants* and the strings the *variables*. The strings travel over fixed points (nodes, such as a 'bridge' or 'nut') allowing each string to have a set playing length – giving it a specific pitch. However, these pitches can be lowered or raised ('tuned'). The strings, therefore, symbolize the *cultural forms* of worship, since strings can be intentionally altered ('re-tuned') for effect and/or style (*genres*). Guitarists and sitarists regularly do this and I, too, re-tune my violin for Indian style. This illustrates how worship can 'flex' to express different cultures. At times, strings also need to be replaced. Much 're-tuning' and 'replacement' in worship has taken place over two millennia, such that the church now 'exhibits an astounding array of worship patterns' (GEN, 2025) and in today's culturally diverse world, the church is again in a time of re-evaluation, re-tuning and replacement, while honouring the worship of the church through history. First, though, what are the 'transcultural' (LWF, 1996, pp. 24–5) constants of Christian worship regardless of time and place?

Constants Part 1: Core Elements

> They devoted themselves to the apostles' teaching and to fellowship, to the breaking of bread and to prayer. ... praising God and enjoying the favour of all the people. And the Lord added to their number daily those who were being saved. (Acts 2.42, 47)

This passage in Acts provides an account of what the first followers of Jesus did when they gathered for worship. It includes four or five elements that we see in every Christian tradition and era:

1 the word of God
2 fellowship
3 the Lord's supper
4 prayer
5 praise.

'These seem to be non-negotiable elements that define and characterize truly Christian worship' (Man, 2023, p. 407). Jamaican-born professor Pedrito Maynard-Reid extends this picture: 'The basic forms of Christian worship ... were developed from the Jewish synagogue services and other Jewish rites. ... From these emerged the Christian eucharistic or love feast and weekly worship services' (Maynard-Reid, 2000, p. 43). He further summarizes 'the ageless, universal, common and core factors in worship' as:

1 an assembling of the people of God to experience the presence of God in encounter with their neighbours
2 a celebration of festivals and sacraments
3 the word of God in Scripture readings, study and sermon
4 prayer.

Contextualizing Worship

If the above are constants, Maynard-Reid emphasizes the need for contextualizing worship (Maynard-Reid, 2000, p. 44), in the same way that theology needs to be contextualized. He cites Stephen B. Bevans: 'The contextualization of theology ... is really a theological imperative ... part of the very nature of theology itself' (Bevans, 2015, p. 3). This is true of worship too, agreeing with what ethnodoxologists across the continents have reported for many decades (*Mission Frontiers*, 1996, various) that thoughtlessly transporting *forms* and *models* of worship across the world into different cultures is presumptuous and fails to follow the incarnational pattern demonstrated by Jesus. Rather, it is time to give space for the emergence of worship expressions created by Christ-honouring believers in their own communities, so that their voices can be heard. This is ultimately more effective for worship, witness and discipleship. It has been my experience as a missionary ethnomusicologist, as I have watched new worship expressions emerge both in Asia and Europe, including the first ever Christian songs in certain languages – set to musical styles chosen by the local songwriters. This is a common story in ethnodoxology (Fortunato, Neeley and Brinneman, 2006, various). For our present discussion, contextualization applies equally to multi-ethnic congregations (Collinge, 2022b, pp. 91, 94, 98).

'Intercultural worship' is typically more than 'multicultural', 'multilingual', 'multi-ethnic', 'multiracial' or 'multigenerational', since all such 'multi-', 'poly-', or 'plurality' terms tell us nothing about power dynamics and who makes decisions. By contrast, 'intercultural worship' starts with mutual listening and the sharing of stories, songs and other forms. It focuses on what emerges from this kind of respectful 'interaction' among culturally diverse Christians seeking to worship as equals before God (for more, see Collinge, 2022a, pp. 121–9). It could be defined as worship that creates a space where three things can happen:

1 Worshippers from diverse cultures listen to one another and shape worship together.
2 Pre-believers hear God speak in their voice.
3 Individual churches discover their unique, Spirit-enabled worship culture.

How, then, might the core elements of Christian worship be contextualized ('re-tuned') for intercultural settings? The answer lies not in the *components* themselves but in the *way* each is expressed and what *forms* are used:

- *how* we gather
- *how* we celebrate events, festivals and sacraments
- *how* we read, teach, preach, study and engage with the word of God
- *how* we pray and praise.

How we gather: architecture, clothing, volume and layouts

For example, how we gather demonstrates what we think worship is for, including architecture. A Moravian church I know in India engaged in a creative design for their building to reflect eastern aesthetics more appropriate for peoples in their area (Johnson, 2020). Dress codes (including protocols about shoes) also vary, as do volume levels and the functions of music. Similarly, the physical layout shows leaders' (ultimately, theological and cultural) priorities in worship, whether it is simple or elaborate, lectern-centred, round-table-oriented, campfire-shaped, stage-focused or a ceremony with honoured persons, for example. 'Re-tuning' for intercultural worship will require discussion, willingness to adjust and experimentation around these matters.

How we pray and praise: musical instruments

What guidance does the New Testament provide on instruments in worship? Realistically, scholars find very little evidence for musical instruments in early church worship. Donald P. Hustad concludes that in both synagogue services and Christian gatherings, the Scriptures were chanted and sung but 'no instruments were involved' (Hustad, 1994, p. 192). Despite some evidence for occasional use of the plucked *kithara* (lyre) in segments of the early church (Alikin, 2010, p. 253), the consensus drawn from documents in the early church period is that singing was enjoyed in various formats but was usually unaccompanied (McKinnon, 2001, p. 20). To music-filled churches today, this may be a surprise. However, it highlights the primacy of the *message* over the *medium* (Col. 3.16) and that the ways in which Christian truths are sung, prayed and taught change over time, according to context. Indeed, just as Jesus taught that worship is no longer limited to places but is to be 'in spirit and truth' (John 4.21–24), similar principles apply to cultural forms. Man emphasizes that, 'We search the pages of the New Testament in vain for detailed instructions, much less structures or liturgies' (Man, 2023, p. 17). This liberates (and requires) the church in each age and place to seek God for *how* to glorify him, including in musical expressions, while not diverging from the core elements and, as we now discuss, biblical principles of worship.

Constants Part 2: Core Principles of Worship

Specialists in Worship Studies present 'biblical principles' of worship (Man, 2023, pp. 437–96; Maynard-Reid, 2000, pp. 43–4). Six are offered by Professor Constance M. Cherry (Cherry, 2010, pp. 5–17). To Cherry's six, I add one by Ron Man (Man, 2023, pp. 278–86; 464) and another inspired by John Piper (Piper, 1993, p.11).

1 Worship is a transformational journey.
2 Worship is a dialogue, patterned in revelation and response.
3 Worship is corporate in nature.
4 Worship is trinitarian in nature.
5 Worship is scriptural, centred in God's acts of salvation.
6 Worship is covenantal in nature.
7 Worship is motivated and empowered by the Holy Spirit.
8 Worship is missional, the goal and fuel of missions.

In the following section, I examine each of these, reflecting on how each might be 're-tuned' for intercultural settings. Furthermore, since the primary *mode* of Western theological discourse is intellectual, it is self-evidently limiting, since it requires audiences attracted to dissecting concepts intellectually. As John Piper says, 'a congregation learns its theology and takes it down into the crevices of their soul by the songs that they sing, not just by the preaching they hear' (Piper, 2017).

We also engage with theology in fellowship, creeds, liturgy, story, videos and many other ways. As human learning styles are diverse, including many non-written, oral methods, I suggest we expand this to recognize that *the whole act of intercultural worship is a primary mode of theologizing*. It allows for multiple avenues of regular and participatory theological discourse. This includes sermons, prayers and song but also storytelling, poetry, drama, movement, visual and digital images and music – engaging congregations holistically: interpersonally, culturally, aesthetically, physically, emotionally, spiritually and intellectually. We will observe all of these as we assess how biblical worship principles can be greatly enhanced by intercultural worship.

Worship Is a Transformational Journey

As mentioned earlier, true Christian worship, including intercultural worship, is God-centred. 'Worship is first and foremost for God' (Man, 2023, p. 442), a response to the injunction, 'Worship God' (Luke 4.8; Rev. 19.10; 22.9), since:

> Only the Creator is worthy to be revered and praised by his creatures. It is corporate worship which calls men and women to throw off the engulfing self-absorption … and … refocus on him who is the Giver and Sustainer of life and of life eternal. Our worship must be relentlessly theocentric. (Man, 2023, pp. 443–4)

Intercultural worship facilitates transformational discipleship

Such 'relentlessly theocentric' worship faces two realities: God is God, and we are not. All true Christian worship should turn us from self to God. Enthroning God and dethroning our egocentric dispositions is profoundly transformational – both personally and communally. Paul recognized this: 'we all, who with unveiled faces contemplate the Lord's glory, are being transformed into his image with ever-increasing glory, which comes from the Lord, who is the Spirit' (2 Cor. 3.18). The problem is we easily fall into our 'comfort zones' and become less challenged about cultural idols. Therefore, intercultural worship is well-placed to address this by engaging us with someone else's preferences as part of inclusive worship. In doing so, we turn from our preferences and 'look to the interests of others' – and then to Christ (Phil. 2.4–6). Of course, this can be unsettling at first, because it shines a spotlight on our reliance on familiar practices. We are challenged to worship in a new way, not only learning something from another culture but unlearning the tendency to prioritize our own. While this picture appears to expect congregations to be unrealistically selfless or 'mature', let us first consider what we gain: more ways to encounter God!

Intercultural worship facilitates more ways to encounter God

Since worship is to be with all our heart, soul, mind and strength (Mark 12.30), culturally diverse congregations can draw on a range of expressions to enable us to grow in more of these areas. For example, Eurocentric church cultures may shine in areas such as the cerebral, inward and personal, while those with a holistic and communal orientation are more likely to excel in worship with heart, soul, body and community. In congregations exploring liturgical diversity, an increasingly polycentric approach to worship can be adopted, where no one cultural group determines everything and each culture has a voice. This is enriching to all. In the Pentecost Sunday example above, it was the physicality and exuberance of the African-style drummers that released a freedom in others to respond to God in new ways.

Worship is a Dialogue of Revelation and Response

> The most foundational of all principles underlying true worship is the principle of revelation and response. It is the pattern of all true worship; in fact ... it is the pattern of all God's interactions with humankind ... We can worship God because he has first revealed himself to us. (Man, 2023, p. 23)

There are multiple examples of this revelation-response cycle throughout the Bible (Cherry, 2010, p. 45; Man, 2023, pp. 23–49). We highlight one here: Isaiah's call in the Jerusalem temple (Isa. 6.1–8):

- God appears to Isaiah (vv. 1–4).
- Isaiah responds, confessing his sin (v. 5).
- God cleanses Isaiah from sin (vv. 6–7).
- God asks, 'Whom shall I send?' (v. 8a).
- Isaiah responds, 'Send me' (v. 8b).

Intercultural worship facilitates response to God

Our worship should facilitate this dialogue. In intercultural worship, some cultures may excel in certain types of *response*, like lament, confession, intercession, giving, communal acts, 'high praise', dance, prostration or corporate devotion. For example, the Indian *bhajan* song form is especially suited to calm hearts and focus minds in communal, devotional worship. It is a deeply spiritual genre, resonating with many South Asians (Hale, 2001, p. 16–17; DwaarDelhi, 2014). Additionally, the setting for these, known as a *Satsang* (LSTheology, 2016), sometimes includes opportunity for the biblical practice of prostration (Ps. 95.5; Num. 24.4; Deut. 9.18; 2 Chron. 20.18; Matt. 2.11; 26.39; Rom. 12.1; Rev. 7.11), submitting each part of our being to God, a moving way to express worship (Robertson, 2017) as the body of Christ.

Worship Is Corporate in Nature

> Christian worship is what happens when the body of Christ assembles to hear with one heart and speak with one voice, the words, praises, prayers, petitions, and thanks fitting to Christian worship (Cherry, 2010, p. 13).

Christ created his Church as a multi-ethnic, multilingual 'body' – made up of many parts, each with different functions. In intercultural worship, individuals bring their language, culture, strengths, stories, gifts and insights. Paul lists the diversity of believers in Colossae, 'Here there is no Gentile or Jew, circumcised or uncircumcised, barbarian, Scythian, slave or free, but Christ is all, and is in all' (Col. 3.11), encouraging them to share the word of Christ with one another: 'Let the message of Christ dwell among you richly as you teach and admonish one another with all wisdom through psalms, hymns, and songs from the Spirit, singing to God with gratitude in your hearts' (Col. 3.16).

What kinds of songs did these ethnicities bring? Clearly, as well as Jewish-style 'psalms and hymns', there were Greek-style 'Christ hymns', hints of which we might glimpse in the New Testament (Hustad, 1994, p.195). Additionally, the (often spontaneous) 'spiritual songs' of believers from around the Roman empire would have resounded with their accents, cultures and musical backgrounds. Alec Robertson considered this probable: 'one may well believe that these converts sometimes used folks-songs familiar to them for their inspired utterances' (Robertson, 1960, p. 141). Cherry stresses that the environment of these pluralistic cities would have 'fostered a breadth of song' (Cherry, 2010, pp. 157–8) and Man agrees that this likely included 'musical expressions indigenous to the various groups' (Man, 2023, p. 253).

Intercultural worship facilitates cultural diversity in song

As with the churches Paul knew, songs from different parts of the world can bless today's culturally diverse congregations. However, in some cultures, people wait to be invited, so leaders need to be sensitive and proactive. If we ask, 'do you have a song from your background that we could use in worship?', we might discover invaluable resources. In addition, there are many existing multilingual songs created in multi-ethnic worship settings. Our Pentecost Sunday songs included a trilingual song from the Philippines, a multilingual chorus from Zambia and a song from South Africa. Nigerian songs like 'Waymaker' (Sinach, 2019),

'*Nara Ekelemo*' (Godfrey, 2019) and 'I Have Seen the Future' (Oyekan, 2024) exist in translation, as does the Hindi '*Ek Naam*' (Bangera, 2020). Other songs are available from Arts Release, Eric Lige Music, the Iona Community (Bell, 2000), Proskuneo Ministries, the Royal School of Church Music (Weaver, 2008), Songs2Serve and SongSelect. Regular events by All Nations Christian College, Proskuneo Ministries, Resonance, and Songs2Serve offer training in how to introduce multilingual songs. Today there is no lack of local, global and glocal song resources to praise Father, Son and Holy Spirit.

Worship Is Trinitarian in Nature

Cherry makes a remarkable statement: 'The beautiful mutuality so evident in the relationship of Father, Son, and Spirit, is profoundly at play in worship' (Cherry, 2010, p. 5). How is this true? First, in Christian worship, we have access to the Father through the Son by one Spirit (Eph. 2.18), glorifying Father, Son and Holy Spirit in prayer and adoration (2 Cor. 13.14; Rev. 5.12–14). Second, in the Scriptures, we glimpse a mysterious interrelationship between the persons of the Godhead in which each honours the others (John 13.31–32; 16.13–14; Phil. 2.9–11). Timothy Keller explains:

> Each of the divine persons centres upon the others ... That creates a dynamic, pulsating dance of joy and love. The early leaders of the Greek church had a word for this – *perichoresis* ... It means literally to dance or flow around. (Keller, 2008, p. 215)

Intercultural worship rejoices in relationships of mutuality

Intercultural worship can reflect this divine 'dance' in worship when each worshipper contributes their strengths, gifts and insights – recognizing and honouring each other (1 Cor. 12.21–26). Native American author Richard Twiss considers that, in such diversity, 'we get a glimpse of God ... a reflection of the diverse, interrelated community of God' in the Trinity (Twiss, 2009, p. 172). The authentic levels of mutuality this requires may seem idealistic but, in the same chapter, Paul highlights what we need for this to happen: 'Be completely humble and gentle; be patient, bearing with one another in love. Make every effort to keep the unity of the Spirit through the bond of peace' (Eph. 4.2–3). First, humility is required for intercultural worship, to give opportunity to people we do not easily relate to culturally. Second, patience is needed, because such mutuality takes time, even years, to cultivate. However, I have noticed that once a congregation makes room for diversity of cultural expressions, the hearts of worshippers expand to embrace people different from themselves. This openness points to the next principle of worship: realizing we are all recipients of God's grace, regardless of culture.

Worship Is Scriptural, Centred in God's Acts of Salvation

> God initiates worship ... Worship is fundamentally the result of, and response to, great saving events performed by God. (Cherry, p. 6)

In both testaments, worship arises as a response to God's saving acts for his people. In the Old, it centres on the Exodus (Ex. 15.1; Ps. 136). In the New, it focuses on Christ (Phil. 2.6–11). It is worth observing that the Scriptures that relate God's saving acts can be used in every part of the service. Indeed, 'The word of God must be central in our worship' (Man, 2023, pp. 449–54), as it was in the early church. Worship services filled with God's word equip believers to counteract influences in today's self-absorbed culture and to be part of God's story in this world.

Intercultural worship facilitates engagement with God's word

In intercultural worship, we can engage with the Scriptures in more ways. Some cultures are accomplished at storytelling God's word, others at poetry, yet others have song forms that help Scripture memorization, while many excel at teaching or powerful preaching. This diversity connects different parts of our brains and engages people of varied personalities and abilities. For example, hand actions provide a way to focus on the biblical truths of songs. Second, cultures that value poetry (such as West Africans and Persians), calligraphy (Arabic, Persian, Chinese, and so on) or visual expression can demonstrate how Christian poetry, writing and art offer great insights. Third, those who pray using memorized Scriptures build others' faith (Heb. 4.12). Finally, leaders who share preaching rotas cross-culturally with competent speakers not only exhibit humility but also enable more people to lay hold of Bible truths – through different lenses.

Significantly, diversifying a preaching rota is one way to break out of a monocultural theological mindset, since people whose circumstances require them to interact with different questions bring new insights. Maynard-Reid highlights: 'One important aspect of relating worship to life involves forging a liturgy that addresses the social injustices and pain that rack the society in which God's people live' (Maynard-Reid, 2000, p. 49). For example, in our church, non-Caucasian preachers have spoken openly of the pains of the racism they have encountered in a white-majority society, bringing authentic messages in a loving, biblical way. Fortunately, breaking out of monoculturalism (theological or liturgical) is made possible because Christ made his people one – in a radical new covenant fundamental to our worship.

Worship Is Covenantal in Nature

> Christian worship, ... is covenantal worship – worship that flows from a formal relationship between God and God's people. (Cherry, p. 10)

As we observed, biblical worship is built on a covenantal relationship between God and his people (Gen. 12.1–3). Through Christ's 'new covenant' established by his death (Luke 22.20; Heb. 9.15), his Church is ethnically diverse but one (Gal. 3.26–29; 6.16; 1 Peter 2.9–10). This is symbolized and experienced in baptism and communion (Acts 2.41–42) and this unity is particularly highlighted in breaking bread (1 Cor. 10.17; 11.25). Japanese missiologist Ken Christopher Miyamoto writes: 'God draws nearest to the world in the midst of worship, particularly in the Eucharist. There the broken relation between God and human beings is healed, and ... the people of God are transformed into the true people of God' (Miyamoto, 2008, p. 161).

Intercultural worship facilitates communion practices

There can be a heightened sense of being 'transformed into the true people of God' when breaking bread in multi-ethnic congregations, since all differences are levelled at the Cross. We each come crying, 'have mercy', and in breaking bread we receive fresh grace. Likewise, communion can be conducted in various cultural ways, such as levels of formality, forms of 'bread' and 'wine' and who does what, where and when. Third, communion provides a deep encounter with God with very few linguistic barriers. A multi-ethnic Anglican church considered observing a monthly communion but chose a weekly practice instead, for worshippers to meet with God in ways not dependent on English ability. This eucharistic encounter happens, of course, by God's Spirit moving, as we see in our next biblical principle.

Worship Is Motivated and Empowered by the Holy Spirit

> For we are the circumcision, who worship by the Spirit of God and glory in Christ Jesus and put no confidence in the flesh. (Phil. 3.3 ESV)

As Man says, 'Our response of worship is enabled, motivated, and empowered by the Holy Spirit.' (Man, 2023, p. 464). The New Testament is clear that it is the Holy Spirit who is active in the believer enabling us to worship the Father and the Son, that by the Spirit we cry, 'Abba, Father' and 'Jesus is Lord' (Rom 8.15; Gal 4.6; 1 Cor. 12.3). Believers are given gifts through the Spirit, many of which Paul lists for use in worship (1 Cor. 12—14). The Spirit's role is seen in Corinth, where 'each of you has a hymn, or a word of instruction, a revelation, a tongue or an interpretation' (1 Cor. 14.26). In Ephesus, Paul expected that, being 'filled with the Holy Spirit', disciples would speak 'to one another with psalms, hymns, and songs from the Spirit' (Eph. 5.18–20), enabling them, as in Colossae, to thank God and share the message of Christ with one another through song (Col. 3.16).

Intercultural worship facilitates the sharing of spiritual gifts

Believers from different backgrounds may be gifted in many areas, such as sharing words from God or praying with discernment and effectiveness. Likewise, some carry a freedom to worship that rubs off on others. Similarly, a healthy lack of expressive inhibition or a greater respect for elders can become countercultural forces for good in churches dulled by the secularism, cynicism and apathy of a Euro-centric spiritual climate. Some people need to be actively invited to contribute or, alternatively, guided in how to contribute, but we all need the gifts of fellow believers to 'spur us on' in our faith (Heb. 10.24) and in God's mission, to which we now turn.

Worship Is Missional, the Goal and Fuel of Missions

John Piper set out the relation between worship and missions in these striking phrases: 'Missions exists because worship doesn't ... Worship is the fuel and goal of missions ... Missions begins and ends in worship' (Piper, p. 11).

We see this demonstrated in Acts 2. People responded to the gospel and were gathered into the church. Then, they encountered the Spirit of Christ through the word of God, breaking of bread and prayer, being equipped to impact others, so that, 'the Lord added to their number daily those who were being saved' (Acts 2.42–47). True Christian worship, then, results in mission and true mission results in worship.

Intercultural worship equips for cross-cultural mission

In my experience overseas, I found that worship using the language and idioms of the people reduces barriers. In intercultural worship this can work in several ways:

- If visitors hear a song, prayer or Bible-reading in their language, it can be eye- and heart-opening. If a song is also in their musical style, I have seen people respond with gratitude and tears in their eyes. They feel accepted by the church and by God. Some turn to Christ in faith (Davis and Lerner, 2021, p. 201–2).
- Congregations can be equipped for cross-cultural conversations outside church. As part of a service, leaders can invite everyone to use a greeting in someone's language. Even one phrase can become a conversation opener. I recently heard of a Methodist lady who came across a distressed Iranian refugee in her town – but she knew a simple greeting in Farsi, learned from a takeaway shopkeeper. This created an instant connection and a welcoming church community for the Iranian family.
- Songs learned at church can open conversations. You can ask for pronunciation help or sing to a speaker of that language. A Nigerian pastor learned an Indian song from our team, later singing it for a despondent Muslim man in a London market. The song created a bridge and he came to faith in Jesus (Collinge, 2022b, p. 94).

Practicalities

Your church may be advanced in intercultural worship or just starting out. In either case, a few practical tips might help. Let's take the Pentecost Sunday example. There are several things to note:

1 **Take time.** Our service was part of a process over several years of building intentional cross-cultural dialogue. We have taken gradual steps, faltered, paused and kept reviewing. Our leadership team has begun to diversify, expanding our capacity. We now more frequently include various languages in prayer, readings and songs.
2 **Seek God and plan.** Our worship trajectory results from the vision of our leaders, especially Dan Chadwick and Matt Hatch, and discussions with various subgroups. Details of the event itself were co-planned by the pastor, preacher, service host and music leader.
3 **Invite help, if needed.** Pentecost Sunday gave us opportunity to request help from a drumming group we have links with. Their vibrancy undoubtedly generated an atmosphere of participation and freedom to contribute.
4 **Rehearse well.** For special events, pre-service preparation and rehearsal are vital. Also, multilingual songs from around the world work well and familiar songs can be translated into appropriate languages (see resources listed on pages 92–3).
5 **Build diversity one element at a time.** Learning a Middle Eastern prayer gesture, engaging in cross-cultural discussion, being led in intercession for certain countries and hearing insights from a Nigerian diversity expert all contributed to our worship and mutual understanding.
6 **Delight in God and his people.** Worship like this shows that intercultural worship is supremely about the praise of God and therefore also about building a community that glorifies him through loving, respecting and celebrating one another.
7 **Keep building – keep praying.** The intention of our Pentecost service was to help us keep moving towards intercultural community and worship, realizing it's about what happens after the service not just in the event itself.

Conclusion

This chapter has highlighted that intercultural worship provides the church in our day with an expanding range of ways to encounter the God of the Bible. Far from overriding the core elements and principles of New Testament worship, each of these is enhanced, since we can now call on diverse cultural strengths – multiplying our modes of theological discourse. For this to happen, leaders need to find ways to de-centre the dominant culture and to ask, 'whose cultures could shape our worship?', allowing all voices to be heard. The answer, surely, is that it will not be any one culture. Rather, as the Holy Spirit leads, a 'culture of many cultures' (Kwiyani, 2020, p.113) and a new 'shared worship culture' will gradually arise (Collinge, 2022a, p. 139; Seevaratnam, 2020, p. 19). This emerging culture is not a 'melting pot' where individual flavours get lost in the whole, but it combines shared commonalities (biblical, global, societal and congregational) with each culture's distinctives. In such an environment, we anticipate the vision and sounds of the future, as in Revelation 7.9–10:

> After this I looked, and there before me was a great multitude that no one could count, from every nation, tribe, people and language, standing before the throne and before the Lamb. They were wearing white robes and were holding palm branches in their hands. And they cried out in a loud voice: 'Salvation belongs to our God, who sits on the throne, and to the Lamb.'

Bibliography

Alikin, Valeriy A., 2010, *The Earliest History of the Christian Gathering: Origin, Development and Content of the Christian Gathering in the First to Third Centuries*, Leiden: Brill, 2010, pp. 211–54, available at https://www.jstor.org/stable/10.1163/j.ctt1w76wv6.11 (accessed 20.2.25).

Bevans, Stephen B., 2015, *Models of Contextual Theology: Revised and Expanded Edition*, New York: Orbis Books.

Black, Kathy, 2000, *Culturally-Conscious Worship*, St Louis, MO: Chalice Press.

Cherry, Constance M., 2010, *The Worship Architect: A Blueprint for Designing Culturally Relevant and Biblically Faithful Services*, Grand Rapids, MI: Baker Academic.

Collinge, Ian, 2022a, 'Intercultural Worship: A Contemporary Understanding of Church and Worship in the Global Age', in Beattie, Warren R., and Soh, Anne M. Y., eds, *Arts Across Cultures: Reimagining the Christian Faith in Asia*, Oxford: Regnum.

Collinge, Ian, 2022b, 'Intercultural Worship: Liturgical Diversity for the Sake of Unity, Mission and the Glory of God', in Spohn, Elmar and Werner, Eberhard (Hg.), *Polyphone Klangraüme, edition missiotop, Jahrbuch 2021*, pp.85–99.

Cosper, Mike, 2013, *Rhythms of Grace: How the Church's Worship Tells the Story of the Gospel*, Wheaton, IL: Crossway.

Davis, Josh and Lerner, Nikki, 2015, *Worship Together in Your Church as in Heaven*, Nashville, TN: Abingdon Press, p. 201–2.

Fortunato, Frank, Neeley, Paul, and Brinneman, Carol, eds., 2006, *All the World Is Singing*, Tyrone, GA: Authentic.

GEN – Global Ethnodoxology Network, 2025, https://www.worldofworship.org. Also see: https://www.worldofworship.org/core-values/ (accessed 20.2.2025).

Hale, Chris, 2001, 'Reclaiming the Bhajan, Ancient musical styles of India transform modern worship of Christ', in *Mission Frontiers*, June 2001, pp. 16–17, *Worship that Moves the Soul: Recognizing the critical role of indigenous worship in church planting*.

Hustad, Donald P., 1994, 'A Brief History of Music in Worship', in Webber, Robert E., ed., 1994, *Music and the Arts in Christian Worship, Book 1*, Nashville, TN: Star Song Publishing Group.

Johnson, Ajaye, 2020, 'Moravian Church Building, Dehradun, India': https://tinyurl.com/2p9hnvp2 (accessed 20.2.25).

Keller, Timothy, 2008, *The Reason for God: Belief in an Age of Scepticism*, London, Hodder & Stoughton.

Kim, Jaewoo, 2013, 'The Whole World Has Gone "Glocal"', in Krabill, James, gen. ed., and Fortunato, Frank, Harris, Robin, and Schrag, Brian, eds., *Worship and Mission for the Global Church: An Ethnodoxology Handbook*, Pasadena, CA: William Carey Library, pp. 46–8.

Kwiyani, Harvey, 2020, *Multicultural Kingdom: Ethnic Diversity, Mission and the Church*, London: SCM Press.

LSTheology, 2016, 'LST Host Satsang': https://artsrelease.org/en/resources/lst-host-satsang (accessed 20.2.25).

LWF – Lutheran World Federation, 1996, 'Nairobi Statement on Worship and Culture: Contemporary Challenges and Opportunities', in *Christian Worship: Unity in Cultural Diversity*, pp. 23–8: https://lutheranworld.org/sites/default/files/2022-02/lwf_studies_christian_worship_unity_cultural_diversity.pdf (accessed 20.2.25)

Man, Ron, 2023, *Let Us Draw Near: Biblical Foundations of Worship*, Eugene, OR: Wipf and Stock.

Maynard-Reid, Pedrito U., 2000, *Diverse Worship: African-American, Caribbean and Hispanic Perspectives*, Downers Grove, IL: Intervarsity Press.

McKinnon, James W., 2001, 'Christian Church, music of the early', in *Grove Music Online*: https://doi.org/10.1093/gmo/9781561592630.article.05705 (accessed 20.2.25).

Mission Frontiers, May–Aug 1996, *Worship and Missions*.

Miyamoto, Ken Christoph, 2008, 'Worship is Nothing but Mission: A Reflection on Some Japanese Experiences', in Walls, Andrew and Ross, Cathy, eds, *Mission in the 21st Century: Exploring the Five Marks of Global Mission*, Darton, Longman and Todd, pp. 157–64.

Piper, John, 1993, *Let the Nations be Glad! The Supremacy of God in Missions*, Leicester: Inter-Varsity Press.

Piper, John, 2017, in Desiring God, *Ask Pastor John*, 'When Worship Lyrics Miss the Mark' in Interview with John Piper: https://www.desiringgod.org/interviews/when-worship-lyrics-miss-the-mark (accessed 20.2.2025).

Robertson, Alec, 1960, *The Pelican History of Music, 1: Ancient Forms to Polyphony*, Harmandsworth: Penguin Books.

Robertson, Andy, 2017, 'Becoming Pentecost People', in Baptists Together, Summer 2017: https://www.baptist.org.uk/Articles/495752/Becoming_Pentecost_People.aspx (accessed 20.2.2025).

Seevaratnam, Mohan, 2020, 'Worshipping Together Interculturally at Mosaic', in Aldous, Ben, Dunmore, Idina and Seevaratnam, Mohan, 2020, *Intercultural Church: Shared Learning from New Communities*, Cambridge: Grove Books Limited, p. 19.

SEM, no date – Society for Ethnomusicology, https://www.ethnomusicology.org/page/AboutEthnomusicol (accessed 20.2.2025).

Twiss, Richard, 2009, 'Imaging God's Diverse Unity' in *Holy Bible: Mosaic NLT*, Carol Stream, IL: Tyndale House Publishers, Inc., p. 172.

Walls, Andrew, 2007, 'The Ephesians Moment in Worldwide Worship: A Meditation on Revelation 21 and Ephesians 2', in Farhadian, Charles E., ed., *Christian Worship Worldwide: Expanding Horizons, Deepening Practices*, Grand Rapids, MI: Eerdmans, pp. 27–37.

Musical References

All Nations Christian College: https://www.allnations.ac.uk/ (accessed 20.2.2025).

Arts Release: https://artsrelease.org/en/music-worship (accessed 20.2.2025).

Bangera, Sheldon and others, Jaago Music: 2020, *Ek Naam – JaagoAcoustic*: https://youtu.be/Nx_m6KP4AJY; The SelahVideos, 2021, *Selah – One Name (Ek Naam)*: https://youtu.be/RRH4M0A3BkE (both accessed 20.2.2025).

Bell, John L. (compiler), 2000, *One is the Body: Songs of Unity and Diversity*, Wild Goose Publications, Glasgow.

DwaarDelhi, 2014, *Bhajo Naam by Dwaar Satsang*, https://www.youtube.com/watch?v=jyiTyYflhF8 (accessed 20.2.2025).

Elevation Worship, 2023, *Praise (feat. Brandon Lake, Chris Brown & Chandler Moore), Elevation Worship*, by Chris Brown, Steven Furtick, Cody Carnes, Chandler Moore, Michael Brandon Lake, Joseph Patrick Martin Barrett: https://www.youtube.com/watch?v=f2oxGYpuLkw (accessed 20.2.2025).

Eric Lige Music: https://www.youtube.com/channel/UCbQXso55k7sBXSPEECvVK_g (accessed 20.2.2025)

Godfrey, Timothy 2019, covered by Arts Release, 2020, *Nara Ekele Mo (Global Version) – Resonance and Friends*: https://www.youtube.com/watch?v=hxSvSmjmCmE (accessed 20.2.2025).

Hillsong, 2019, by Jason Ingram, Scott Ligertwood, Brooke Gabrielle Fraser.

Makai, Paul, c.1970, 'God is So Good'; Translator: Marilyn Foulkes (c. 1970). See: https://hymnary.org/text/god_is_so_good_god_is_so_good (accessed 20.2.2025).

Oyekan, Dunsin, 2024, in The Praise Court, 2024, *I Have Seen the Future*, Dunsin Oyekan feat. Naomi Raine, Sheldon Bangera, Matt Marvane and Joseph Espinoza: https://www.youtube.com/watch?v=x_3voPKWslo (accessed 20.2.2025).
Proskuneo Ministries: https://proskuneo.org/music (accessed 20.2.2025).
Resonance Band UK: https://artsrelease.org/en/music-worship (accessed 20.2.2025)
Sinach (Osinachi Okoro), 2019, *Waymaker*.
Songs2Serve: https://songs2serve.eu/songs (accessed 20.2.2025).
SongSelect: https://songselect.ccli.com/search/language (accessed 20.2.2025).
Tomlin, Chris, 2004, *How Great is Our God*.
Victory Worship, 2019, *Victory Worship – Tribes (Official Music Video)*, by Jose Villanueva III, Sarah Bulahan, Bryson Breakey and Elizabeth Cabiling Tumaliuan: https://www.youtube.com/watch?v=66H4mLGgZ54 (accessed 20.2.2025).
Weaver, Geoffrey (compiler), 2008, *In Every Corner Sing – Songs of God's World*, London: RSCM.
Worship Central South Africa, 2018, *Come Holy Spirit (Uthando) Lyric Video – LIVE at LIV*, by Denise Counihan, Mark Counihan and Langelihle (Langa) Mbonambi: https://www.youtube.com/watch?v=UKAlsYb2V6o (accessed 20.2.2025)

5

Intercultural Church as a Direction of Travel: Exploring the Journey of a Korean Diaspora Church (KDC)

MIJA WI

Introduction

Diverse diaspora churches have breathed new life into post-Christian Western society while addressing the needs of diaspora people moving into new contexts. While the meaning of diaspora will briefly be discussed later in the chapter, here and throughout the chapter diaspora broadly refers to 'peoples living outside of their places of origin'. See the statement of 'The Seoul Declaration on Diaspora Missiology', Lausanne Movement (2009). This statement requires no further explanation in the current landscape of Christianity in the UK, where many fast-growing churches belong to diaspora communities (Jenkins, 2007, pp. 92–3), such as Nigerian, Ghanaian, Chinese and Brazilian congregations, to name a few.

As Harvey Kwiyani aptly puts it, any discussion of European Christianity, or, for that matter British Christianity, must acknowledge the presence and impact of diaspora churches, referred to as 'the blessed reflex' (2020, p. 51). However, despite their evangelical fervour and phenomenal growth, ongoing concerns about diaspora churches persist both from within and outside. While serving the constant influx of newly arrived immigrants, many diaspora churches have often produced replica communities of their homelands, which increasingly widens intergenerational gaps (Koo, 2019, p. 2; Kwiyani, 2020, p. 145). Also, they tend to focus on in-group ministries while remaining as ghettoized homogeneous units with little impact on the wide society (Kim and Hershberger, 2020).

In this context, the chapter critically reflects on the journey of a Korean diaspora church (KDC), taking approaches to an intercultural model.

As the title 'Intercultural Church as a Direction of Travel' indicates, becoming an intercultural church is not simply a final destination, but a journey or ongoing process. I aim to offer a realistic picture of what it looks like when an established mono-ethnic church takes a journey toward an intercultural one, exploring key issues and themes that need consideration along the way. The KDC under discussion has not fully transitioned into an intercultural one. But it has taken intentional approaches and directions toward an intercultural church. Before reflecting on the KDC's intercultural journey, I will firstly provide brief overviews of perspectives on diaspora churches in the UK. Following that, I will discuss the intersection of the homogeneous and diaspora church, given the current state of the KDC, which is a homogeneous diaspora church. Finally, I critically reflect on a slow but continual journey toward an intercultural church as a direction of travel of the KDC, suggesting that these steps may offer a future direction for diaspora churches in the UK.

Perspectives on Diaspora Churches in the UK

Christianity in the UK has been on the decline for the past few decades. The 2021 Census indicates that it has now become a minority religion. The percentage of those who identified as Christians in England and Wales fell from 59.3% in 2011 to 46.2% in 2021 (ONS, 2022) In Scotland, over 50% said they had no religion according to the 2022 census (Scotland's Census, 2024). However, as with any statistical data, these figures require interpretation, as raw numbers or trends alone do not tell the full story. While it is true that the number of white Christians in Britain continues to decrease, the overall trend shows an increase in the number of Christians among non-white populations, mainly driven by migration. When examining the data in the context of shifting ethnic demographics of Christians in the UK, this trend becomes more revealing (Church of England, 2014). This pattern mirrors a global trend. According to the 2015 World Christian Database, over half of the world's migrants identify as Christian (Zurlo, 2020, p. 55). The recent wave of migrants from Hong Kong to the UK, following the introduction of the British National (Overseas) immigration route in 2021, points to this trend. Over 40% of Hong Kong migrants under this scheme are Christian (UK Hong Kongers, 2021). This ratio is strikingly high compared to the religious demographics of Hong Kong where only 16% of the population identifies as Christian (*Hong Kong Yearbook*, 2021).

The analysis of the ethnic shifts among Christians in England (2001–11), conducted before the recent migration from Hong Kong, still provides valuable insights into this ongoing trajectory. Christianity in the UK is becoming increasingly ethnically diverse, 'thriving, vibrant and on the increase among white (other), mixed, Asian and Black Christians, and rapidly so in the Asian population' (Church of England, 2014). In the wider European context, Philip Jenkins argues that the influx of immigrant Christians not only offsets the rise of immigrant Muslims but also revitalizes Christianity, with the potential to re-evangelize Europe (2007). The growing presence of diaspora churches and their impact has undeniably altered the face or perhaps the fate of European and British Christianity.

Many diaspora church leaders express both their genuine recognition and deep gratitude for British mission works despite the painful and complex colonial history associated with it. They now see it as their turn to support their British brothers and sisters, who face the challenges of rising secularism and the decline of Christianity. Perhaps revival is already under way in Britain, though it remains largely unrecognized. The late Swiss theologian Walter Hollenwerger once remarked, 'Christians in Britain prayed for many years for revival, and when it came they did not recognize it because it was black' (1992, p. ix). To this statement, Kwiyani adds, moreover, 'It came dressed in Pentecostal clothes' (2020, p. 54). The diverse colours, expressions, and flavours of Christianity brought by diaspora churches are often treated as little more than 'a footnote' (Kwiyani, 2020, p. 51) or 'an appendix' (Kim, 2022, p. 10) in discussions of British Christianity.

What might explain this marginalization? First and foremost, there remains strong scepticism – perhaps even 'disdain' – towards the beliefs, practices and expressions of diaspora churches, both from the general public and, at times, from other Christians in the UK (Jenkins, 2007). Their enthusiastic expressions of Christianity are often seen as unfit or even potentially harmful to British society. This reaction is not entirely surprising. Christianity, when it arrived in East Asia, clothed in Western cultural forms, was similarly met with suspicion despite its Asian origins (Chia, 2022). The unfamiliar expressions of diaspora Christians, deeply intertwined with their faith and culture, can be off-putting to non-religious people and sadly often evoke similar sentiments among fellow Christians. Moreover, there is increasing fear and hostility toward the rising number of immigrants in the UK, as evidenced by recent anti-immigrant riots and the growing popularity of far-right movements across Britain and Europe (BBC, 2024). Unfortunately, the narrative of the British nationalistic agenda is shared by some Christian circles to promote their own Christian causes (Paynter and Power, 2024). Immigrant Christians are often viewed with suspicion, perceived as people coming to the UK primarily for their economic benefit while masking their intentions with claims of spiritual zeal. In certain Christian communities, there are even calls for white British church leaders to focus on evangelizing their *own kind* (Rah, 2009). This sentiment can be interpreted as a subtle way of saying 'No, thanks' to those who come to the UK to work in partnership with British fellow Christians.

Second, limited interaction has existed between British local churches and diaspora ones, with Sunday services largely remaining segregated. Martin Luther King's speech over 60 years ago still resonates today as Sunday continues to be one of the most segregated days in the multi-ethnic and multicultural UK. Many Asian and Latin American churches have opted to form homogeneous congregations, primarily because of the practical challenges of language and cultural differences, which can make collective worshipping difficult (Rah, 2009). Similarly, Black African and Caribbean Christian communities have established their congregations, despite the separation prompted by the historical alienation and marginalization of these Christians from British churches (Jenkins, 2007). Many of these communities do not seem to bother any more with the integration into British churches but happily remain separate, exercising autonomy and power while celebrating their cultural identities within their worship settings (Kwiyani, 2020). Over the decades, many growing diaspora churches have been preoccupied with serving their ever-growing communities, often remaining isolated and thus unseen from the wider Christian network in the UK. Meanwhile, local British congregations have been grappling with their challenges in navigating their present and future in the rapidly shifting post-Christian UK. Hence the core issue is not merely segregation but a lack of meaningful interaction. The pain of displacement literally experienced by diaspora communities remains largely misunderstood, just as the metaphorical sense of displacement felt by British Christians is not fully empathized with (Marzouk, 2019).

Diaspora and Homogeneous Church

I have used the term 'diaspora church' interchangeably with mono-ethnic or homogeneous church, although it may or should not always be the case. However, it is somewhat true that many diaspora churches have become homogeneous to the point where these terms are often used interchangeably. The term 'diaspora', coined by the Septuagint, originally referred to the Israelites scattered among the nations or living in exile in the Old Testament (e.g. Deut. 28.25; 30.4; Isa. 49.6; Jer. 41.17) (Barclay, 2004). In the New Testament, it describes (Jewish) Christians scattered across Asia Minor (1 Peter 1.1; James 1.1). One of the most striking aspects of Israel's history through the lens of migration is 'recalled and interpreted in Stephen's speech in Acts' (Stenschke, 2016). Each key point in Israel's past is marked by migration and exile. Furthermore, the diaspora is characterized by its mission-shaped identity (Carroll R., 2020). While migration and diaspora became an integral part of God's people's identity in the Bible, they almost always evoked missional purposes while living in a foreign land. They were called to be a blessing to the land where they resided (Isa. 49.6) and scattered to share the message of good news to the nations. The scattering of early Christians and the proclaiming of the message go hand in hand (Acts 8.1).

In contemporary discourse, diaspora has become a trendy term, or better put a 'concept', widely used in anthropological, cultural, political and religious studies. Robin Cohen's story of an Israeli professor who lamented yet another 'stolen' term from his Jewish heritage well-illustrates the gist of its popularity (Cohen, 2005). Regardless of its broad usage, the discussions of diaspora revolve around the themes of home (either making or imagining it), displacement, exile, identity and movement.

On the contrary, the term 'homogeneous' unit (HU) was birthed and gained its popularity in mission theory in the late twentieth century, thanks to Donald McGavran who defined it as 'a segment of society in which all members have some characteristics in common' (McGavran, 2018). It could be based on ethnic, socio-economic status, class or language. At its core, McGavran argued the growth of church should be prioritized. To this end, crossing of any barriers or differences for people to become Christians should be removed. He further stated that 'Men like to become Christians without crossing racial, linguistic, or class barriers' (McGavran, 1970, p. 178). Furthermore, he adamantly defended why the HU was not unbiblical, but solidly grounded in the teachings of Paul, particularly drawing from Ephesians 2.11—3.19 and Galatians 3.28. He argued that Paul taught each church to preserve its cultural heritage and its distinct identity without blending everyone in one pot (McGavran, 2018, p. 413–16).

In response to McGavran, C. René Padilla stated that 'The breaking down of the barriers that separate people in the world was regarded as *an essential aspect of the gospel*, not merely as a result of it' (Padilla, 1982, p. 29). Padilla further points out that there were no biblical examples of building homogeneous churches to maintain culturally distinctive identities of people. Instead, the unity of the church was portrayed through how members lived out the oneness in Christ amid cultural, socio-economic or ethnic differences (Padilla, 1982). If this were not the case, what would have been the point of wrestling with differences to embody their 'in Christ' identity? While learning to genuinely accept one another, this process at times involved giving up one's cultural identity to seek others' interest first despite potential misunderstandings and disagreements (e.g. 1 Cor. 8—10; Rom. 14.1—15.6). Moreover, the coming of the Holy Spirit enabled and empowered different socio-economic, ethnic and cultural groups to cross the barriers for the unified formation of communities of believers (Wi, 2019a, 2019b). McGavran either underestimated the multi-ethnic and cultural contexts of the Roman Empire where Paul planted and nurtured churches or overemphasized the 'indigeneity' of each church at the expense of crossing barriers that defined being part of the body of Christ (McGavran, 2018).

Fifty years on, the HU principle or strategy remains highly controversial, yet popular. On the one hand, Soong-Chan Rah accuses the HU principle of consolidating racial segregation with the dominance of Western white culture, especially within American Christianity (Rah, 2009). On the other hand, one cannot deny its effectiveness, particularly in (quantitative) church growth. Thus, it has been adopted and adapted by many churches around the world. Here, my interest lies in the intersection between diaspora churches and homogeneous ones. Strangely enough, the critique of in-group focused ministries always lingers in the background in discussions of diaspora churches, missions and missiology. However, the HU principle rarely comes to the fore in these conversations (Tira and Yamamori, 2020; George, 2018; Wan, 2011). The focus tends to remain on the roles of diaspora communities in the expansion of Christianity in the Bible and today, alongside the themes of identity formation in exile, the experience of displacement, the imagination of home, and the shaping of faith across cultures. It might be an uneasy reality that diaspora churches where the majority of believers share similar experiences of displacement, identity crisis, longing for home and linguistic and cultural challenges, have somewhat naturally evolved into homogeneous churches. Their growth to some degree can be attributed to the HU principle, whether or not they have consciously embraced McGavran's strategy.

The intersection of diaspora churches and the HU principle needs further consideration. While growth is often seen as a positive outcome, it does not justify the process, that is, how we build the body of Christ. As discussed, the HU principle is not biblically, and for that matter, theologically, grounded. However, I do not want to underestimate the realities and needs of diaspora communities, which the HU principle, albeit unwittingly, seems to address. For instance, homogeneous diaspora churches play a key role within immigrant communities to meet spiritual longings of those who find themselves in new places as well as their practical needs, such as finding houses and schools, opening a bank account or registering at a GP. Rah's description of the Korean-American church aptly mirrors the situation in the UK. 'Evangelism is the engagement of life on all levels – serving a community in need and providing the services that demonstrate the kingdom of God to those who may be experiencing a sense of displacement in the kingdom of this world' (Rah, 2009, p. 177). For many immigrants, particularly struggling with a new language, homogeneous diaspora churches are often the only places where they can freely and fully express themselves, not to mention the appreciation of worshipping in their mother tongue. For those working within British society during the week, these churches provide a haven for them to relax in a culturally familiar territory to regain strength to return to their daily lives. Most crucially, in times of crisis and death, these churches offer invaluable support and comfort to their fragile communities. The deep sense of 'intense community' and mutual care seems to play a greater role in church growth than the HU principle itself, echoing sociologist Rodney Stark's classic study on the rise of Christianity, which emphasizes the power of close-linked networks (1996, p, 208).

Nevertheless, the goodness of serving marginalized and displaced communities can no longer be justified if it results in creating an exclusive, self-serving bubble and thus becomes an unwelcoming place (Kim and Hershberger, 2020). As noted earlier, diaspora cannot be discussed apart from its missional purpose. In the book of Acts, diaspora believers not only played a key role in spreading the gospel as they moved (11.19–30), but they also planted a multi-ethnic church, the church in Antioch which was truly intercultural in its structure and missional in its dynamic (13.1–3) (Chang, 2020). At its core, Christian identity formation and growth almost always took place in the process of crossing cultures. With that in mind, what might be the way forward for homogeneous diaspora churches? The next section will offer a critical reflection on the KDC's intercultural journey.

A Case Study of the KDC: Critical Reflections

The KDC is one of many Korean diaspora churches in the UK, located in the north-west of England. Established in 2017, it was initially planted to serve a small number of Korean immigrants, which comprised both permanently settled families and temporary immigrants such as students. Homogeneity is a deeply embedded cultural reality of Koreans, and it is not surprising that Koreans and the KDCs are known for their 'ethnic detachment' or 'ethnocentric tendencies' (Koo, 2019, p. 4). Historically, Korea, as a small country, surrounded by global powers, strived to survive and preserve its autonomy and identity by keeping others out. Assimilation was seen as a threat that could erase its unique and distinctive identity. For centuries, it remained as the 'hermit kingdom', maintaining minimal contact with the outside world till the Japanese occupation of Korea in 1910 (Seth, 2008, p. 28). Some of the most distinctive features of Korean identity today, including cultural and linguistic homogeneity, were shaped during this period of isolation. As a result, Koreans living abroad often find that preserving their culture and forming tight-knit communities is key to their survival strategy. In this context, diaspora churches like the KDC naturally become focal points for cohesion, providing cultural and spiritual support to Koreans navigating life in a foreign land.

The Journey

The KDC began as a homogeneous church, both ethnically and socio-economically, though the latter was not intended. The Korean immigrants in north-west England generally represent a narrow spectrum of Korean society – middle class and highly educated – and most of them live in affluent suburban areas to ensure good educational opportunities for their children. In its early years (2017–20), the KDC was mainly concerned about its socio-economic homogeneity, as it could be perceived as an unwelcome place for anyone who did not fit into this so-called middle-class Christian category. However, as the church grew, it has grown not only in number but also its diversity both ethnically and socio-economically. It started welcoming people from a broad spectrum of socio-economic groups, from North Korean asylum seekers to single parents, although these groups remained relatively small. The KDC evolved with the joining of new people and began to reshape its dynamics. It took a journey in a new direction as more of the under-represented group took leadership roles.

After the pandemic, the KDC saw a growing influx of non-Koreans, ranging from non-Korean spouses and friends to those who were interested in Korean culture, many of whom were not Christians. Alongside this, the increasing number of students and young adults are so-called Global Nomads or Third-Culture Kids, who spent a significant part of their lifetime elsewhere outside of Korea and moved to the UK, either for their studies or jobs. As a result, a simple bilingual service through translation gadgets seems no longer enough to meet the needs of the growing presence of non-Koreans and the changing faces of ethnic Koreans in the church. The shifts in the demographic of the KDC have posed some exciting, yet challenging, questions among its members. A few of these are:

1 Is it not a *Korean* church? If it were not, why would we choose it over a British local church? Where is the uniqueness of the KDC?
2 Do we want our children to learn the Korean language and culture since the church is the only place where they can truly engage with their Korean heritage (Marzouk, 2019)?
3 Is the mission of our church to serve non-Koreans? Are there other churches better suited for this mission?

These are all legitimate concerns. The first-generation Korean immigrants still struggled with British culture and language, went through the trauma of displacement, and sought to find safety, boundaries and belongingness in the church. More importantly, this change was not what they signed up for when they came to the KDC. Nonetheless, the creation of a cultural island of the Korean diaspora is not helpful for them while living in a multi-ethnic and cultural society like the UK. The monocultural KDC is becoming inadequate or irrelevant to the growing number of the second generation and young people. Most importantly, it is detrimental to, and to some degree a denial of, their Christian identity which is always formed and shaped alongside others (Kwiyani, 2020). The complex realities of diaspora experience and the evolving demographics of the KDC have prompted the church to consider a potential intercultural journey. Before reflecting on the intercultural steps taken by the KDC, it seems fair to address some key issues in light of the current state of the KDC, which is marked by its East Asian diaspora identity.

East Asian Diasporic Identity

First, certain cultural characteristics of East Asian-ness, such as its group-oriented and hyper-relational tendency, should be taken seriously when discussing the KDC's intercultural practices. On the one hand, it is easier to communicate the importance of the corporate identity of Christians and Paul's community-focused teachings to East Asians, as they are naturally relational, interconnected and interdependent, not individualistic (Jackson, 2019). In addition, East Asians who think and behave under collective societal norms find it particularly challenging to adjust to the more individualistic UK society, where they may feel disconnected or unwelcome. As individuals, they often feel intimidated or disempowered in a setting where they remain as foreigners and minorities. However, they as a group find strength and empowerment, making it easier for them to engage with mainstream society.

Another cultural aspect that should be acknowledged is the East Asian approach to hospitality. They feel unwelcomed, not because of explicit hostility, but because they assume the host must proactively offer hospitality. One of the common frustrations, shared by East Asians attending local British churches, is the persistent feeling of remaining as guests indefinitely or never fully included with opportunities to take on the role of hosts within the church. Once they feel secure in their own group, however, they can play the role of hosts and offer hospitality to others. These unique cultural characteristics of the KDC should be taken seriously, not dismissed, as the church takes on a journey toward an intercultural church.

Second, as discussed earlier, while the strong homogeneous ties may have facilitated the growth of the KDC to some degree, a more crucial factor that contributed to the growth lies in its provision of holistic ministry that shows genuine care and concern to the immigrants, Christians and non-Christians alike. The KDC, like many other Korean diaspora churches around the world, has not merely served as a religious place but also functioned as a hub for long-lasting relationships, connection to their roots, and social networks (Rah, 2007; Song, 2020). The KDC has provided 'an immediate basis for attachments' and 'a new and expanded sense of family' to those living in a strange land, particularly in times of crisis, which have been some of the key sociological factors of the growth of early Christianity (Stark, 1996). Hence the diasporic existence of 'uprootedness', loneliness, or 'loss' of belonging, shared among the KDC members, should not be so quickly disregarded in the discussion of its intercultural journey, although I fully agree with Kwiyani's critique on monocultural churches.

> Monocultural churches, especially in contexts of cultural diversity, go against everything we read in the New Testament. ... Migrants who say that worship feels better and more authentic in their mother tongue need to be reminded that mission only works in the language of the strangers that you are trying to evangelize. A commitment to stick to 'home languages' automatically excludes all who cannot speak the language – and this often includes their own sons and daughters. (Kwiyani, 2020, p. 146)

Finally, the preservation of cultural identity remains an important issue, as raised by KDC members (George, 2018, p. 2018). Diaspora communities often wrestle with the tension between assimilating into their host culture and preserving their home culture. Interestingly, diaspora communities sometimes maintain cultural artefacts more diligently than their homelands, which continue to evolve. Hence any intercultural approach needs to address these concerns in a way that does not feel threatening to cultural preservation. After all, the goal of building an intercultural church is not to get rid of cultural distinctiveness, but to 'add to' the celebration of our corporate identity in Christ through our differences (Song, 2020). Marzouk is spot on when he argues: 'Forming an intercultural church is not about the loss of identity, and fellowship does not mean loss of boundaries' (2019, p. 41). Having considered the 'East Asian' and 'diaspora' identity of the KDC, I will now move on to reflect on the steps that the KDC has taken as part of its journey toward an intercultural church.

Intercultural Steps on the Journey Toward an Intercultural Church

The KDC from the outset has taken intentional steps to build meaningful connections with the wide British Christian community through various partnerships, especially in charitable works. For instance, the KDC actively collaborated with British churches in the area in serving asylum seekers. It organized several groups to prepare and serve meals. In the process, their cultural strength in group-oriented work and hospitality was fully utilized. Serving meals with warm hospitality, embedded in their cultural DNA, opened up opportunities for the KDC members to step out of their comfort zones. Their lived experience of being strangers has shifted to becoming hosts to others. This was truly empowering in that this simple act of service reminded them of God's calling.

Additionally, what began as simple food donations to a local food bank, organized by another British church, soon developed into a deeper partnership particularly in the areas of worship. At first, a group from the KDC became long-term volunteers, serving the community alongside others. Through the ongoing partnership with the British church in serving the local food bank, the KDC became aware of the challenges of the partner church, which struggled to find worship leaders. The KDC, being a relatively young church with abundant musical resources, agreed to send its music team to lead worship regularly. As this relationship grew, the KDC encouraged its members to visit and worship alongside their British brothers and sisters, fostering a sense of shared community.

The KDC has also built partnerships with other East Asian churches in the region, creating spaces particularly for young people to have fellowships. These gatherings initially focused on discussions around shared experiences, such as living with multiple identities, and then developed into prayer meetings where young people from different East Asian churches worshipped and prayed together. Although these partnerships are still evolving and to be further strengthened, the significance of partnerships between the diaspora and British churches cannot be emphasized enough. It is through these partnerships that the KDC has found a deeper sense of its calling and mission as a people of diaspora and started to have a wider perspective on what it means to be Christian alongside others. Perhaps, most crucially, partnerships allow the KDC to shift its focus from 'self-serving church' to becoming 'a truly missional church' (Song, 2011, p. 124).

While partnerships with various churches were being proactively cultivated, another change was taking place within the KDC. The increasing presence of non-Koreans, global nomads, and second-generation Koreans meant that business as usual for the KDC might not be an option any more. Language, once a significant barrier for the first-generation Koreans, is no longer an issue for younger members. As Enoch Wan observed, 'simultaneously living in multiple identities' and in a liminal space is a norm for the majority of them (2011, p. 126). They are seeking home and a sense of belonging, but not in the sense that they are looking to reconnect with their home back in Korea, but instead they seek to create a new sense of home – a place where they feel accepted, included and present. In response, the KDC has made intentional efforts to welcome non-Korean speakers by organizing small group gatherings and occasionally offering a separate service in English rather than relying on interpreters. Non-Koreans are also invited to actively participate in worship by reading and praying for the community during services. These efforts represent crucial steps in the KDC's intercultural journey, but they also raise challenging questions. Where will these intercultural practices and approaches ultimately lead the KDC? Embracing others may mean that the KDC will have to change, perhaps fundamentally and forever, as it truly welcomes and embraces others. Indeed, 'becoming [an intercultural] church is easier said than done' (Song, 2020). What then is the ultimate goal of welcoming, crossing boundaries and creating these spaces?

In many ways, the KDC has been on this journey toward a more inclusive and intercultural church. Yet, like many other diaspora churches, it is still grappling with what the road ahead looks like. One of the most frequently taken directions of travel is to create an English-speaking congregation within the KDC. This is one of the most popular models among diaspora churches around the world (Rah, 2007). Alternatively, there have been some successful models of building intercultural churches by second-generation immigrants (Song, 2020). Nam Soon Song's interviews with second-generation Canadians of Asian heritage reveal their aspirations for multi-ethnic and multicultural churches (2020, pp. 177–83). It might be a natural way forward particularly for them in that their lived realities of living in-between or multiple worlds of cultures, languages and perceptions as insiders and outsiders have shaped their unique identity. They feel at home in a multicultural environment. As Stuart Hall puts it, cultural identity is not simply about recovering something of the past, but also about producing something new as it 'undergo[s] constant transformation'(1990, p. 225). The lived experience of second-generation immigrants or global nomads allows them to connect across cultures and cross boundaries without losing their identity, which is being formed and produced in the process (Rah, 2007). An intercultural church is almost certainly a way forward, particularly for the new generation.

Conclusion: Intercultural Church as a Direction of Travel

As I conclude, the KDC is still on the journey, navigating its future while residing in a liminal space. It is clear that the KDC will continue to embrace deeper intercultural approaches while fully appreciating their unique condition of being a Korean diaspora congregation. Here

I envision two directions, travelling alongside each other. The KDC, while navigating to build deeper partnerships with British churches as a Korean diaspora congregation and continuing to serve temporary immigrants, nurtures a vision of planting an intercultural church, possibly in partnership with like-minded churches. After all, planting an intercultural church is 'not only for theological, Biblical, and sociological reasons, but also for existential and missional reasons' for many diaspora churches (Song, 2011; Song, 2020). Then, how can the KDC prepare its congregants for this further journey?

First and foremost, the KDC needs to identify and equip young leaders, but more importantly, it must empower and release them into ministry. The first-generation members of the KDC need to learn to see them as their partners and co-workers, not as their children. This is often the case in Asian immigrant churches, where intergenerational dynamics often take on a parent–child relationship, which can hinder the younger generation from assuming full responsibilities and leadership roles (Song, 2020). These young people should be acknowledged as the key leaders in this intercultural journey, who 'have capabilities to go beyond their cultural group and form bonds with outsiders' (Song, 2011).

Second, the intentional fostering of a strong sense of God's calling should come to the fore in the ecclesiological conversations of the KDC. Their diasporic experience is not incidental, but has a purposeful role in God's mission, as seen in many biblical narratives (Fröchtling, 2013). Diaspora Christians navigate the purpose of life together while living as aliens and sojourners in a foreign land. However, the strong ties among themselves may hinder them from living out their missional identity as diaspora people. Minho Song's warning speaks the truth here.

> [The] homogenous pull brings and binds them together, but ultimately bans them from meaningfully participating in the lives of those who are outside of the group. Unseen boundaries are drawn between the diaspora church and the people outside the church, and the church forfeits the opportunities of ministering to them. (Song, 2011, pp. 125–6).

Hence, it is fundamental to constantly remind the KDC of the calling to take part in God's mission and to move on with a missional heart as diaspora people, being sent to this multi-ethnic and cultural society to live out their corporate Christian identity (Song, 2011).

Lastly, yet most importantly, the KDC should reflect on their Christian identity, which is formed and shaped by others alongside them. In simple terms, others who are different from them are essential for the KDC to find its Christian identity and to be shaped by corporate Christian identity. As Kwiyani puts it, those who are different from us will remind us that 'we are not at the centre of the universe, ... [but] the centre is out there – in God' (2020, p. 111). Or, put another way, the process of being built as the body of Christ together inevitably results in 'mutual inconvenience', which is perceptively phrased by Israel Oluwole Olofinjana in his discussion of intercultural church (2024). This mutual inconvenience ironically reminds us of our belongingness to one another and will eventually help us build an interdependent Christian identity in Christ together. In a practical and theological sense, I suggest that eating together around the table and gathering together around the Lord's Table are the best practices to cultivate our corporate identity (Marzouk, 2019; Kwiyani, 2020; Fröchtling, 2013). Our belongingness alongside one another is nurtured when we share meals, being hosts and guests at the same time; our corporate identity is reminded when we all together as guests come to the Lord's table and partake in his body and blood. To this end, the KDC will continue to celebrate sharing meals not only among themselves, but also with others. We shall see where the Spirit leads the KDC in its journey.

Bibliography

Barclay, John, 2004, *Negotiating Diaspora: Jewish Strategies in the Roman Empire*, London: T&T Clark.
BBC News, 2024, 'Anti-racism protesters rally after week of riots', 7 August (updated 8 August), https://www.bbc.co.uk/news/articles/czxlgwl28gyo (accessed 21.2.25).
Carroll R., M. Daniel, 2020, 'Diaspora and mission in the Old Testament' in Tira, S. J. and Yamamori, T., eds, *Scattered and Gathered: A Global Compendium of Diaspora Missiology*, Carlisle: Langham, pp. 109–10.
Chang, Steven S. H., 'From opportunity to mission: scattering for the gospel in the New Testament story', in *Scattered and Gathered: A Global Compendium of Diaspora Missiology*, Carlisle: Langham, pp. 136–7.
Chia, Edmund Kee-Fook, 2022, *Asian Christianity and Theology: Inculturation, Interreligious Dialogue, Integral Liberation*, London: Routledge.
Church of England Council for Christian Unity, 2014, 'Changes in the Ethnic Diversity of the Christian Population in England between 2001 and 2011', pp. 5–7, 25, https://www.churchofengland.org/sites/default/files/2017-10/north_west.pdf (accessed 21.2.25).
Cohen, Robin, 2005, 'Foreword', in Sigona, N., Gamlen, A., Liberatore, G. and Neveu Kringelbach, H., eds, *Diasporas Reimagined: Spaces, Practices and Belonging*, Oxford: Oxford Diasporas Programme.

Fröchtling, Andrea, 2013, 'Crossing the waters of Babylon: Diasporas between glob/calizations and spiritual homelands', in Asamoah-Gyadu, K., Fröchtling, A. and Kunz-Lübcke, A., eds, *'Babel is Everywhere!' Migrant Readings from Africa, Europe, and Asia*, Frankfurt: Peter Lang.

George, Sam, ed., 2018, *Diaspora Christianities: Global Scattering and Gathering of South Asian Christians*, Minneapolis, MN: Fortress.

Hall, Stuart, 1990, 'Cultural Identity and Diaspora', in Rutherford, J., *Identity: Community, Culture, Difference*, London: Lawrence & Wishart.

Hollenweger, Walter J., 1992, 'Foreword', in Gerloff, Roswith I. H., *A Plea for British Black Theologies: The Black Church Movement in Britain in its Transatlantic Cultural and Theological Interaction with Special Reference to the Pentecostal Oneness (Apostolic) and Sabbatarian Movements*, Frankfurt: Peter Lang.

Hong Kong Yearbook, 2021, Chapter 21, 'Religion and Custom', pp. 314–18, https://www.yearbook.gov.hk/2021/en/pdf/E21.pdf (accessed 21.2.25).

Jackson, W., 2019, *Reading Romans with Eastern Eyes: Honour and Shame in Paul's Message and Mission*, Downers Grove, IL: IVP.

Jenkins, Philip, 2007, *God's Continent: Christianity, Islam, and Europe's Religious Crisis*, Oxford: Oxford University Press.

Kim, S. Hun, 2022, *Diaspora: Divine Conspiracy*, South Korea: ARILAC Books.

Kim, S. Hun and Hershberger, Susie, 2020, 'Korean diaspora ministries', in Tira, S. J. and Yamamori, T., eds, *Scattered and Gathered: A Global Compendium of Diaspora Missiology*, Carlisle: Langham, p. 475.

Koo, Byoung Ok, 2019, *Transitioning from an Ethnic to a Multicultural Church: A Transformational Model*, Eugene, OR: Wipf & Stock.

Kwiyani, H., 2020, *Multicultural Kingdom: Ethnic diversity, mission and the church*, London: SCM Press.

Lausanne Movement, 2009, at https://lausanne.org/statement/the-seoul-declaration-on-diaspora-missiology (accessed 21.2.25).

Marzouk, Safwat, 2019, *Intercultural Church: A Biblical Vision for an Age of Migration*, Minneapolis, MN: Fortress.

McGavran, Donald, 1970, *Understanding Church Growth*, Grand Rapids, MI: Eerdmans.

McGavran, Donald, 2018, 'The Homogeneous Unit in mission theory', *Papers*, 140, p. 403, https://place.asburyseminary.edu/firstfruitspapers/140 (accessed 21.2.25).

Olofinjana, Israel Oluwole, 2024, 'A mutual inconvenience: why pursue intercultural church in the UK today?', *NextGen*, 13 July 2024, https://www.nextgenevents.org/resources/a-mutual-inconvenience-why-pursue-intercultural-church-in-the-uk-today (accessed 21.2.25).

ONS (Office for National Statistics), 2022, 'Religion, England and Wales: Census 2021', released 29 November 2022, ONS website, statistical bulletin, https://www.ons.gov.uk/peoplepopulationandcommunity/culturalidentity/religion/bulletins/religionenglandandwales/census2021#religion-in-england-and-wales (accessed 21.2.25).

Padilla, C. René, 1982, 'The unity of the church and the Homogeneous Unit Principle', *International Bulletin of Mission Research*, Vol. 6, Issue 1.

Paynter, Helen and Power, Maria, eds, 2024, *The Church, The Far Right, and The Claim to Christianity*, London: SCM Press.

Rah, Soong-Chan, 2009, *The Next Evangelicalism: Freeing the Church from Western Cultural Captivity*, Downers Grove, IL: InterVarsity Press.

Scotland's Census, 2024, 'Scotland's Census 2022: Ethnic group, national identity, language and religion, published 21 May 2024, https://www.scotlandscensus.gov.uk/2022-results/scotland-s-census-2022-ethnic-group-national-identity-language-and-religion/ (accessed 21.2.25).

Seth, Michael J., 2008, 'Korea: from hermit kingdom to colony', *Education about Asia*, 13, No. 2.

Song, Minho, 2011, 'The diaspora experience of the Korean church and its implications for world missions', in Kim, S. Hun and Ma, Wonsuk, eds, *Korea Diaspora and Christian Mission*, Minneapolis, MN: Fortress.

Song, Nam Soon, 2020, 'People of Jeong (Qing)', in Song, Nam Soon et al., eds, *People of Faith and People of Jeong (Qing): The Asian Canadian Churches of Today for Tomorrow*, Eugene, OR: Wipf & Stock, pp. 81–92

Stark, Rodney, 1996, *The Rise of Christianity: A Sociologist Reconsiders History*, Princeton, NJ: Princeton University Press.

Stenschke, Christoph, 2016, 'Migration and mission: According to the Book of Acts', *Missionalia*, Vol. 44, No. 2, pp. 129–51.

Tira, Sadiri Joy and Yamamori, Tetsunao, eds, 2020, *Scattered and Gathered: A Global Compendium of Diaspora Missiology*, Carlisle, UK: Langham.

UK HongKongers' Demographic report, 2021, https://www.ukhk.org/surveys (accessed 21.2.25).

Wan, Enoch, ed., 2011, *Diaspora Missiology: Theory, Methodology, and Practice*, Portland, OR: IDS-USA.

Wi, MiJa, 2019a, *The Path to Salvation in Luke's Gospel: What Must We Do?*, London: T&T Clark, pp. 18–19.

Wi, MiJa, 2019b, 'You will receive power to cross boundaries: an examination of Acts 1.8', the paper presented at Love, Boundaries, and Sacred Texts Colloquium, The University of Manchester (2–3 May 2019), pp. 1–18.

Wu, Jackson, 2019, *Reading Romans with Eastern Eyes: Honour and Shame in Paul's Message and Mission*, Downers Grove, IL: InterVarsity Press.

Zurlo, Gina A., 2020, 'Migration, diasporas, and diversity: a demographic approach' in Tira, S. J. and Yamamori, T., eds, *Scattered and Gathered: A Global Compendium of Diaspora Missiology*, Carlisle, UK: Langham.

6

Feeling Welcome and Accepted: A Case Study of Greenford Baptist Church

DAVID WISE

Introduction

From October 1987 until January 2019, I was a pastor at Greenford Baptist Church (GBC) in West London. During this time the church transitioned from being a white British congregation, to one with people from approximately 45 nationalities regularly attending. During worship, different languages were used with songs, dance and prayer in styles that were used 'back home'. Every aspect of congregational life reflected the cultures from the different ethnicities that made up the congregation. GBC was considered to be a good example of an inter-ethnic church. I use the term 'inter-ethnic church' for a church where aspects of the different ethnic cultures of those in the congregation are expressed and seen throughout the life of the church.

In the autumn of 2017, I commenced doctoral research into how this transition took place. One of the key findings was that people from overseas experienced GBC as a community of faith that was welcoming, safe and fully accepting of them. This chapter explores aspects of that transition largely through the eyes of members of the congregation.

Overview of the Transition

In 1987, GBC was a traditional white British Baptist church. All the members who attended were white British apart from five Caribbean teenagers and the mother of two of the teenagers. The services lasted around 75 minutes. The sung worship was drawn from the *Baptist Hymn Book* supplemented by a contemporary song or two from *Songs of Fellowship*. The instruments used were the organ and piano. Almost everything was led from the front by the minister.

Some of those who took part in the research recalled that the atmosphere was not friendly; there was fear of what other people might be thinking. Grace recalled (all research participants have pseudonyms that reflect their own description of their ethnicity and gender) that 'nobody talked to you much and it wasn't friendly'. One of the first Africans to attend recalled: 'You would come to church, but you would be really fearful and you would be looking to see people's reactions. I would say it was awful to be thinking, "Oh my goodness, what are they going to say." We were wary and looking over our shoulder at everybody's faces just to see reactions, and I didn't think that was right.'

So, in 1987, GBC was a traditional Baptist church: formal, not very friendly and suspicious of anyone who was different.

In 2017, and for several years before, around one-third of the church members were white British. The majority of adults attending had been born outside of Europe, and the majority of children and teenagers attending had been born in the UK to parents who had migrated to the UK from outside of Europe.

In 2017, the Sunday morning meeting lasted around two and a half hours. The first section consisted of sung worship, prayer, testimonies, celebration of birthdays and anniversaries, an offering and sometimes communion. Each week several different people were involved in leading various parts of the gathering. All ages were together. Music was provided by a small group of musicians, usually there was a drummer, keyboard and guitar. Songs were mainly contemporary but were drawn from a wide range of ethnic backgrounds and were sung using the language, style and accompaniment of their origin. For example, when a song in Hindi was used, the singers and musicians, along with many of the congregation, would sit on the floor. The only instruments used were a tabla drum, bells and a drone sound. When a song in Yoruba was used, only drums accompanied it and there was a lot of dancing. When someone led in prayer, either from the front or from the congregation, they were free to use whichever language they were most comfortable with. During prayer ministry (when individuals came forward to be prayed for by members of the prayer ministry team), those praying were free to use their first language, whether or not the person they were praying for understood it.

Using First Language at GBC

I asked questions about the freedom to use first language and the significance of this for people attending GBC in both focus groups and interviews. Here are some of the comments. Lavanya: 'My first language is Punjabi, so when I hear the worship in Punjabi, I understand all the words ... I am uncomfortable to pray in English with some words I don't understand. So, I start praying in my own language and I say that's good.' Panha: 'I think like, you know, people feel free to talk in their languages, you know. Like, people pray in their languages, you know. People are not ashamed or shy. They will say it in their languages, you know. And people don't feel exclusive also, you know, like you will all be included. I think it's the freedom to speak. The freedom to worship in the way that you want to worship. Yes, so I think that is what make people comfortable.' Bunmi: 'If you want to pray in your language, then pray in your language. If you want to prophesy in your language, then prophesy in it. It is not everything needs to be made more British to be acceptable.'

For Bunmi, Lavanya and Panha, the use of other languages at GBC was a clear indication that one did not need to use English to be welcome and accepted at GBC. The way they talked about this implies that in other contexts they had felt that they had not been accepted. They each talked about being free to be themselves in worship and prayer at GBC, free to be the person God had created them to be. At GBC, a way of being together had been established that recognized both that English was shared as a common language and that alternative languages were valued.

For Jayanti, who moved to the UK from India as an adult, hearing a Hindi song the first time she attended GBC was very significant. 'When I came to Greenford Baptist, the first time the congregation sang *Amrithawani*, I said, "Oh gosh, I can't believe it" because that is a typical, Indian worship song, and the style is typically Indian whereby people sit on the floor and one person is leading while others join in it. And the music, the sitar, the guitar, all that music, it just took me by surprise. I couldn't believe it, because in this country I'd never, ever heard an Indian worship song like that in the same style as they do in India, sitting on the floor with everybody joining in. That was awesome'. She immediately felt that she was welcome at GBC as an Indian.

For some the significance was profound. Ronke: 'To be able to be part of a church ... [that] ... allows people to worship and pray in their first language and also puts a system in place to embrace different types of songs in different languages to allow me to come on stage to the podium and share testimony and break out in choruses in my language ... That is huge, that is deep. So, it's very refreshing and has been very helpful.'

I was deeply moved by a comment from Tambara: 'When you speak or when you sing in somebody else's language, when they are not expecting it, it is such a wonderful, beautiful feeling. They think "Oh!" (voice raised excitedly). "He is singing in my language." It is just so lovely, such a beautiful feeling. So, to have a church where your language is being spoken in the songs and the prayers, you feel welcome ... [people] feel like they are human beings and not just second-hand citizens or whatever.'

Tambara's description that people 'feel like they are human beings not just second-hand citizens' when their language has been used is striking. Her phrase calls to mind the experience of many Black people as being treated as less than fully human. At GBC, through the use of songs and prayers in languages other than English, people felt that they were recognized as being fully in the image of God, fully accepted, fully human. Ronke described her experience as 'huge' and 'deep'. This sense of acceptance was not superficial but something that resonated at a very deep level.

Dancing

By autumn 2017, dancing during the Sunday meetings was a normal component of the worship. When songs were used that had a Caribbean or African rhythm, members of the congregation would dance in their places. Often people would also use the space in front of the platform or behind the congregation to dance. It was common for the offering to be received accompanied by the entire congregation in turn dancing down the aisle to place their gifts in the offering plate or to touch the plate in recognition that all they had was given to God. Members of the congregation, especially those who had grown up in West Africa, saw this as an important part of their worship, presenting themselves and their gifts before God. The style of dancing was exuberant, drawing particularly on movements usual in West Africa and the Caribbean.

For most GBC members who had grown up outside of Europe, dancing at home as well as in church is a normal part of expressing their devotion to God. Lavanya: 'Even at home when I get up in the morning ... I put on my Indian worship. Sometimes I love my worship. I'm dancing with it and I enjoy it, all the worship that God gives us.' So enabling dance to be a part of congregational worship was important. Alvita noted that 'in Jamaica you are accustomed to lots of the tambourine, lots of drumming, lots of clapping ... I'm accustomed to seeing people running around in the Spirit and things like that, shouting Hallelujah.'

Alvita, a worship leader at GBC, uses Caribbean rhythms such as calypso and reggae. She commented that when she is at the front, she sees 'people dancing, people raising their hands. It's just the whole-body movement that you don't get if they are maybe just doing a normal English song.' From her perspective when people are physically moving they are more engaged with God than when they are static. She talked about a specific incident she remembered: 'A couple of months ago, when I just changed the rhythm to "It is well with my soul" and there was one particular Jamaican lady. She would just come to church and she'd be sitting there and just talk to who she wanted to talk to and that's it. That Sunday was the very first time I'd heard her. She jumped up, she uttered out and that's because that connected with her. So, for me that meant she was really engaged in the worship ... There was another African lady and she just ran straight up to the front and she's not somebody who would normally be doing that, but there was something that connected with them. So, the movement that you are seeing there would say people are actually engaging with what is going on.'

In his interview Oluwasesan commented: 'I think a lot of Yorubas, Nigerians and maybe Africans generally like to express themselves, and when we really express ourselves, we do it by dancing. We see a lot of that in the church, and I think it is the same for the people from the Caribbean as well. There is a lot of movement, a lot of joy. I see that in the church, and that is one of the reasons I've stayed for so many years now.'

Tabia commented: 'It shows that you are happy. It shows you are delighted, you are comfortable, so you are able to move your body freely because if you are not, if you are in a strange place and you feel frightened, you're not going to move your body ... they feel connected. So, they express their worship through their movement, not only of their mouth, but all their body.'

For Alvita, Lavanya, Oluwasesan and Tabia, coming to GBC from three different continents, dance was a normal part of their worship. Being allowed to express worship via the medium of dance meant that people felt accepted and included. There is a connection here with Tambara's view, already quoted above, that when the first language of people in the congregation was being used, people 'feel like they are human beings not just second-hand citizens'. Dance as a bodily language seems to function in a similar way to first language. Being able to dance as a part of their congregational experience was therefore a significant aspect of being accepted.

Opposition to Change

So, how did these changes in the nature of Sunday morning gatherings come about? The early stages of the journey were not without opposition. In the mid-1990s, there was sustained conflict between the church leadership and the leadership of the church Music Team. This conflict was long running, multifaceted and very unpleasant. There were numerous issues raised. Relevant to this chapter is that the leaders of the Music Team held a European understanding of music/worship that prevented participation by people from other ethnicities. At the time I was only aware of the lack of cooperation with me in my attempts to introduce worship material that had originated in other cultural contexts, or to involve people that were not white British as singers or musicians. In the spring of 1999, the LT decided to disband the existing Music Team entirely and to remove its leaders from their leadership roles. The three music team leaders left the church with a few supporters. After their departure, as people from a range of ethnic backgrounds became involved in worship leadership, Africans told me that it had been made clear to them that they were not welcome as musicians or singers by the previous leaders. Other Black people told me of having been refused auditions to join the singers' team. This was a key moment in the transition because the sudden departure of people who had tightly controlled music in all our corporate meetings created a need, and a lot of space, for others to become involved. Many were enthusiastic to take part.

Developing Prayer and Worship

In the summer of 1999, the Leadership Team decided to try to introduce into the life of GBC prayer in styles drawn from other ethnic contexts. In the autumn the first prayer night vigil at GBC was held. It was led by some of the Nigerian members of the church and drew on the styles and practices that they had used 'back home'. Naturally many of those from West Africa who attended GBC were present, but so were many of the white British members, as well as people from other ethnic contexts. The event was considered a success, and subsequent prayer night vigils were organized.

In addition to special prayer events, the Leadership Team decided to try and introduce praying styles and practices that had originated from outside of the UK into the Sunday morning meetings. The initial approach taken was a very gradual one with only the occasional experiment always with some explanation and initially only in English. Examples were encouraging everyone to pray out loud together at the same time and inviting a church member to lead prayer in a similar style that they would have done 'back home' but in English. Very gradually these sort of practices began to take root in the church and slowly the use of a person's first language when praying, which enabled a much closer engagement with the 'back home' style, was introduced.

In 2003, there was a significant development that led to a much more focused and intentional move towards the development of worship (sung, spoken, dance and visual arts) that drew on, and incorporated, styles and material that originated from outside of Europe and North America. The GBC church members unanimously appointed a part-time 'Prayer Co-ordinator and Worship Facilitator'. Among the responsibilities for this role was 'to integrate and develop multicultural prayer and worship'. The person appointed served in this role until 2017. His ministry, under my direction, was the main driver for the gradual but sustained increase in the inclusion within the Sunday meetings of material and practices from other cultures. A key component in these developments was working with the singers and musicians. There were workshops where, as well as learning new material in different styles and languages, usually led by someone for whom the new material was used 'back home', there were discussions around theory, practice, and experience of multi-ethnic church. In 2008, a Worship Co-ordinating Group was created. Apart from the GBC staff member, all the initial members had been born outside of Europe. At this stage there were also visits to workshops on 'multi-cultural worship' and the staff member attended a week-long course that was a part of a module of an MA in Ethnomusicology.

There were two further staff appointments that helped the slow but continuous transition in Sunday meetings. First, also in 2003, a part-time church evangelist was appointed. He was British born but of Jamaican parents. As GBC's evangelist, he was often the first person from GBC that people met, he was usually greeting people, especially visitors, on Sundays, and he was at the front at most GBC outreach events. Having Jamaican parents he was obviously not white British, which made a visible statement about the church's welcome and inclusion of people from other ethnicities.

In 2010, GBC appointed a female Brazilian Assistant Pastor who had been previously involved in leadership roles in a Baptist Church in Brazil. She worked part-time initially, but full-time from February 2011. Her cultural preferences had a major impact on the rest of the male British-born ministry staff team that, by this time, also included a white British Assistant Pastor. For example, the *pastora* was very passionate, emotional and loud in her prayer and worship. She was very physical when she greeted people with hugs and kisses. She interpreted the biblical text with a much more literal approach than we were used to. In essence, she confidently challenged the staff team norms.

Restructuring Sunday Mornings

At the start of this chapter, I described what a Sunday morning at GBC was like. I have already described what a Sunday morning looked like in 2017. But how did the change in the structure of the meeting come about? In the summer of 2003, I took my second sabbatical that lasted for three months. The aim was to explore cross-cultural ministry. I spent time in Albania, Italy and Jamaica exploring how British and other European nationalities had, and were currently, working across cultures. The most significant outcome for GBC from my sabbatical experiences was the transformation of the structure of our Sunday morning meetings. Sitting on a hillside overlooking Vlore in Albania, thinking and praying about what I had so far seen and learnt, I heard God speak to me in an almost audible voice. I wrote down what I heard, 'You have been putting the new wine at Greenford into an old wine skin; if you do not change the skin, the wine will be lost.' I understood this as expressing the need for us to completely change the structure of our Sunday meetings, which is what I had been thinking about at that moment.

In December 2003, the Leadership Team began considering what changes to the format of our Sunday meetings might look like. We put a big blank sheet of paper in the middle of the room and asked the question: 'If everything was possible, what might feature in our Sunday morning meetings?' Over a couple of months, we looked at a number of different possible combinations of the various ingredients. In the spring of 2004, there was discussion about the possibilities at the meeting of church members. To my surprise there was strong enthusiasm for experimenting with changes. I had proposed that initially we took it slowly, occasionally trying one of the different formats, but the church members disagreed. They decided that starting in two weeks, we would try one format for four weeks then we would try a different one for another four weeks, and then meet to consider the way forward. At that subsequent meeting the decision was made to adopt a format that was a mixture of the two formats that had been tried and not to review again for six months. The final outcome was that the new format continued unchanged.

In summary, the morning meeting was extended from around an hour and a quarter to around two and a half hours, which included a 25-minute 'connection time' in the middle when refreshments were served and people were encouraged to talk to each other. Newly added weekly ingredients in the meeting included time for testimonies, celebration of birthdays and anniversaries, and a time for 'prayer ministry'. Prayer ministry refers to the practice of inviting anyone who would like to be prayed for to come to the front during the meeting. One of the church leaders or staff would invite two others from the congregation to pray for each person who came forward. There was increased time for singing, praying, creative activities (such as dance, poetry, drama) and more time for Bible teaching and age-specific groups. Eating together after the service became a monthly event.

Connection Time

In my research there was a lot of comment made about the significance of the 'connection time'. The intention had been to create a space and an opportunity for people to interact and get to know each other. Using this title to describe this 25-minute period each week reinforced the objective of people intentionally initiating or building on relationships with other people in the congregation. There were drinks available and some snacks. There were always plenty of biscuits, but if people were celebrating a birthday or other special event, they often brought along cake and sometimes savoury snacks such as samosas for everyone to share. Other than the physically infirm (who were provided with chairs) everyone stood while they ate and drank and talked to people. The fact that people were standing made it easier for them to wander around and to talk with multiple people during the 25 minutes available. During the first section of the meeting, people who were present for the first time were always asked to raise their hands so they could be welcomed. GBC had a small team whose task it was to remember who these people were and to ensure that they were helped to get their refreshments and engaged in conversation during the connection time. The importance of looking out for, and including in conversation, anyone who was standing on their own was regularly emphasized to church members. I, and other staff, kept a look out for people on their own or looking uncomfortable and either engaged with them ourselves or made sure someone else did.

Kunle was a member of the Leadership Team when it proposed the introduction of connection time. He commented: 'It [the previous pattern] did not give us that opportunity to actually connect with people that were in the building as a lot of people just go out immediately [the meeting ends] ... So, the new system with the connection time provided us with the opportunity to connect with each other, to relate to each other and ask questions about how people have been.' Natalie, who was a part of the church when the change was introduced, commented: 'The connection time in the middle meant that people couldn't escape. When it was at the end of the meeting then people, and particularly people who were new and didn't know each other, tended to look around and nervously leave. But, because it was in the middle of the service, it meant people had to stay, they had to engage, and I feel connecting is an important part of the service. It is not just drinking tea and coffee and having a chat – I think it is an important part and the new format literally reinforced that.'

Both Kunle and Natalie, who were part of the GBC congregation when connection time was introduced, believe that people connecting with each other 'is an important part of the service'. During the previous format, people could, and often did, leave without speaking to anybody. With the new format, 'people had to stay' and engage.

Felix, in his interview, contrasted his experience at GBC (where he had grown up) with that of other churches he had visited after moving away from Greenford. 'It also means you have an enlarged portion of the congregation that is going to be there for that connection time. So, it is going to make people feel welcome. I've had it when I've been trying to find new churches. You wait until the end of the service to try and catch people or see how you fit in with the church, and people are in a rush to go, or they've got their own friendship groups already.' In Felix's view, 'connection time' led to people feeling welcome, in contrast to his experience at other churches.

Several interviewees recalled their first visit to GBC. Alvita said: 'And my very first time coming here, I was welcomed in during connection time. The people who met me, there was just this sense that people were genuine about what they were saying to you.' Shanice was asked specifically about her first visit to GBC and whether at connection time people had come up and talked to her and made her welcome. 'Yes, they did, yes. People just came and talked to you, so it was easy to just mix and talk to people and have coffee.'

It was clear from some of the interviewees that the impact of connection time went beyond simply feeling welcome when they first attended, but that it was a context from which friendships had developed. For example Harnoop commented: 'What I really liked about the people in the church is when we had a connection time that was one of the best times within the church ... you can actually relate to another member of the church.' Panha commented: 'In connection time when you get a chance to speak to people and you kind of build relationships from there ... just to get to know a bit about them and them about you. You build in from there.' Finally Oluwasesan commented: 'The one thing I did enjoy was connection time ... it was an opportunity to actually talk to people. A lot of churches, you go in, you walk in, you have the service and you walk straight out. That doesn't help build relationships ... that [connection time] in itself then was somewhere where you could start building relationships, by getting to know people.'

For Harnoop, Oluwasesan and Panha, connection time was a context where their initial conversations with people led to the forming of deeper relationships. For Kunle there was a particular significance for 'non-white' people. 'I will harp back to when I was in Nigeria when after the church meeting you would have your different groups that you had meeting ... part of the meeting was for people to relate and find out how people were doing. Yes, there was ... a business context to it, but also it enabled people to actually relate with each other, do things together, celebrate with each other and in a way, having the "connection time" brought that aspect back into the life of the church rather than come in, finish meeting and shoot out. It brought back into context for a lot of the non-white, particularly for the Nigerians, the opportunity to be able to meet and talk and relate and interact with other people.'

Tabia, in her interview, gave an illustration of how this worked. 'I knew somebody else who comes to church now, who when they came, they were introduced to us because as soon as they knew they were from Cameroon they came and told me there was a Cameroonian here, so I went to speak to them. And because I've been here for a long time, they asked me: "How can I find a job – what can I do?" I asked: "What do you want to do?" And they said they wanted some kind of help like working in a care home. I knew someone who was working in a care home inside the church, so I connected them up and straight away they see the benefit of the "connection time". It is not only helping them spiritually, but economically and socially.'

For Kunle and Tabia, both from West Africa, connection time enabled the sort of interaction between people that they were used to from their home context. It gave the space for interaction between people that 'at home' had been a normal part of meeting on a Sunday at church.

The research highlighted the significance of connection time for visitors feeling welcome at GBC, for the starting of friendships and for interaction with others. Set within the wider context of an emphasis on making sure visitors were welcome, and the culture of creating community within GBC, the weekly 25-minute connection time set in the middle of the morning meeting was a key component that encouraged and facilitated relational connection between people from all ethnicities who attended GBC.

There were other features of the changed format of morning meetings that were mentioned by research participants as being significant for developing relationships. Several mentioned the fact that every week the congregation celebrated the birthdays of people present. People with birthdays either in the previous or in the coming week were invited to the front; they were asked their name, when their birthday was/will be and how old they will be. 'Happy Birthday' was then sung to all those assembled, and the worship leader then prayed for them. Janice: 'I think recognizing people and their birthdays is something that was positive and good for the church for bringing people closer and connecting people more so together.' Natasha: 'It's a family thing celebrating the birthdays of people, and it is good to have knowledge of people's anniversaries and to pray for them. I think that was significant.' For Janice and Natasha, the celebration of birthdays was a 'family thing' that brought 'people closer' and connected people. Other interviewees commented that they would talk to people whose birthdays had been celebrated during 'connection time'. There were similar comments about the practice of allowing people to 'give a testimony'. This is where there was an 'open microphone' for people to share something about what they had experienced of God's activity in or around their lives recently. Interviewees commented that during 'connection time', there would be conversation around what had been shared.

Food

Earlier I mentioned that when the Sunday morning meetings were restructured, the congregation eating together became a monthly event. In my research, food was often mentioned as a significant component in people's experience of GBC. For Sunday lunches the most common format was 'bring and share' where people were invited to bring some food that would be put out on tables for people to take. Generally, people brought food that reflected their own ethnic background. The numbers of people who stayed for lunch varied but it was rarely less than 60 or more than 100. Eating together was mentioned as a significant aspect of the way that people connected with one another. In the view of some of the research participants, eating each other's food meant accepting each other's culture.

Oluwasesan said: 'I like my food and I like tasting different things, different food from different places. It was another way of getting to know people and different cultures as well ... And then I'm happy to explain what it is, when it is eaten, how it is eaten, how it is prepared. So, it's just ... sharing my experience of Nigeria and just letting people know a bit more about the foods and the culture. I'm very happy when people try Nigerian food and then ask questions about what it is and how you actually prepare it.' Tabia commented, 'It makes you feel very proud. You feel appreciated. They don't just like me; they like what I eat and they are eating it too, so they are connecting with me. They are connecting with me; they are acknowledging me. It's very important.' Food from different cultures was not only significant for those born outside of Europe but for white British people too. For example, Graham commented: 'I think we have embraced things like church lunches and international evenings which always express integration and something of an introduction to other cultures ... I think the fact we have a long table with food from however many cultures on offer and people fill their plates with it, for those who are bringing and preparing the food there is massive acceptance. A massive sense of belonging.'

For Oluwasesan, Tabia and Graham, eating food prepared by different members of GBC led to a 'massive sense of belonging', united in their diversity through eating together. For Tabia, when someone ate her food, they connected with her and acknowledged her. So sharing her food involved being accepted in her ethnicity by others. As Ronke expressed it, 'So, the impact of food is very, very significant. I think it brings people together.'

Flags and Art

On three sides of the rectangular worship space at GBC, there were (in January 2019) 47 full-size national flags on display. Each of these flags represented a country that at least one member of the congregation had come from. Each year the flags were reviewed. Flags from countries where no one now attended were removed, and members of the congregation whose flags were not on display were given the opportunity to pay for their flag to be purchased and displayed. On the left-hand wall behind the platform, where the meeting was usually led from, was an art installation consisting of 28 large hand-painted canvases. The canvases were painted during a workshop at GBC. Each has the name of God in the first language of the person/people who painted the canvas surrounded by colourful decoration; from top to bottom the canvases reflect the colours of the rainbow. On the right-hand wall behind the platform was a plain wooden cross that from time to time was surrounded by a colourful seasonal display. Additionally, on the walls of the worship area there was other art on display painted by people who attended the church, usually drawing on their own ethnic cultural styles. For example, there were two paintings using traditional Chinese artistic forms and Chinese letters illustrating Bible stories that were painted and donated by a Chinese attendee.

There was no flag displayed on the wall that people usually faced during Sunday worship. This was a deliberate choice. In some churches, the national flag of the dominant ethnicity is on display at the front. At GBC, we wanted the displayed flags to be a marker that people from all ethnicities were equally welcome; the flags in a sense marked out their space. Although at GBC God was addressed in different languages, everyone came to relationship with God through Jesus' death and resurrection (the bare wooden cross represented this). GBC was diverse in its ethnicity but united in its acceptance and worship of God through Jesus Christ.

Bunmi was at the workshop that produced the large artwork: 'I remember we made some artwork with different languages demonstrating God's name. And it was so beautiful the work that everyone did because everyone worked independently, yet created a rectangle decorated beautifully with the name of God in their native tongue. Then we put it all together ... all working together to create that artwork.' Each person contributed something unique drawn from their own ethnic heritage, but built together, it made something 'really beautiful'. There is here an obvious link to the tapestry metaphor, discussed in Chapter 2, that underpinned GBC's understanding of congregational church life.

Tabia was one of those who paid for her national flag: 'We were the only Cameroonians before and we paid for the flag. So, when the other Cameroonians came and they found the flag, it was "ooh, our flag is there", and I'm always beating my chest – I paid for it (laughter). So, when they find their flag there, they also have that feeling of "they know my country here – I belong here". I think that also makes them feel at home because they can see their flag here and they are represented here. So, my identity is here.' For Tabia, having her national flag on display was a marker that at GBC her ethnic identity was welcome and accepted. It was her view that, at least for Cameroonians, seeing their own flag on display meant that they felt welcome 'at home'.

Harnoop related an account of a visit to GBC by some Nepalese guests: 'I brought some like people whom I know who are Christians and Nepalese ... And the first impression they had was that it was a traditional kind of a British ... church and also, they were a bit taken aback because they didn't see much Nepalese except us, but then something caught their eye. It was the Nepalese flag and that really you know brought: "I've never ever seen a church in the UK that has got a Nepalese flag, you know, hung on the wall". So, I told them that ... not just the Nepalese flag, but all these flags they bow down to the cross at the front, so they were like: "Wow, really?" ... And every time I see that flag, I feel like I am a member of this church and part of Christ's family.'

In his account, Nepalese people who had never attended GBC before noticed the Nepalese flag on display, and it was significant for them to see their flag displayed in what they felt was a traditional British church. For Harnoop, seeing his national flag on the wall meant that he felt that he was welcomed and accepted as part not just of GBC but of 'Christ's family'.

Several others expressed the view that the display of flags meant that even people whose flag was not displayed felt welcome. Oluwasesan: 'One other thing that caught me was the flags as well. I thought, "Yes, okay, there are representatives from all these countries." It gives you that feeling that, yes, you are welcome here whatever country you come from.' Anthony commented: 'If someone comes in ... if you saw a load of flags, even if it may not be yours personally, but you saw other ethnic groups represented or nation's flags, you would feel more welcome. You know, it's that significance in what you see visually.' The visual impact of the flags, in Oluwasesan's and Anthony's view, meant that people felt welcome whether or not their own national flag was on display.

Third-Culture Kids

Some of the first-generation migrants who became part of GBC arrived with very young children; others soon started families. People born in the UK to parents who were born and grew up in a different country are called 'Third-Culture Kids' (TCK). These children grow up in a different culture to the culture of their parents; they draw on elements of their parents' culture and of the culture where they now live. However, they do not fully identify with either culture, hence 'Third-Culture Kids'. In my thesis, there is a long section that explores the view expressed by GBC TCK that their experience of growing up as a part of GBC had given them advantages over their peers who had not had a similar experience. However, here I want to explore only one aspect, which is the experience TCK had at GBC of it being a safe space for them, where they felt fully welcome and accepted. This, in their view, helped them form a positive self-identity.

Gbemisola commented: 'Being part of a multi-ethnic church has inspired me ... seeing Greenford Baptist Church so mixed and some of those from other cultures being in areas of leadership, talking at the front, or praying at the front and having different roles, that has just inspired me in life.'

Bunmi's comments are very helpful in understanding the way that GBC helped form her self-identity, so I will quote her at length.

> I think being brought up in this type of church, it really helped me to kind of navigate my way through that third-culture kind of space because we were loads of people from different countries, with that shared identity ... I think it was a place where you felt safe and that you are not on your own. I definitely struggled with that third-culture identity through my teens because, especially because of the school I went to as well where there were white British people and there was only one other Black person in my year. So, you don't really feel you fit in that well ... at school you are not as British as the other people there. They know you pronounce things differently, eat different food, or you can't go and do the same things that they do. So, it was quite tricky, but I think things like being at this church and at university helped me to accept myself for who I was. It helped me to know you aren't the same as everybody else. You have your own unique experience, and that is what makes you, you ... [at school] until they get to know you well, they have a certain perception of you. Whereas, people in church ... never made me feel like I was lesser or I was different.

They acknowledged we had different cultural backgrounds, but we were family and it didn't matter where you were from. Actually, we embraced it. It was celebrated rather than a bad thing. So that is why I would say this was a safe place for me because we acknowledged there were differences … that really differed from my school experience where … at the beginning it was very, very hard to adjust to where you felt you didn't really belong and you weren't the same as other people and that was seen as a bad thing, rather than a good thing, whereas in church I always felt differences were celebrated and you worked together in grace to have an understanding.

This acceptance and celebration of difference is explored theologically in Chapter 2.

Bunmi's experience at school and in wider society was that for people who were a bit different from the average person in England or came from a certain type of background, it was a case of: 'You are not included, and so you are kind of invisible in a way.' However, at GBC, the situation was very different for her: 'I felt very visible in this church. I felt like the unique things about me were great, God-given and to be celebrated. That gave me a sense of belonging and a sense of feeling loved and … like I mattered … knowing that within myself, I then have that confidence that this has value and maybe not everyone else believes it but my church family believes there is value in it. It just gives you that confidence to think I can overcome a lot and I am not by myself. And actually, it is God-given, it is not just an opinion. God actually loves that we are all different.'

Although not a TCK, as she arrived in the UK and at GBC in her twenties, Honoria's experience was also transformational for her life. She said:

I came from a quite closed society … so my family is … quite closed … my mother is quite a racist person … she is very traditional, having been brought up in a very traditional Portuguese cultural background … then I came here and been spoilt with all this beauty of differences. So, for me it has helped me to develop a passion to understand human beings and why you behave the way you behave… understanding why the person behaved like that and why their culture is that way, it is amazing. It is a fabulous way of looking into God's creation with all of its diversity because it's from God who created the world in that way. So yes, it really contributed to the person I am today, definitely and for my career choice [as a mental health nurse] as well because I couldn't do the work I do today if I didn't have this passion for these things from my early years in London. So today, all I do is about that. It is about acceptance. It is about respecting people the way they are … For me it is an amazing thing, and it is such a wonderful journey to be involved in this, to be honest with you, to understand God doesn't see those things as a barrier that we struggle with as human beings. For God, it is nothing because he created all of us and all those differences. So, actually we contribute to each other.

Bunmi, Gbemisola and Honoria each attribute a key part of the positive development of their self-identity to their lived experience of being welcomed and accepted as a part of GBC. One aspect of this was seeing people who looked like them in leadership/ministry roles at GBC encouraging them to aspire to leadership in their careers. Another component was the positive message that they were different from white British norms, but that this was good and to be celebrated. They felt welcomed and affirmed in their difference. Together these things helped the formation of a strong and positive self-identity. This enabled them to be confident and secure in themselves.

Conclusion

In this chapter I have explored how the culture of welcoming and accepting people from different ethnicities developed at GBC. We have explored the way that the use of a person's first language became normal and the significance of this for those in the congregation. We explored the way that dance became a normal vehicle for people to express their adoration of God, and the significance for many in the congregation. We have looked at prayer and how the use of styles of prayer from 'back home' became a normal aspect of church life. We have looked at the restructuring of Sunday morning meetings, and in particular the significance of 'connection time'. We have looked at the role of food and the significance of eating food from many ethnicities in helping people to feel accepted. We have explored the way that the flags and artwork on display helped people feel welcome. Finally, we looked at one aspect of how some of those who arrived at GBC as new-borns or children and who grew up within the GBC family viewed their experience.

GBC was a space where people felt safe, a place where they could be themselves, knowing that they would be accepted with all their ethnic differences. Honoria expressed this very clearly: 'to have this acceptance was something that captured me ... I didn't need to be tense or pretending ... I could always be myself here. It was always a place where I really felt at home ... everyone is really open to accept people.'

Bibliography

Wise, D., 2022, 'Developing a genuinely multi-ethnic local church congregation: an auto-ethnographic investigation into Greenford Baptist Church 1987–2014', https://pure.roehampton.ac.uk/portal/en/studentTheses/developing-a-genuinely-multi-ethnic-local-church-congregation (accessed 7.2.25).

7

Among the Nations, for the Nations: Championing Diversity in the Church in Edinburgh

MÀIRI MACPHERSON

Introduction

The movement of people has been used by God throughout history to bring about the growth of his kingdom and the worship of his name. The Bible traces the continual movements of God's people and the coinciding blessing of the nations. We see it from Abram's call to leave his country and be a blessing to the nations (Gen. 12.1–3) to Jesus calling his followers to go and make disciples of all nations (Matt. 28.16–20); from the exile of Judah in Babylon (2 Kings 25.1–26) to the scattering of the church in Acts because of persecution (Acts 8.1–3); from the captivity of a little Israelite girl serving Naaman's wife in Aram (2 Kings 5) to an Ethiopian eunuch returning to his homeland and being baptized by Philip on the way (Acts 8.26–39). We are shown time and again how God uses migration, be it voluntary or forced, to bring glory to his name. And he has not ceased to do this, even in twenty-first-century Scotland. Over the past 20 years, Scotland has seen a higher increase in net migration than other parts of the United Kingdom (National Records of Scotland, 2025). Simultaneously, it has witnessed the springing up of a plethora of church plants by individuals and communities from other places in the world.

However, this is not the story that we see in headlines or read about in census reports. Instead, we are presented with a narrative of decline when it comes to Christianity in Scotland, with onlookers wondering how Scotland 'lost the faith' (Lloyd, 2023) and asking 'Is the church running out of disciples?' (Healey, 2023). We as Christians feel a sense of despair and disappointment when we read that the majority of people in Scotland claim that they have no religion (Carrell, 2024). But we must remember that narratives of decline are hugely complicated. The status of Christianity in Scotland is often equated with the health of the Church of Scotland as a denomination, limiting how 'Christianity' is defined and not taking into consideration other denominations, theologies and traditions. We rarely hear about the minority-ethnic churches who are buying the buildings of historic churches that are going on sale (Akomiah-Conteh, 2021). And while it is indeed true that 'the majority of people in Scotland said they had no religion in the 2022 census' (Scotland's Census, 2024), it is also true that this does not indicate a rejection of all forms of Christianity, but perhaps only certain forms of what is conceived as traditional organized state religion. So what does Christianity actually look like in Scotland today? How are historic church denominations and Christian organizations acknowledging and reacting to the increasingly diverse global church in Scotland?

In an attempt to answer these questions, this chapter will serve as a case study for Nations, a ministry of Edinburgh City Mission that is working to stimulate and strengthen the mission of ethnically, linguistically and culturally diverse churches in Edinburgh. Edinburgh City Mission is an example of a historic Christian mission organization that has recognized the need for intentional intercultural work among Christians in Edinburgh in order to promote unity and extend God's kingdom. We will initially set the scene of the church in Edinburgh today and then go on to look at Edinburgh City Mission and how it is responding to this contemporary context with its Nations ministry. We will do this by examining how Nations represents the five core values of Edinburgh City Mission, the barriers it encounters, and its invitation to engage with the multicultural church in Scotland.

A few points of preface also ought to be included in this case study. First, this chapter will focus primarily on the city of Edinburgh, as this is where Edinburgh City Mission works. What is experienced in Edinburgh does not necessarily reflect the reality of the church in other places in Scotland, but at times it will be helpful for us to consider the context of Christianity in Scotland as a whole. Second, this kind of ministry is relatively new in Scotland, and it is continually adapting and developing. I request grace from those reading in cities and contexts where the following thought processes are perhaps old-hat or are simply part of the world-view already. I hope that for these readers this case study will be both a challenge to reflect on the initial stages of such ministries and an opportunity to celebrate the progress that may have been made by God's grace.

The Church in Edinburgh Today: A Movement Going Unnoticed?

Edinburgh is a city renowned for its history. Tourists travel from across the globe to wander the cobbled streets and marvel at the architecture, galleries and museums. It also has a rich Christian history that has left an indelible mark on the global church. In 1910, it witnessed the first world missionary conference, which aimed to see 'The Evangelization of the World in This Generation' (Ponraj and Devasahayam, 2010). At this conference, there was a recognition of the need to work ecumenically to do mission, but there was little representation of the global church with only 17 out of the 1,200 delegates being from outside Western Europe and North America (Sunquist, 2013). 100 years later, another world missionary conference was held in Edinburgh, and the number of Global South representatives was intended to present the reality of the global church of the time, with 60 nations represented by the delegates (Fox, 2011). This increase in diverse Christianity in the world is now reflected in the church in the city of Edinburgh itself.

A 2024 research report published by the Centre for the Study of World Christianity (CSWC) at the University of Edinburgh states that there are 'at least 80 global Christian groups' in Edinburgh (Chow, Wild-Wood and Hatzaw, 2024). We estimate that 29 nations are represented among these churches as majority nationalities (not including all nations represented by individuals within each church). Around 26 languages are being worshipped in regularly as the sole majority language or as an equal majority language with English. The CSWC report breaks down the 'global Christian groups' into three helpful categories: autonomous churches, international churches, and sub-congregations (i.e. fellowships within existing mainstream churches) (Chow, Wild-Wood and Hatzaw, 2024). This final category makes it difficult to tell exactly what percentage of Edinburgh churches are 'global Christian groups', but we can estimate that minority-ethnic and/or minority-language groups represent roughly 16% of the churches and Christian groups in Edinburgh in 2024. This figure is taken from the assumption that there are 80 groups out of the 500 Christian organizations that are mainly minority ethnic and/or linguistic. These are the statistics used in the *Global Christians in Edinburgh* report, 2nd edition (Chow, Wild-Wood and Hatzaw, 2024).

Whenever I share these statistics with church leaders and members in Edinburgh, I am usually met with surprise. Majority white Scottish church members might be aware of two or three Chinese churches. Their church leaders might be part of a city-wide prayer meeting with a few

African pastors. An Indian church leader might know about one other Indian fellowship that uses the same language in worship. But there is little awareness of the real number of Christians from other places in the world living and worshipping in the city.

I have noted three common reasons for this lack of awareness. First, there has been a lack of intercultural networking. Church planters often arrive in Edinburgh with no prior connection to existing local churches, or their only connection is with churches and organizations from their own ethnic or linguistic groups. Second, local church leaders can find themselves overburdened and under-resourced, meaning that they are working so hard in their own churches that it becomes a tall task to lift their heads from the plough. Intentional intercultural ecumenical engagement does not come high in the list of priorities. These leaders may start to consider it only when their own churches become more ethnically diverse. Third, there is the rather simple explanation that nobody actually knew how many of these churches there were until very recently.

Dr Sheila Akomiah-Conteh's 2018 PhD thesis on new churches created in Glasgow between 2000 and 2016 showed that the majority of new churches during that time were set up by minority-ethnic groups (Akomiah-Conteh, 2018). This discovery ignited an interest in global Christianity as it exists in Scotland more widely. The CSWC Global Christians in Edinburgh project aimed to find out what global Christian groups were active in the capital in 2023 and released a second edition of their project report in August 2024. Brendan Research initiated a research project on minority-ethnic Christian mission in the whole of Scotland and released their results in October 2024. As we will now come to see, Nations was created in the midst of this wider movement and has benefited greatly from the insights gained from the pioneering research by these individuals and organizations.

Edinburgh City Mission: A Brief History

Since it began, Edinburgh City Mission has been a truly pioneering charitable organization, making it the ideal setting for developing an innovative ministry like Nations. Edinburgh City Mission was founded in 1832 by David Nasmith. Scotsman Nasmith had founded the first City Mission in Glasgow six years earlier in 1826 and was passionate about caring for the poor in urban areas. Nasmith's approach was groundbreaking in its time. He emphasized the role of building relationships between the City Mission workers and those suffering from exclusion, isolation and deprivation in the city. This promoted a sustainable form of charity that encouraged the poor towards better education and consequently better opportunities rather than solely providing for immediate material needs without consideration of a person's wider circumstances (Orchard, 2020; Shaw, 2004).

Additionally, Nasmith was a proponent of ecumenical cooperation across the evangelical spectrum. Church of Scotland, Episcopalian, Free Church of Scotland, Baptist and Methodist (among others) were united in support of the City Mission as it paired evangelism to those living in deprivation with holistic care. The City Mission created united prayer meetings for the theologically diverse church leaders, encouraging them to work together to run facilities such as food and clothes banks and evangelistic events in the mid-nineteenth century. Thus, Edinburgh City Mission became known for its positive impact on the society of Edinburgh through caring for the people's spiritual welfare by sharing the gospel of Christ with them. It has continued to have this reputation for the following two centuries (James-Griffiths, 2016).

Although we may now be living in an Edinburgh that is almost 200 years older, many of the core issues that existed in Nasmith's time sadly persist. Edinburgh City Mission continues to serve those suffering from exclusion, deprivation and/or isolation, with a vision to help to create a mission movement across Edinburgh. Our strategy to achieve this is to stimulate and strengthen churches through prayer, community engagement and befriending schemes. This strategy is in keeping with Nasmith's original approach, but we also seek to be highly contextualized for twenty-first-century Edinburgh. One aspect of this contextualization is the recognition of the impact of migration and globalization on the capital over the past century in particular. As we have seen, there are now many nations represented by Christians in Edinburgh, and we have the opportunity as Edinburgh City Mission to harness the energy, passion and gifts of the diverse church to serve our increasingly globalized city.

But Nations did not find its origins in attempting to achieve an intercultural church model for mission. Rather, when Edinburgh City Mission joined many others across the world in lamenting the killing of George Floyd in May 2020, it recognized a need for an initial discussion about racial justice – and, more specifically, how the wider church in Edinburgh should provide a safe place for people of every ethnicity and language to have their voices heard and their cares listened to and addressed. Nations therefore started out as an event called 'A Place at the Table', where minority-ethnic Christian leaders and academics in

Edinburgh were interviewed and provided with a platform for them to share their experience of living in Edinburgh and/or elsewhere in Scotland. While beneficial as a limited online series during the Covid-19 pandemic, this format did not satisfactorily transfer into an in-person event. Concurrently, a local pastor and missionary, Russell Phillips, who had just returned from leading a church in Siberia, had passed on the 'Acts 2.11 Edinburgh' project to Edinburgh City Mission in April 2020. 'Acts 2.11 Edinburgh' was a database containing contact details for Christians who speak different languages. This database was able to be used to connect non-native English speakers to someone with whom they could speak about Christianity in their first language. As these two strands of racial justice and linguistic diversity weaved together, Nations began to take shape.

Nations: Among the Nations, for the Nations

As I stepped into the role of Mission Strengthener for Nations in April 2022 and connected with various church leaders across the city, the ministry saw a slight shift in focus. It became apparent that the felt need of the global Christian groups was not necessarily a project to talk about racial justice, but rather practical demonstrations of unity and love among God's diverse people, which in themselves promote racial justice. And although GDPR guidelines made the growth of a database of contact details difficult (we did not share this database or contact details without the relevant permissions), I was still able to find out about many groups worshipping in different languages whose meeting details and contact information could be shared publicly. I compiled a database of public meeting information for the global Christian groups in Edinburgh that could be circulated around the Edinburgh City Mission team and other contacts with the purpose of raising awareness of the diversity of the church in the city. I also created a vision document for Nations, which could demonstrate how this ministry would contribute to Edinburgh City Mission's aim to help to create a mission movement in Edinburgh. Thus, the two distinct areas of racial justice and minority-language fellowships were blended into an overarching ministry to promote unity in diversity.

After 18 months of development, we set our mission statement for the Nations ministry: 'to stimulate and strengthen the mission of ethnically, culturally and linguistically diverse churches in Edinburgh', along with our accompanying vision statement: 'to champion diversity and build unity in the wider church through creating meaningful and mutual engagement between local and global Christian communities in Edinburgh, reflecting the heavenly vision of Revelation 7.9'. We wanted to ensure that the ministry was representative of the people whom it sought to support, so we ran the first 'Nations Gathering' on Saturday 2 December 2023. This gathering aimed to bring global church leaders together to meet one another, share breakfast, be introduced to Nations and be given the opportunity to give feedback on the vision document and the ministry in general. There was then a time of prayer together, giving the leaders space to share their burdens with one another. This event was the first time some church leaders had met others who were also working with minority-ethnic groups and wrestling with similar issues such as worshipping in multiple languages and maintaining connection with younger generations in their churches. The feedback on the vision document was positive overall; we were encouraged to continue to develop the ministry and were offered support by those present (as well as by those who were unable to make it to the gathering). Since then, we have witnessed relationships developing between churches and have held subsequent Nations Gatherings with the same aim to bring the nations together, reflect on unity, and pray with and for one another.

As the ministry grows, we have recognized the need to ensure that it continues to reflect the needs of those it aims to advocate for and attempt to fulfil these needs lovingly and sustainably. This includes continual reflection on the language of Nations. The terminology used by charitable organizations is key to promoting understanding and presenting aims and objectives effectively. Nations therefore moved away from using negatively framed terms such as 'non-English' and 'non-white majority' to the positively framed terminology of 'ethnically, linguistically and culturally diverse'. This positive language fulfils two main purposes. First, it acknowledges the diversity that exists in groups that are presumed to be 'homogeneous', for example a majority-Nigerian church that in fact has a multitude of languages represented by its members. Moreover, it allows space for church communities that may have previously been majority white but now represent a variety of different ethnicities and languages, and seek to intentionally celebrate this diversity. In other words, this terminology is flexible enough to handle the fluid nature of migration. Second, it avoids the use of the term 'diaspora', the interpretation of which can differ from person to person. According to Narry F. Santos, the term 'diaspora' now describes 'any religious or racial minority living within the territory of another religious or political society' (Santos, 2004). It is also often associated with a maintained connection with the territory of origin, in other words maintaining culture and language representative of this territory. This is where the terminology of 'diaspora' could have become problematic for Nations. We recognize that a common concern among global Christian communities in the UK is keeping their children in the church and in the Christian faith. This becomes more and more difficult as their children may prefer to speak English rather than the language of their parents, or as they begin to feel more comfortable in social settings that are more culturally 'Scottish' rather than culturally reflecting their parents' nation of origin. The phrase 'ethnically, linguistically and culturally diverse' therefore describes the felt experience of individuals and individual families as well as larger communities found in churches. It includes those who live in the 'hyphenated space', operating within and in between ethnic, linguistic and national identities (Ybarrola, 2012).

The ministry title 'Nations' was itself selected in February 2021 by the current CEO of Edinburgh City Mission, Duncan Cuthill, in collaboration with María de los Ángeles Reyes Mesa, Mission Strengthener at the time for what was soon to become the Nations ministry. They viewed 'Nations' as the ideal catch-all term to reflect the diversity of people that exists in Edinburgh, and María, originally from Colombia, felt that the term represented her well as a Christian from another country living in the city. We will soon come to see how this term is used in the Bible. For now, it is worth noting that the title 'Nations' provides us with a fresh vocabulary that we can mould to fit the context of Edinburgh. Rather than using the terms 'global Christian groups', 'migrant churches' or 'diaspora Christian communities', we can use the terms 'Nations churches' or 'Nations Christian groups'. Here, 'Nations' reflects a community where white is not the sole majority ethnicity, English is not the sole majority language and Scottish/British is not the sole majority nationality. It enables an intercultural perspective where ethnic, linguistic and cultural groups can interact and work with one another within a larger entity instead of becoming more established in potential individual enclaves. This sense of living among one another has informed the tagline for Nations. Edinburgh City Mission seeks to be 'In our city, for our city'. Nations has embraced this model and sees itself as being 'Among the Nations, for the Nations'.

Our Values Inform Our Ministry

We have established a picture of what the church in Edinburgh looks like in the 2020s, hopefully capturing an idea of its ethnic, linguistic and cultural diversity. We have also witnessed how Nations was moulded in the context of Edinburgh; it sought to listen to and learn from church leaders in the city and develop terminology for the ministry that was both clear and malleable. As we desire for the ministry to be built according to God's will, it is vital to build it upon the foundation of God's word. Edinburgh City Mission is shaped by five core biblical values: love, generosity, unity, justice and being pioneering. These five values are also therefore foundational to the Nations ministry. We will now consider how Nations thinks through the theology of each of these values and how the ministry then works out this theology practically. (More information on Edinburgh City Mission's values can be found on the Edinburgh City Mission website: https://edinburghcitymission.org.uk (accessed 24.2.25).)

Motivated by love

Nations seeks to live out the self-sacrificial love that we learn about in the Bible. 1 John 4.7–21 tells us that 'God is love' and that this revelation calls us to action; it calls us to actively love one another as God has loved us. But God does not love us half-heartedly or temporarily when it suits him. He loves us with a fully committed and eternal love; we see this in the Father sending the Son to be the saviour of the world. Not only does he achieve everlasting salvation for us, but he also gives us his Spirit, which enables us to love others self-sacrificially.

While working with churches representing a plethora of ethnicities, languages and cultures, we desire to love one another in a way that reflects God's love. Throughout the Bible we see God calling his people both to bless others as they themselves move to different lands and to love others who move into their land, for all the earth and its dwellers belong to the Lord (Gen. 12.1–3; Ex. 22.21; Ps. 24.1). And so the love worked out in God's intercultural church ought to be multidirectional. It is not simply a case of 'welcoming' the Christian who has moved to our country (although this is obviously very important); it is a willingness to allow that brother or sister who has moved to your country from elsewhere to bless you as they are called to do. And it is not a case of simply discounting Scotland and its churches for no longer being Christian; it is rather a willingness to come alongside Christians living in the local context to support them practically and prayerfully. It is in this multidirectional love for one another that Jesus tells us we will show the world that we are his disciples (John 13.34–35).

We are therefore all called to discerning and loving humility as we live in this globalized world and in the intercultural church. The Nations ministry loves people as it acknowledges and celebrates the diversity in our city and offers space for Christians to share their ethnic, linguistic and cultural riches with others, such as multilingual prayer meetings and worship events.

Committed to generosity

Edinburgh City Mission has made a commitment as an organization to be wisely generous to the people in Edinburgh. In the city, it continues to be known for its holistic provision through partnering in ministries such as food banks, a clothes bank, befriending services and English conversation cafés. Nations likewise has been committed to generosity, however this has been worked out differently in this ministry given the relative lack of accessible material resources to support this kind of work. (Although we do always endeavour to provide food at every event since it is such a powerful touchstone for almost every culture!) What Nations may lack in material generosity, we seek to make up for in generosity of spirit, seen more specifically in a generosity of attention, open-mindedness, and networks.

Many Nations churches have not previously been recognized or acknowledged by other churches or Christian organizations external to their ethnic and linguistic groups. This disconnectedness can lead to a sense of isolation among church members and discouragement among the leaders. Nations therefore serves the purpose of connecting Nations church leaders with one another, providing a space to find fellowship and encourage one another. Sometimes a church's mission can even be strengthened and stimulated simply by giving the church attention; I have done this through meeting with leaders and members and through attending regular worship services in the churches.

Not only do we seek to give churches fresh attention, but the Nations ministry also wants to be generous in its outlook, not making presumptions about what to expect from church leaders or church services. At the very beginning of my role with Edinburgh City Mission, I remember a representative from another Christian organization warning me that I would not receive engagement from certain groups of churches because they chose to remain distant from the rest of the Christian scene in the city. This perception is sadly not uncommon among Scottish churches and Christian organizations. However, I found these generalized assessments of Nations churches to be incorrect and unfounded, and instead they wanted to show generosity in being open-minded. Approaching the plethora of ethnic and linguistic groups with a posture of true interest, learning and celebration, encouraging the spread of the gospel rather than just academic research or ideas of 'integration', has meant that Nations has been welcomed by all kinds of churches and groups.

In order for this ministry to be truly effective and sustainable, a generosity of resources is indeed required, and at this stage in its development Nations can offer the resource of networks. Culturally, the Scots are known to be a very interconnected people; they get to know a stranger often through finding mutual acquaintances and shared locations. This means that Scotland is an ideal place to create networks, particularly among churches and Christian organizations that are feeling isolated. Nations has been able to plug church planters from other countries into existing church planting networks, connect Nations church leaders with local highly trained practitioners and invite Nations church members to volunteer with Christian charities in the city. We do not want to gatekeep any networks or resources that could strengthen the mission of God's global church.

Pursuing unity

The vision statement for Nations is 'to champion diversity and build unity in the wider church through creating meaningful and mutual engagement between local and global Christian communities in Edinburgh, reflecting the heavenly vision of Revelation 7.9'. We believed it was key to include a biblical motivation for this ministry in the vision statement, ensuring that the foundation for Nations was based not on our own understanding but on the plans and character of God.

Revelation 7.9 says: 'After this I looked, and there was a vast multitude from every nation, tribe, people, and language, which no one could number, standing before the throne and before the Lamb.' This verse is often used in the promotion of church unity and is presented as a future hope. Of course this is true, and we will surely see God's church united perfectly and eternally in the new heaven and earth, but we can also experience a taste of this blessing today in Edinburgh. What are the people before the Lamb doing? The next verse tells us: 'And they cried out in a loud voice: "Salvation belongs to our God, who is seated on the throne, and to the Lamb!"' They are worshipping Jesus together while maintaining their ethnicity and language; God does not expect us to give these up in order to enter the kingdom of heaven. And so today, in Edinburgh, we have the opportunity to witness the worship of the Lamb by people from all over the world in a multiplicity of languages. Nations desires to raise awareness of this beautiful image that exists in our city.

It should of course be noted that we seek to promote Christian unity in the midst of theological diversity. This is by no means an easy task and requires consistent prayer and guidance from God. But we can trust that our God, who perfectly models unity in diversity for us in the Trinity of Father, Son and Spirit, desires us to live alongside one another in unity. We are still in the early stages of what unity in theological diversity means as a ministry. The Nations ministry recognizes that theology is contextual, and that one group cannot claim to have the only 'correct' theology, for all humans are fallen and their thinking requires redemption and restoration that can only be made complete in heaven. With this in mind, we can approach the theological diversity in Edinburgh positively rather than warily. We can recognize that we are able to be one body of Christ with different parts that have different strengths, and which can inform one another and keep one another alive and moving forward. Ultimately, we want to recognize Jesus as the gate to the salvation (John 10.7–10), not a specific theology, and certainly not a specific culture or heritage.

Striving for justice

As we have seen previously, the Nations ministry finds its roots in the interweaving of two thematic strands: racial justice and linguistic diversity. The idea of striving after justice is therefore already embedded in this project, just as it is embedded in the identity of Edinburgh City Mission. This is reflected in one of Nation's charitable goals: 'Nations recognizes, engages with, and provides relief for communities who have suffered historic exclusion and isolation in Scotland due to their ethnic, cultural and linguistic heritage.' To bring about justice in the context of Nations is consequently to bring about inclusion and fellowship among the Church of Christ in Edinburgh.

It is part of our fallen human nature to become exclusivist and exclusionary; we gravitate towards building our own groups with specific ethnic, social and/or linguistic attributes. Dutch missiologist Johan Herman Bavinck (1895–1964) wrote during a time when the world was witnessing unspeakable injustices during the Second World War. He helpfully frames these injustices in the history of the world as symbolic of the 'terrible rival' of the kingdom of God, which he calls 'the empire of humanity'. Humanity continually strives after unity, and subsequently justice, by building homogeneous kingdoms, attempting to find identity and worth in these unified kingdoms. Bavinck argues: 'World history is nothing but the ever-repeated attempt to build empires and the stubborn striving to rediscover humans' lost unity in such an empire' (Bavinck, 2014). These homogeneous kingdoms never satisfy humanity's craving for unity, identity and justice because they are not God's intention for his creation. He teaches his people to be just and caring towards all people, not just those within their own ethnic and linguistic groups.

Pioneering for the future

Edinburgh City Mission holds to the understanding that Jesus was a pioneer, in the sense that he pioneered our salvation through his death and resurrection. The groundbreaking nature of this gospel message led to the early church turning the known world upside down in how they taught about Jesus and lived out their lives for him. We have already considered how Edinburgh City Mission was a pioneering work when it was set up by David Nasmith in 1832 and how it continues to be so. God has continued to bless the work of Nations through providing us with people, organizations and churches who share in our vision. In these early days of ministry development, we have sought out groups who cherish the value of diversity in the wider church. These include the One People Commission (Evangelical Alliance), OMF International, Latin Link, Intercultural Church Planting UK, Asian Concern and Integrity Languages.

Using the resources and networks now available to us, we want to organize pioneering city-wide events that intentionally celebrate the diversity with which God has blessed us. These will take the form of more Nations Gatherings (prayer meetings for Nations church leaders) – specifically, multilingual prayer meetings, and interdenominational, intercultural times of worship. These events could come alongside training and equipping opportunities for the Nations churches – for example, training in how to provide effective language interpretation in a church service, or how to speak to secular white Scottish neighbours about Jesus. Our network includes organizations and professionals who specialize in these areas of work. Additionally, we are considering the idea of a mentoring programme for Nations church leaders who perhaps do not already have a wider pastoral care network.

In order to best fulfil the needs of the churches we wish to serve, Nations needs to continually be up to date with key trends in the study of migration, justice and missiology. These areas of study are constantly shifting and developing on both a local and a global scale, and it is helpful for Nations to always be aware of the issues most relevant to its network of churches and organizations.

Barriers to Unity

As Nations continues to grow by the grace of God, we must ensure that our goals are not idealistic or unachievable. We bow to God's ways, which are higher than our own, and accept that we will not experience perfect unity in diversity until we see heaven, although we have the privilege of enjoying a taste of it today. And so it is helpful to now look at three elements of the churches in Edinburgh that have been and could be barriers to unity within the diverse wider church of the city.

First, the issue of prejudice and discrimination is particularly pertinent to this kind of ministry. As people from a multitude of different ethnic, linguistic, socio-economic, ecclesiastical and theological contexts gather together, they bring with them their own perceptions of others from those various contexts. This leads to presumptions about other people's theologies and priorities. Some Christians from the Global South would avoid white Scottish churches by arguing that they are just 'religious' and are no longer preaching the true gospel. Some white Scottish Christians are inexcusably surprised when they realize that not all 'African churches' preach a prosperity gospel. Very real tensions exist between groups whose representative nations are in conflict with one another outside the UK, leading to theological rifts. Individuals and groups who may have a strong stance on a specific conflict can struggle to worship alongside those who have either a different stance or a stance that is not strong enough. These varied perceptions of conflict can be informed by, and can result in, differences in ecclesiology (for example, the role of church and state) and eschatology (for example, the idea of tribulation). Suspicions about others in the church can therefore arise when such theological differences begin to rise to the surface during times of conflict; the seeds of disunity are given fertile soil in this context. I can give no solutions to these problems outside inviting people together in fellowship. At times, we feel powerless when faced with engrained discriminatory perspectives, but we give thanks that we have a God who already knows people's thoughts and who can transform our hearts and renew our minds.

Second, we note that simply busyness can hamper the active pursuit of unity. As mentioned previously, local church leaders are working extremely hard to maintain their congregations and encourage growth in their members. Dedicating time to participate in a supplementary activity promoting church unity might not be at the top of their to-do list. Similarly, Nations church leaders often have one or two other jobs alongside their work in ministry. Their free time in the week is extremely precious and must be spent wisely. However, as with many things, this kind of ministry requires the investment of time if it is to reap sustainable rewards. We can only pray that God would grant us capacity for this.

The third barrier to mention here is the lack of understanding surrounding the communal outworking of unity. By this I mean that many Christians in Edinburgh see the work of church unity in ethnic and linguistic diversity as something to be done by a small minority of people who are interested in 'international missions'. Often the white Scottish people showing interest and investing time in Nations are those with experience in mission organizations working in other countries. While this may be a great place to start, and we can learn many things from them, this does not promote sustainable growth for the ministry. When celebrating the diversity of God's church in unity is seen as something only for a certain group set aside to do so, then it becomes exclusivist and consequently disunited from the rest of the church. We lament when discussions about ethnic and linguistic diversity take place with only white and English-speaking people sitting around the table (or only Black and Yoruba-speaking people, or only Indian and Malayalam-speaking people), for we are missing out on the riches that God has gifted to other nations.

An Invitation to be Empowered and to Engage

As we conclude this case study of Edinburgh City Mission's Nations ministry, we identify the invitation that this ministry offers to Christians of every tribe, tongue and nation to be empowered by the Holy Spirit and engage with one another as the multifaceted body of Christ. Many Nations churches have emerged over the past 20 years with a fresh energy for the task of mission in 'post-Christian' Scotland. Christians from more historically 'Scottish' churches can be encouraged by this energy and can harness it, for example in joint evangelistic events. And Christians belonging to ethnic and linguistic minority churches can learn about the culture of Edinburgh from the historically 'Scottish' churches. This could be vital to them better understanding how they can witness in the workplace to their Scottish colleagues. For such collaboration to take place, we must adopt the view that ethnic, linguistic and cultural diversity in the church is part and parcel of God's mission in Edinburgh in the twenty-first century.

And as we encourage one another as the diverse body of Christ, we acknowledge that it is ultimately the Holy Spirit that empowers us in this work. Every Christian has already been empowered by the Holy Spirit to be a missionary witness and be taught by this Spirit of Truth (Tennant, 2010). We have already been freed by the Spirit and do not need to give or be given permission to be part of the kingdom of God; no one group of us is the gatekeeper to the kingdom because of our ethnic, linguistic or cultural heritage. It is with this spirit (and by the Holy Spirit) that I challenge all those I speak to about Nations to attend a service or event at a church in Edinburgh where their ethnicity is not the majority ethnicity, and where their language is not the majority language. I invite all to take a moment to experience this taste of heaven, learn humility by seeing how each nation is only a small part of a huge world church, and be encouraged that God has provided us with such well-equipped fellow workers in mission.

Bibliography

Akomiah-Conteh, Sheila, 2018, 'The changing landscape of the church in post-Christendom Britain: New churches in Glasgow 2000–2016', PhD thesis, University of Aberdeen.

Akomiah-Conteh, Sheila, 2021, 'Rivers in the desert: The story of African Christianity in Britain', *ANVIL*, Vol. 37, Issue 3, https://churchmissionsociety.org/anvil/rivers-in-the-desert-the-story-of-african-christianity-in-britain-sheila-akomiah-conteh-anvil-vol-37-issue-3/ (accessed 24.2.25).

Bavinck, J. H., 2014, *Between the Beginning and the End*, translated by Bert Hielema. Grand Rapids, WI: William B. Eerdmans.

Brendan Research, 2024, *Churches without People, and People without Churches*, Edinburgh: Brendan Research.

Carrell, Severin, 2024, 'Majority of people in Scotland have no religion, census shows', *The Guardian*, 21 May, available at: https://www.theguardian.com/uk-news/article/2024/may/21/majority-of-people-in-scotland-do-not-believe-in-any-religion-census-shows (accessed 24.2.25).

Chow, Alexander, Wild-Wood, Emma and Hatzaw, Nuam, 2024, *Global Christians in Edinburgh* (2nd edn), Edinburgh: University of Edinburgh, available at: https://era.ed.ac.uk/handle/1842/40766 (accessed 24.2.25).

Fox, Frampton F., 2011, 'A Participant's Account of Edinburgh 2010', *Evangelical Missions Quarterly*, Vol. 47, No. 1, pp. 88–93, available at: https://missionexus.org/a-participants-account-of-edinburgh-2010/ (accessed 24.2.25).

Healey, Derek, 2023, 'Special investigation: Is the Church running out of disciples?' *Sunday Post*, 1 October, available at: https://www.sundaypost.com/fp/churches-attendance/ (accessed 24.2.25).

James-Griffiths, Paul, 2016, 'David Nasmith: A Dynamic Founder of Missions (1799–1839)', Christian Heritage Edinburgh, 23 August, available at: https://www.christianheritageedinburgh.org.uk/?s=david+nasmith (accessed 24.2.25).

Lloyd, John, 2023, '"No congregation, no church": how Scotland lost the faith', *Financial Times*, 19 August, available at: https://www.ft.com/content/a690a5b6-7c4a-4501-9974-a7502327b5c8 (accessed 24.2.25).

National Records of Scotland (NRS), 2025, 'Migration flows', available at: https://www.nrscotland.gov.uk/statistics-and-data/statistics/statistics-by-theme/migration/migration-statistics/migration-flows#:~:text=Main%20Points,was%2028%2C100%20in%202018%2D19 (accessed accessed 24.2.25).

Orchard, Stephen, 2020, 'David Nasmith (1799–1839), Philanthropy Expressed as Campaigning', in Binfield, C., Ditchfield, G. and Wykes, D. L., eds, *Protestant Dissent and Philanthropy in Britain, 1660–1914*, New edition [Online], United Kingdom: Boydell & Brewer, pp. 95–112.

Ponraj, S. Devasahayam, 2010, 'Edinburgh 1910 and Christian Mission among Other Faiths', in Frampton F. Fox, ed., *Give Us Friends! An Indian Perspective on 100 Years of Mission*, Bangalore: Asian Trading Corporation, pp. 60–79.

Santos, Narry F., 2004, 'Survey of the Diaspora Occurrences in the Bible and of Their Contexts in Christian Missions', in Pantoja, Luis, Tira, Sadira Joy B. and Wan, Enoch, eds, *Scatter: The Filipino Global Presence*, Manila: Lifechange Publishing, pp. 53–66.

Scotland's Census, 2024, 'Scotland's Census 2022 – Ethnic group, national identity, language and religion' (last updated: 21 May 2024), available at: https://www.scotlandscensus.gov.uk/2022-results/scotland-s-census-2022-ethnic-group-national-identity-language-and-religion/ (accessed 24.2.25).

Shaw, Ian J., 2004, 'Thomas Chalmers, David Nasmith, and the Origins of the City Mission Movement', *Evangelical Quarterly*, Vol. 76, No. 1, pp. 31–46.

Sunquist, Scott W., 2013, *Understanding Christian Mission: Participation in Suffering and Glory*, Grand Rapids, MI: Baker Academic.

Tennant, Timothy C., 2010, *Invitation to World Missions: A Trinitarian Missiology for the Twenty-first Century*, Grand Rapids, MI: Kregel Academic.

Ybarrola, Steven, 2012, 'Anthropology, Diasporas, and Mission', *Mission Studies*, Vol. 29, No. 1, pp. 79–94.

8

What Even Is My Culture? Exploring Identity in an Intercultural Church

JESSIE TANG

I'm really confused sometimes about who I am or what I want to be. I wish Mama were here, she would know what to do. She always told me to be proud of being Chinese ... If I weren't Chinese, I wouldn't have so much pressure to be good at Maths ... I wouldn't have to worry about people not saying my name correctly ... I don't know – it's confusing. (Wong, pp. 44–5)

The Challenges of Minoritized Experiences

The Life of a Banana, published in 2014, is the first book of its kind – written by the first British-born Chinese author to be published in the UK, detailing the life experiences of a second-generation immigrant who was born and brought up in England (Wong, 2014). It struck me as significant because as I read this novel, which draws on the author's own experiences, I realized it expressed something within me that I did not have the tools to articulate. I felt seen and known. Throughout time, I have discovered that this cultural identity tension that the character Xing Li faces is not unique or unusual, but is held by many second-generation immigrants, Third-Culture Kids and those who have a bi-cultural identity or come from mixed heritages. It is not particular to the East Asian experience – my friends and contacts from a variety of ethnic backgrounds and faith backgrounds share this commonality. We have this cultural affinity, an understanding of a minoritized experience, of having to constantly navigate and construct our own identity. Some of us have been ashamed of our heritage or have attempted to hide our cultural differences relative to the white normative culture, due to experiences of othering and racism, whether in covert or overt ways. In addition, almost all of us are required to assimilate into the white dominant culture in Britain, to self-edit, and fall into the 'temptation to take up as little room as possible, to dial down any parts of ourselves that might make us conspicuous or allow anyone to notice too much that we are in any way different' (McDonald, 2021, p. 58). Chine McDonald adds that the white person is the 'default human' as described by Andre Henry (2021, p. 58). Writing from the US context, Daniel Lee states that: 'Only White people are truly human, and the members of other racial groups are only human to the extent that they resemble White people.' Failure to do so results in otherness (Lee, 2022, pp. 166–7).

It is therefore unsurprising that we have been taught to assimilate. Ben Lindsay, in his book *We Need To Talk About Race* (2019), suggests that assimilation presents a 'false dichotomy for the person of colour – you're accepted by a white majority culture, but it is not authentic to your own experiences/background' (Lindsay, 2019, p. 109). If a person has had to 'fit in' for their entire lives, it is probable that there may be a lack of knowledge of one's culture, and a risk of not knowing who oneself is apart from assimilation. One may even struggle to express what cultural authenticity is. Does that matter, when a second-generation person like me can fit very easily and well into a white majority space? After all, Western society has been operating in this way, so why should the church be any different? In this chapter I argue that intercultural church is a third space, where the cultures in the church shape the shared culture of the church. This dynamic and ever-developing space paints a beautifully messy picture but can cause the identity challenges of a rootless second-generation immigrant, like myself, to be exposed and come to the surface.

The Bring-and-Share Dilemma

At Mosaic, an intentionally intercultural church plant in Harrow, London, which I joined in 2020, we often had 'bring and share' meals after the service, where each was encouraged to bring a dish – 'heart food' – from their culture. I considered what I thought I knew how to cook: egg fried rice, fried noodles, a meat in black bean sauce, char siu chicken wings. But when I sat down (or stood up) to cook a dish, I would momentarily freeze in realization that I did not know the 'authentic' way of cooking these dishes. I was paralysed and wondered if what I brought would be acceptable, and whether I would represent 'my people' properly. This almost always turned into me asking for tips from my dad, who sometimes would cook the dish for me! But such an event caused me to question how much I knew of my own culture, and I was caught between worlds – perhaps I was not 'Chinese enough' to even attempt to cook this. McDonald also shares her experience of questioning herself – 'Was I British or Nigerian?' – at International Sundays held at her church in her book *God Is Not a White Man* (McDonald, 2021, p. 194). She describes that fellow Nigerians in the church would bring dishes such as nkowbi, containing cow's foot, or abacha, with dried fish, causing those who were white British to feel awkward at these more 'exotic' dishes (McDonald, 2021). Instead, in choosing to bring an acceptable dish, she records how she felt as follows: 'We were making our dishes, our cultures and subsequently ourselves more palatable to our white British friends, toning ourselves down to fit the tastes of the majority' (McDonald, 2021). I suggest that in such instances, people with non-white British backgrounds are not able to genuinely choose what to bring, because our contributions have already been 'chosen' by what is considered appropriate. This is masked by the perception that there is openness to receive everything, but in reality, only what is palatable is accepted.

Such are the dangers of tokenism and white supremacy, which, if we are not careful, can be pervasive in an intercultural church. White supremacy declares that the white race is superior (Merriam-Webster, 2025); it refers to the way society, socio-economic and political systems enable white people to hold power over others. If white supremacy is in the fabric of society, and has been the driver of the Western Church's contested history, it is not a surprise that it exists in our churches today if left unchecked. In instances such as the above, self-awareness, particularly of one's culture and identity, is key to guard against tokenism and knowing what one can offer. However, awareness of one's own culture and identity is very difficult with a white assimilationist orientation in white spaces, which is why such a positioning should be acknowledged and expressed in order for it to become conscious. Tokenism is often regarded as a symbolic effort where minoritized people are recruited to tick a box rather than given equal opportunities or being heard as a full member of the body. Lindsay describes this as 'having [his] individuality instrumentalised for the sake of a white diversity agenda' (Lindsay, 2019, p. 108). Sadly, this is a criticism of the intercultural church, International Sundays, and other events that may paint a picture of cultural diversity but do not allow these cultures to affect a church's life, mission and worship. For example, the church's worship style may remain entirely Western, with hymns and contemporary Christian music in English, even though there are a number of people on the worship team and in the congregation from various nations who would prefer to sing in their own languages. Additionally, a minoritized person in the leadership team may have their views and opinions disregarded or struggle to bring their voice to the table, especially where the culture is not conducive to allowing this.

Defining Intercultural

An article from the Lausanne Movement in 2020 on uncovering discrimination in missions highlights that people do not realize or even notice that the founding culture of an organization continues to dominate thinking and practice (Rievan, 2020). Since the dynamics of race are always at play in society, with the dominance of whiteness in Britain, it is unsurprising that such a thing often goes unnoticed. This could be dangerous in an intercultural church if the congregation assumes there is equality in cultures, but in fact there exists a dominant culture. If this culture, often the host culture, is not recognized as dominant, it may have a damaging effect on those who are minoritized, and this damaging effect also goes unrealized. Therefore, it is imperative that such a dominance needs to be exposed and acted upon.

A telling article from *Christianity Today* revealed that 'large, multiracial churches with largely white pastoral leadership can unintentionally pressure worshippers to conform to culturally white behaviours', adding that some people of colour are rejecting white-led multi-ethnic spaces and choosing to return to the immigrant church (Ding, 2021). In Black-majority spaces, a wholly white leadership, when the rest of the church are Black or ethnically diverse, is collectively understood as the Guinness effect (Lindsay, 2019, p. 105), borrowing the image from the draught stout beer whose liquid is dark in colour, sitting under a thick white foam. I argue that diversity in leadership is an important way to guard against the damaging effects of a church, who on the surface may look intercultural, towards those of the Global Majority Heritage.

In addition to this, culture needs to change. Marzouk, in his book *Intercultural Church* (2019), puts forward three models of church: an assimilation model, segregation model and intercultural church model. I suggest we must properly move from an assimilation model, where minorities are expected to take on the dominant culture, to a truly intercultural church model, where the cultures of the church adjust and adapt and 'together give birth to something new' (Marzouk, 2019, p. 38). In a Grove booklet on *Intercultural Church*, it is helpfully explained in a diagram referenced to Anthony Gittins, which demarcates intercultural from multicultural (Aldous, Dunmore and Seevaratnam, 2020, p. 4). We live in a multicultural society in multicultural Britain, where diverse people groups coexist in the same spaces. Some have relationships, but many live alongside one another without allowing their cultures to shape each other. In contrast to this, an intercultural community is commonly considered as a place where there are interactions between cultures. Further to this, in a church context, these interactions include the mutuality of sharing one another's cultures and gifts for the blessing of the whole body. This means that an intercultural worship service may have songs in various languages, different styles of praying and a diverse array of foods to share. In intercultural fellowship, intentional friendships and relationships occur across cultural boundary lines. Hospitality is shared organically without discrimination, and yet every person's culture is acknowledged, redeemed and transformed for the betterment of one another, and to display God's glory in community. I agree with Cole Arthur Riley's statement, that: 'If we bear the image of God, that means we bear the image of a multitude. And that to bear the image of God in its fullness, we need each other' (Arthur Riley, 2022, p. 73). This need of one another must occur to see more of who God is, and for fresh perspectives about God. This need must also be remembered when living and ministering in an intercultural church in the face of challenges and trials that are present. The collective is an important component in the church that functions as a Third Space, or Third Culture – where the cultures in the church form the culture of the church.

The Third Space

Postcolonial theorist Homi Bhabha has written about the Third Space, suggesting that it is an in-between space that arises between the colliding of cultures. It is an intervening space, a middle passage, a borderline which carries tensions and 'resists the binary opposition of racial and cultural groups' (Bhabha, 1994, p. 207). Jenny Wang, in *Permission to Come Home*, calls it 'a space between worlds and within margins' (Wang, p. 212). Similarly, Third Culture is a term used by sociologists to describe a new culture formed by the combining of a first culture – perhaps the culture where a person's parents are from – and a second culture – the place where they grew up. This Third Culture is the liminal space inhabited by such a person, who has their feet in different worlds and world-views simultaneously (Jennings, 2024). Such people are commonly considered to be Third-Culture Kids (TCKs).

Third Culture is beautifully described by Dave Gibbons in *The Monkey and The Fish*:

> Third culture is being able to live in both first and second culture and even adopt an entirely different culture. Third culture is about adaptation, the both/and, not the either/or, mindset. It doesn't eradicate colour or lines but embraces and affirms who we are, regardless of differences in ethnicity, culture, or mindset. (Gibbons, 2009, pp. 39–40)

However, the creation of culture, and the fluidity of it, is not only found in Third Spaces. Bhabha expresses that there is 'no purity of culture' (Bhabha, 1994, p. 37), because no one culture has an essential culture. For example, what is regarded as 'Chinese' by one person may differ from another, which may not necessarily take historical changes and heritage into consideration. Essentialism puts people in boxes and ascribes certain unchanging characteristics to them to describe who they are – promoting stereotypes. Stuart Hall states that diaspora identities are defined by hybridity, 'constantly producing and reproducing themselves anew, through transformation and difference' (Hall, 1990, p. 235). Therefore, this fluidity means that, in addition to the changing nature of culture, no one person has a fixed cultural identity, but the way somebody identifies may change based on the context that they are in. Bhabha predicates that there is a 'problem of identity' in the post-colonial context, where the person who is colonized is 'confronted with its difference, its other' (Bhabha, 1994, p. 46). In the British context, I suggest that it is this othering and difference that causes the minoritized person to either hide that which distinguishes themselves from the white normative culture or to forget that they have such differences, believing themselves to be the same as the majority. Therefore, the task of bringing one's culture in an intercultural church for a second-generation immigrant, TCK and bi-cultural person with mixed heritages often causes a self-conscious tension, and the question arises, 'What even is my culture?', which I have experienced.

What Even is My Culture?

The Burden of Representation and Further Challenges

In the life of the intercultural church, Mosaic, which I was part of, we were encouraged to share from our culture. At times, I was asked to pray or read Scripture in Chinese, and I would also ask others to read in their languages too. Although I speak Cantonese at home, and learnt Mandarin at Chinese-language school throughout my childhood, I do not have the ability, or the confidence, to read Scripture well or pray aloud in any of those languages. In group discussions, most of my church family would easily share their cultural practices, traditions and values, but on occasion I would barely have anything to contribute – either because I was unsure if my family traditions were 'correct' and 'authentic', or I just had no idea! I experienced the burden of representation, where, as a British-born Chinese (BBC), I felt I had to speak for all those who are BBCs, represent all Chinese, all East Asians, South-East Asians, Asians, and those of the Global Majority Heritage. In my mind, the less the difference there was in the space I found myself in, the larger the representation became. Although I do not necessarily still feel this way as strongly, there are others who do.

The aforementioned *Christianity Today* article quotes from an individual, a child of immigrants, who has the following view of the intercultural church, although she never left the ethnic church: 'I feel like when you go to a multi-ethnic church, you're constantly explaining things or holding back, or you're very conscious that you kind of represent your culture' (Ding, 2021). Daniel Lee, in *Doing Asian American Theology*, states that 'Asian Americans end up bearing the heavy burden of trying to find their gift for this multi-ethnic context', especially where others incorrectly believe that 'racial identity functions the same way among different minorities' (Lee, D., 2022, p. 195–6). When I studied the trajectory of Chinese immigration to the UK for my master's degree in Ethnomusicology, I learned that a wave of migration in the 1970s and 1980s led to the dispersed settlement of those from South China and Hong Kong, mainly via the scattering of Chinese restaurants and takeaways (see Benton and Gomez, 2007). As a child of one of these immigrants, I grew up without many BBC or East Asian friends, as we were under-represented in my schools and neighbourhood.

In contrast to this, I saw that my Gujarati Indian friends had a stronger collective and cultural identity, often gathering for cultural and religious celebrations, whereas my communal cultural experience was limited to the monotonous weekly Chinese school sessions or the odd trip to London's Chinatown. In addition, some children of immigrants from an Asian background have noted that there is a prevailing expectation to assimilate to the dominant culture and stay silent in the face of racial discrimination in order to survive, as well as a burden of holding an immigrant parent's hopes and expectations of excelling in education and gaining a respectable job (Toyama-Szeto and Gee, 2006, pp. 37–8). Those of an Asian background may also live in the tensions between the East and West, which have different perspectives on boundaries, family and community, hospitality, dreams and individual pursuits – causing a Third-Culture Kid to constantly have identity struggles where values collide. There is a profound sense of an unknowing of oneself, which contributes to the difficulty of bringing something to the table.

Another difficulty is the act of taking up space. Wang suggests that the dominant culture and colonialist structures have framed the idea of space-taking as an overtaking, overshadowing, overpowering, consuming and reducing space for those with less power (Wang, p. 127). A marginalized person who has been taught to live inconspicuously is unlikely to be able to properly grow into the fullness of what God desires of them, embracing their cultural heritage as part of themselves, without intervention. Furthermore, as a second-generation immigrant grows up disconnected from their relatives, which I have noticed to be more prevalent in East and South-east Asians in the UK, compared to South Asians, there is a sense of rootlessness and other cultural losses that occur without extended family or a thorough knowledge of one's own history. History classes in secondary school hardly chart the histories of those who are not white British. In addition, if there is a language barrier with parents and grandparents, and cultural and generational differences, the bi-cultural individual has a further sense of grief and dismembering of relationship and culture. Some feel as though they have lost themselves, so how are they able to relearn, reclaim and find who they are once again?

Although the experiences and descriptions above are not particular to the British East and South East Asian experience, I highlight such things to show that context and cultural group is a large factor in determining how much somebody knows about themselves and their cultures, and by extension, how much someone is able to contribute to the shared culture of the intercultural church.

Identity Exploration in the Intercultural Church

My belief and hope is that the intercultural church is a unique space that allows the rootless second-generation immigrant to explore culture and identity, compared to a multicultural but white-led majority culture space, which demands individuals assimilate and leave their cultures at the door. Tasha Jun depicts her experiences of assimilation in the church in a poignant and powerful way in *Tell Me The Dream Again*, writing that she had to leave her cultural identity at home and 'sever [her] Koreanness in exchange for a new family' (Jun, 2023, p. 22), and how she must present herself as 'colorless to appease a theology of colorblindness' (2023, p. 24). Sadly, to be colour-blind is to strip those who are not white of their colours and proclaim that 'we are all one in Christ', where in reality, the Global Majority Heritage person has lost something of themselves, which cannot be brought to the church and to God. There is a deep sense of unfairness here, when we must assimilate and erase something of ourselves, when others do not have to. An essay by Masing in *East Side Voices* also expresses something similar: 'I get angry because I work hard in finding a way to articulate my identity, my difference, so that it fits your understanding ... by not seeing race, you have stripped me of my heritage' (Lee, H., 2022, p. 103). If the premise of the intercultural church is for the good of all cultures to shape the culture of the church, then I presume there would be an openness to talk about, display and express culture, and provide ample opportunities for the Third-Culture Kid to explore their cultural identity.

It is therefore imperative that such a space is a safe space, or brave space, where all are invited to participate and be heard (Jones, no date). This kind of setting is only possible through intentional relationships, which I propose are the bedrock of a thriving intercultural church. Relationships during the week and not solely on a Sunday means that people in the church are learning about and supporting one another in day-to-day life. Relationships across cultures also enrich a person, help them to discover different ways of being, and allow them to grow in embodying an intercultural lifestyle. And it is in these relationships that conversations around culture can develop naturally, not forced because it is a mandatory part of the Sunday service, but because cultures and world-views form a person and are the lens through which they exist and operate.

Cultural reckoning will, at some point, come to the surface for the Third-Culture Kid, whether intentionally, accidentally or through triggers. If the individual is already in a space that is open to these explorations, this provides a conducive environment for the arduous yet fulfilling journey of ethnic healing. True friendships and knowing one another also help to guard against tokenism and stereotyping. I have seen this multiple times, where somebody is asked to read or pray in a language that they do not speak, because it was assumed that they were from a particular culture or are proficient in that language. This is often the result of a lack of knowledge and depth of relationship with the person. If somebody knows me, they will know where I am in my journey and how much I am able to contribute. They will listen to me process the highs and lows, tensions and ease of my bi-cultural identity in the church, society and home. Additionally, I would be able to bring the impact that a racist incident, such as a micro-aggression, has caused me, knowing that it will be heard and not negated under a colour-blind theology. This would help me to learn how to not self-edit and default to assimilating but allow more of myself to be known and loved by me, by others and by God.

If such an environment develops and deeper relationships exist, then the third component in this formula is for the second-generation immigrant to show up, learn, and dare to be vulnerable – perhaps stepping into the unknown for the first time, which is simultaneously unsettling, exciting and nerve-wracking. Discovering more of who one is can be painful and exposing, but hopefully the journey helps someone to see how their story and experiences are ordained by God. We must also have the intentionality to learn about our own cultures – talk to our parents, relatives and peers, and read books and watch documentaries about 'our people', with a posture to hear. I am learning to reclaim my culture – to relearn parts of my culture that have been unclear and confusing, and intentionally participate in cultural practices that would allow me to have a deeper sense of my ancestry and heritage, to piece together the fragments of myself and my story that were either lost or undiscovered. I am watching my dad cook and learning how to replicate these dishes, as well as listening to him tell stories of how he grew up in his village in Hong Kong – which I did not always do as a child. At the same time, I am learning about why it is important for me to bring my whole self to God, in my cultural body, so that the whole of me may be embraced, and so that I may discover how 'this part of me needed to show up so that it, too, could experience the love of God' (Jun, 2023, p. 116). In my learnings, I hope to encourage and inspire others in their journey too.

But this isn't just for the bi-cultural or mixed-heritage person to learn, as it is for everyone in an intercultural church to learn. I believe such learning is the call of the whole church family. It is a shared burden, where the body together grows and develops into the church that God desires us to be – one where many colourful threads are noticed, known, loved and flourish, woven together to create a beautiful tapestry. An intercultural church congregation must remember the vision of a diverse church and discover the immense blessing it can be. It must love the richness that diversity brings, stay resilient when cultures collide, and realize that differences may lead to innovative ways of working and being. Furthermore, the intercultural church will learn to have its humility-muscle strengthened, knowing that no one culture has the correct way of expressing Christian principles, and yet choose to serve one another across boundary lines. All parts of its body are to bring their gifts to the table, and each person should be patiently encouraged to bring of the good of their cultures, whatever it may be.

Conclusion

Finally, I suggest that it is the duty of the church to recognize the contributions and blessings that a TCK has, by nature of growing up between worlds: higher sensitivity to different ways of life, increased levels of cultural intelligence, adaptability, unique perspectives, and more (see Jennings, 2024). This means that TCKs are uniquely placed to be bridge-people, which surely is an asset to the intercultural church, if not wider society. As mentioned earlier, these blessings are held in tension with cultural identity challenges.

I am still on a journey of discovering my ethnic and cultural identity, and what that means for where God has placed me in his kingdom. I am learning to embrace my Third-Culture identity and believe that bringing my bi-cultural perspective is intrinsic to the life of the worshipping community. If my contributions are different from that of the first-generation immigrant from one of my parents' countries – that is fine. I bring what I know. Learning my story allows me to travel deeper with God and with my heritage, and importantly, learning my story is for the blessing of the wider body, because my contributions are valid and desired, and they are gratefully received and gently held by my loving Church family.

Bibliography

Aldous, Ben, Dunmore, Idina and Seevaratnam, Mohan, 2020, *Intercultural Church: Shared Learning from New Communities*, Cambridge: Grove Books Limited.
Arthur Riley, Cole, 2022, *This Here Flesh: Spirituality, Liberation, and the Stories That Make Us*, New York: Convergent.
Benton, George and Gomez, Edmund Terence, 2007, *The Chinese in Britain, 1800–Present: Economy, Transnationalism, Identity*, London: Palgrave Macmillan.
Bhabha, Homi K., 1994, *The Location of Culture*, London, New York: Routledge.
Ding, Erin Chan, 2021, 'Why the Children of Immigrants Are Returning to Their Religious Roots', *Christianity Today*, March 2021, available at https://www.christianitytoday.com/2021/02/children-of-immigrants-multiethnic-church/ (accessed 25.2.25).
Gibbons, Dave, 2009, *The Monkey and the Fish: Liquid Leadership for a Third-Culture Church*, Study Resources.
Hall, S., 1990, 'Cultural Identity and Diaspora', in J. Rutherford, ed., *Identity: Community, Culture, Difference*, London: Lawrence & Wishart, pp. 222–37.
Jennings, Nathaniel, 2024, 'Treasures of the Nations: Discipling Multicultural Children and Young People', Intercultural Ministries Ireland, https://www.interculturalireland.org/post/treasures-of-the-nations (accessed 25.2.25).
Jones, Micky Scottbey, no date, 'An Invitation to a Brave Space', Grossmont, https://www.grossmont.edu/faculty-staff/participatory-governance/student-success-and-equity/_resources/assets/pdf/brave-space-poem.pdf (accessed 25.2.25).
Jun, Tasha, 2023, *Tell Me the Dream Again: Reflections on Family, Ethnicity and the Sacred Work of Belonging*, Carol Stream, IL: Tyndale House Publishers
Lee, Daniel D., 2022, *Doing Asian American Theology: A Contextual Framework for Faith and Practice*, Downers Grove, IL: InterVarsity Press Academic.
Lee, Helena, ed., 2022, *East Side Voices: Essays Celebrating East and Southeast Asian Identity in Britain*, London: Sceptre.
Lindsay, Ben, 2019, *We Need to Talk about Race: Understanding the Black Experience in White Majority Churches*, London: SPCK.
Marzouk, Safwat, 2019, *Intercultural Church: A Biblical Vision for an Age of Migration*, Minneapolis, MN: Fortress Press.
McDonald, Chine, 2021, *God Is Not a White Man (and Other Revelations)*, London: Hodder & Stoughton.
Merriam-Webster, 2025, definition of 'white supremacy', https://www.merriam-webster.com/dictionary/white+supremacy (accessed 25.2.25).
Rievan, Kirst (pseudonym), 2020, 'Uncovering Discrimination in Missions: Towards a "Third Culture" of Oneness in Christ', Lausanne Movement, https://lausanne.org/global-analysis/uncovering-discrimination-in-missions (accessed 25.2.25).
Toyama-Szeto, Nikki A. and Gee, Tracey, eds, 2006, *More than Serving Tea: Asian American Women on Expectations, Relationships, Leadership and Faith*, Downers Grove, IL: InterVarsity Press.
Wang, Jenny T., 2022, *Permission to Come Home: Reclaiming Mental Health as Asian Americans*, New York: Balance.
Wong, P. P., 2014, *The Life of a Banana*, London: Legend Press.

9

Laying Firm Foundations for a Healthy Intercultural Church

ADAM AND KARINA MARTIN

Part 1: Our Story

A three-mile missionary journey

It was 2002, we had three small children, were living on a new housing estate on the outskirts of Derby and were busy leading cell groups in our church. In many ways things looked quite settled, and yet in our hearts there was a growing dissatisfaction. We had been back in the UK for about four years, having spent some time in Estonia helping to plant a church. It had been an exciting few years seeing a group of young people come to know Jesus and the church getting established. Increasingly, we were feeling it was time to go again, but this time to more unreached peoples. We'd had dreams about taking the gospel to Muslims, many of whom have never had the opportunity to hear the good news, and some perplexing prophetic words about going not to one nation but to 'many nations'.

As we began to pray about going overseas again, we realized a surprising thing was happening. Into our city, hundreds of young men, and a few families, were arriving from the Middle East and Africa. They were coming from countries such as Afghanistan, Iraq and Iran, some even from 'unreached' people groups. Others were arriving from Eritrea and the Democratic Republic of Congo. It became obvious to us that it was our mandate as the church to welcome the stranger in our midst, and that this was what God was calling us as family specifically to do. In December 2001, he began to speak to us about planting a multiracial church, of doing things differently and not relying on the old ways of doing things. We had no idea what that meant or how we were going to do it, but God seemed to be speaking.

So, in 2003, instead of moving thousands of miles overseas, we moved just three miles down the road, into the centre of Derby, to the area where most of these new arrivals were living. By moving downtown, we were able to exchange our rather modestly sized modern home for an old Victorian property that had a large outbuilding at the back and plenty of space for hospitality and guests to stay. Our street was a wonderful mix of British Asians, new arrivals from Afghanistan, Portuguese, Polish and many African nationalities. Together with a small team from our church, we were commissioned to reach out and welcome these new arrivals to the city.

Offering welcome and hospitality

The challenge was, 'How on earth were we going to connect with people who were so different to us?!' That's when God gave us the idea of taking 'Welcome Boxes' to the newly arrived refugees in our city. The first ones we took at Christmas time, and we were overwhelmed by the welcome that our team received! People said they were so lonely and didn't know anyone in the new city they'd arrived in. From then on, we regularly started filling boxes with small practical items, toys and treats, and taking them to families who had recently arrived. Welcome Boxes opened the door to wonderful friendships and many of those we visited joined our new church community.

As well as reaching out through initiatives like Welcome Boxes, God also sovereignly brought people literally to our door! A story that stands out took place just a few days before Christmas in 2004. Maryam was brought to our door in the pouring rain by a member of the Iranian community. She was in her 50s when she came to know the Lord in Iran, but had to flee when the authorities started to pursue her. What was miraculous about her arrival on our doorstep was that ten years before in Austria, her brother had been baptized by a couple in our small church planting team! This showed us how intimately God was working in the lives of refugees as they moved location, and that he knew about our little church and our desire to welcome them. Maryam continued to be a key member of the church plant for the next ten years and led many others to Christ.

Another precious person God brought to us was 'Behnam' (not his real name). He was in his late teens when he came across a Christian literature outreach in our neighbourhood and wanted to know more. He was from the Kurdish Bahdini-speaking people, an unreached people group (Joshua Project, 2024). His father had been murdered by the military, and he had been put in solitary confinement as a teenager. He was put in contact with us, and we had the joy of leading him to the Lord and baptizing him. He lived with us for the next two years as he began to rebuild his life. Behnam was a joyful member of our church plant who loved to dance Kurdish style!

As God connected us with more individuals, we needed a way to build community together. In February 2002, we had visited 'International House', a community in Loughborough hosted by Peter and Barbie Reynolds, two pioneering church leaders in their 60s. We saw how food brought people together from very different cultures, and we wanted to see a similar weekly international meal in our home. So, as we started to meet more new people, we invited them to a weekly 'Open House' lunch. Before long, we had up to 50 adults and children filling our house and garden every week. Plates would be full of curries and rice dishes, alongside a shepherd's pie or pasta dish! Our three young children (three, five and seven years) joined in enthusiastically, easily navigating language barriers through play, in the way that children do. Alongside our dedicated team, and new friends like Miriam, members of our sending church also came to help cook, serve and wash up. We couldn't have taken on such a big undertaking each week without their help.

Through these weekly meals and our team making visits through the week, deep friendships started to form. Our family loved visiting Ali, whose wife and four young children had recently arrived in the country from Iraq. We would sit on the floor and enjoy a Kurdish feast of dolma, rice and chicken, Bollywood movies playing in the background. These relationships opened doors for us to take teams to North Iraq over a number of years, to serve in the refugee camps and encourage the church there. Twenty years later we still love to visit Ali's family and catch up on news about children's university courses or to meet their latest grandchild!

Starting faith conversations

From this place of friendship and hospitality, it was relatively easy to have conversations about faith and God. We started to have a time after dinner sharing stories about Jesus orally and discussing their meaning. We would pray for people's needs, which were often many, given their difficult circumstances. Each week we would share stories of answered prayers and encouragements. Team members were careful to be respectful and listen to others' faith perspectives without criticizing their beliefs or arguing about contentious issues. Keeping the focus on Jesus and his example was an easy way to share our faith and begin to disciple those from a Muslim background. From this 'open house' lunch a community of mostly new believers began to emerge and, as we will explain, we began to shape 'church life' around the people God had brought us.

Building cohesion in our city

As we began to get established, we wanted a place where we could continue to build connections and reach out to our community. The opportunity to take on the café at our local park emerged, and as a result we started Upbeat Communities (2005) as a social enterprise to run the café, employ refugees and help build cohesion with the local community. The organization gave us the opportunity to catalyse refugee week events in our city and hold world music festivals in the park. We wanted to change the conversation about refugees in our city and for Derby to be known as a welcoming place to live. After a couple of years, we had to close the café for reasons of financial viability, but Upbeat Communities continued to thrive as a charity. It enabled us to meet some of the very practical needs refugees have. We offered English classes and activities for refugee women and children. We ran training courses and started food and sewing enterprises, as well as a language school. Over the years Upbeat grew into an independent and well-respected charity in the city and continues to offer welcome and integration services for refugees today.

Facing challenges and changes

There were also plenty of challenges over this time of experimentation and growth. The needs and trauma we encountered among those who had fled their countries was sometimes overwhelming. Some members of our team missed being in a larger church with the services it provided for kids and youth, so returned to our sending church. Others began to get fatigued with the huge needs and all the activity taking place, and there was a danger of burn-out. On reflection we probably should have done less and taken better care of our team. However, God was gracious, and after ten years he brought a change of direction that would help sustain the ministry we had started and create a bigger impact than we realized.

The transition phase

After ten years, we took time to reflect on where we had got to. International Community Church was a small but vibrant intercultural community of 30–50 believers. Our dream of being a church of many nations had in many ways been realized, but we struggled with the high turnover of people who moved on because of their asylum cases or personal circumstances. At the same time, the leadership of our sending church (Community Church Derby, 2019), which had about 500 members, was becoming increasingly dissatisfied with being a 95% white British church in a multicultural city. Prayerfully and together, the decision was made to bring International Community Church back into Community Church Derby, with a clear vision to transition the larger church into being a truly intercultural one.

The decision was not without its concerns. Would our international members feel comfortable in a large, mainly white church setting? Could we provide as effectively for the needs of an intercultural community in the large church? How would the host congregation respond to large numbers of mainly refugees attending Sunday services? We prepared as well as we could but, in the end, God surprised us, in the way he often does! Workers began to return from overseas to help us with the work, while regular church members got involved with giving people lifts and visiting with Welcome Boxes. Gradually our white congregation (with a few faithful British Asians) began to change. Over the next 12 years, God brought the nations to us. First came Iranians, Kurds and Afghans, then people from various African nations like Eritrea and Zimbabwe. More recently dozens of families from Nigeria and Hong Kong have joined our church family. Our whole church is now about 50% non-white British, and it brings joy to our hearts and the whole leadership to be part of a large intercultural church family!

With this transition came the desire to help other churches experience the same joy and growth that we had, through welcoming refugees. Welcome Boxes had now become a well-respected project in the city, with a training programme for volunteers and various resources, and we wanted to share it with other churches. We approached the Cinnamon Network (2025) for help replicating the project and were awarded a grant and support to help us do that. Over the next couple of years, many other churches started to run Welcome Boxes. Around that time, a young woman, Emily Holden, who was working as an intern with Christians Against Poverty, got in touch. She also had a vision to see the church in the UK equipped to welcome refugees. Emily came to join us, and together we decided to launch Welcome Churches (2015) as a national charity to help churches welcome refugees.

In 2019, I (Karina) left Welcome Churches in the capable leadership of Emily and Sue Butler to pursue further study and ministry back in our local church. Welcome Churches has grown to become a fantastic equipping and resourcing charity with a network of over 1,400 churches who are all welcoming refugees.

Moving from welcome to integration

While we had learnt much about hospitality and welcoming the outsider over the years, the real challenge now was how to fully include different cultural practices and perspectives in our well-established church life. Or would individuals from other cultures always feel like the 'guests' at the table? As we were pondering this challenge, in 2018 we connected with Theo Visser from the Netherlands. He was building a European network called Intercultural Church Plants (now M4 Intercultural, 2025) and was helping church planters grapple with the opportunity and challenge to plant new churches with an intercultural DNA in their roots.

As we talked, we realized we had walked a very similar learning journey over the previous 16 years. The Intercultural Church Plants (ICP) European board invited Adam to become the catalyst for ICP in the UK. As the work in the UK began to grow, however, it was established churches more often than church plants, who were seeking out help to become intercultural. When it came to forming the charity in the UK, the decision was made to expand the remit and form 'Intercultural Churches' (Intercultural Churches, 2025), with a vision to equip both established churches and church plants, in becoming intercultural outposts of heaven.

One of the most effective ways Intercultural Churches has been able to assist leaders has been through running monthly huddle groups. These are online groups of six/eight churches and ministry leaders that are facilitated by experienced practitioners. Each month a topic relating to intercultural ministry is presented and discussed, and members support and pray for each other.

Participants have been enthusiastic in their feedback:

> It has been very rewarding and encouraging for me to connect with others who face similar questions and challenges as we face in our church. I have been encouraged to reflect on the intercultural from

new viewpoints and received concrete tools that have helped me and my church's leadership in an intercultural direction.

Intercultural Churches now has a UK national team of ten experienced leaders, and an established intercultural worship ministry led by the gifted ethnomusicologist Jessie Tang, who leads Songs2Serve. Songs2Serve UK ministry runs workshops and leads intercultural worship at conferences and church gatherings.

Part 2: Our Learnings from the Journey

Growing in relational unity

Paul places a high value on relational unity in the church. Passages like Ephesians 4.16 (NIV) describe the church as a body, 'joined and held together by every supporting ligament, growing and building itself up in love, as each part does its work'. Inspired by this vision, we wanted our church plant to be a loving community, rather than simply a weekly meeting.

Since many who began to connect with us were from deeply relational cultures, it was natural for them to spend time with us over shared meals talking about life, family and faith. Although we often struggled with language, as we found ways to connect, trust and friendship deepened. For our shared meal every Sunday, people would often bring a dish from their homeland. We began to understand the importance of accepting hospitality as well as giving it and would take our young family to eat with new friends from places like Afghanistan, Pakistan or Iran. During such visits, we often had the opportunity to pray for a need, or share a simple Bible story.

Building church family with this level of relational commitment is time consuming, and challenging for many of us used to the fast pace of life in the UK. While the church plant was relatively small, our team was able to invest their time in visiting, hosting and discipling the new believers who had gathered around us. However, when we made the move to become part of our much larger sending church, our focus was drawn into organizing meetings, developing discipleship programmes, and trying to spread ourselves across a much wider breadth of relationships.

Within a few years, we could count a wide array of nationalities gathering together on a Sunday. We were running discipleship groups in several different languages, and many, especially from the Middle East, were coming to faith in Jesus and getting baptized. Despite this, there was a growing sense of dissatisfaction. A comment from one of the Iranians challenged me deeply. He simply asked, 'Will we always be known as the refugees in church?' He simply wanted to be known as an individual, and to form real friendship with members of the 'host' community.

Although some cross-cultural friendships were forming within the church, often through serving together in a ministry team, or offering lifts to the Sunday meetings, these tended to be fairly superficial. People would sit together within their cultural and language groups, and it was telling how, under the pressure of the Covid-19 pandemic, relational circles shrank, and some groups found themselves quite isolated.

As Paul appeals to the church in Rome, 'with one mind and one voice to glorify the God and Father of our Lord Jesus Christ. Accept one another, then, just as Christ accepted you …' (Romans 15.6–7 NIV). While there was a growing acceptance of cultural diversity in the church, we were a long way from the 'one mind and one voice' that Paul calls us to. As a leadership team we had to take responsibility for helping the church develop the relational unity we hoped for. We began to look at ways to create more opportunities for cross-cultural social interactions. By this time, we were welcoming large numbers who had recently arrived from Hong Kong. They enthusiastically began to arrange monthly shared meals after the Sunday morning service, and a special event to celebrate the Lunar New Year. The Iranian and Kurdish groups hosted various Persian celebrations with food and dancing, and of course Christmas and Easter provided further opportunities for extended times of fellowship across the whole church.

Valuable as these events were for helping the cultural groups in the church to mix and appreciate each other's cultural heritage, they were still no substitute for the close 'table fellowship' we had experienced in the church plant. We realized we needed to take a fresh look at our midweek groups. Like many churches, we had a well-established practice of gathering in home groups, even if these weren't always well attended! These groups had remained stubbornly monocultural, despite our best efforts to encourage mixing.

We badly needed intercultural home groups where members of the church could experience what it means to be family together from many nations. These groups would be a place where we could listen to one another's distinct cultural perspectives on faith and life, worship and pray in different languages, and build a depth of fellowship together.

For this to happen, we needed leaders with the skills to foster intercultural community on a small scale. So we invited a culturally diverse group of both new and experienced leaders to meet together for a year, to experiment in a group we called 'Mezze'. We explored what hospitality looks like in different cultures. We learned simple worship songs in one another's languages. We tried different ways to study the Bible together with a multilingual group. Of course, we ate together too, and we enjoyed the process – it was a rich learning environment!

From that 'incubation' group, a number of new intercultural communities have started. It's still early days, and the learning goes on. What is most encouraging is that despite the challenges, people are enjoying being together, they know the names of each other's children, and on a Sunday morning there is much more cross-cultural connection than we have seen before.

Having said that, we also recognize the importance of cultural groups within the church gathering together in whichever way they might choose. Some who have joined us simply don't have sufficient English to participate in a mixed group. Others need some focused discipleship programmes as they grapple with biblical teaching for the first time. Some groups have a cherished tradition of worship and spirituality that they are keen to maintain and which help to anchor their faith during the upheaval and stress of immigration to the UK. We are also keen that each cultural group within the church is able to voice their unique perspective into church life, and for that reason they need to gather together and explore what this might look like.

More important than any arrangement of groups and meetings is the underlying value a church community puts on developing cross-cultural relational unity. There is no doubt it's easier to relate to people similar to ourselves, but Paul's exhortation to 'accept one another as Christ has accepted us' compels us to go beyond merely tolerating the inconvenience of cultural diversity in church life. Instead, we are to love the newcomer as Christ has loved us, and to welcome them as we would want to be welcomed.

Honouring our cultural diversity

When we were a church plant gathering to worship with about 30 people, it was fairly obvious that we needed to acknowledge and include the various languages and cultures present. We could sit in a large circle and learn songs from one another. The music wasn't polished, but we enjoyed moving between a joyful song in Lingala, a moving expression of worship in Farsi, and a simple old gospel song in English.

Introducing different languages and cultural styles to our worship in the larger church was much more challenging. Initially the congregation was overwhelmingly white British with a well-established worship culture. There was an understandable fear that in changing our worship we might lose something very precious to us. Since the newcomers weren't complaining, why not carry on and allow them to adapt to our established worship style? In addition, it wasn't at all clear how we might include other languages and styles while maintaining an uplifting worship experience. Anyway, most of the minority-language groups in the church had their own meetings where they could worship in their own way.

One of the main reasons we decided to embrace 'intercultural worship' was because we became convinced that our corporate worship times are both a foretaste, and a participation in, the worship of heaven. Our Sunday meetings were beginning to look increasingly like the gathering of nations around the throne that John describes in Revelation 7.9. However, we still sounded very English! If the Holy Spirit allowed those gathered in Jerusalem on that first Pentecost to hear the 'wonders of God' declared in their own language, then it seemed reasonable that we should find ways for everyone to participate and express their worship more authentically.

I remember one particular Sunday when our worship leader that week took a bit of a risk. Having led us in the simple chorus, 'God is so good' (Makai, 1970), he invited people to come to the microphone and sing a verse in their own language. I thought we might have three or four brave contributions, but none of us expected what happened next. A line formed at the front of the meeting, and we sang that chorus in language after language for about ten minutes. The atmosphere was electric. We had no idea there were so many native languages spoken in our church! There was a tremendous sense of joy and togetherness that morning, and people were talking about it for weeks afterwards.

Since then, we have slowly developed a more inclusive and diverse worship culture. This has meant encouraging more singers and musicians from minority cultures in the church to join the worship group. It has meant working hard to have several languages on the song word slides, and we have all had the challenge of trying to sing in unfamiliar languages. For everyone this has been costly in different ways, but for this reason, perhaps our worship is becoming a sweeter offering to the Lord.

I have focused on our journey with sung worship, but of course honouring diverse cultures in church has many aspects. These include providing translation and interpretation wherever possible, ensuring that our leaders and preachers reflect the diversity of the church, and celebrating different cultural festivals together. These are the more visible expressions a church can work on. However, it is important that we don't neglect the less obvious but even more important aspect of our differing cultural world-views.

You don't need to spend very long with someone from another part of the world to realize that not only do they behave and speak quite differently to you, they may also think quite differently. An intercultural church is remarkable because we have so much in common despite our different backgrounds. However, that sense of familial unity that we experience can easily blind us to the significantly different values and outlooks we carry because of our cultures.

When we first began to welcome refugees arriving from the Middle East, we would often invite people for a shared meal. Once they had agreed to come, we would make preparations and cook the food. There were times when those who had agreed to come just did not show up. From a British cultural perspective, this was just plain rude! It took us a while to begin to understand that our new friends were from an 'honour/shame' culture (Georges, 2023; Moon and Simon, 2021). It would have seemed rude to them to refuse our invitation even though they knew they were not able to come.

In our church now, we have many people whose outlook is framed by an honour/shame world-view rather than the typical British 'guilt/innocence' lens. Their style of communication is often more implied and indirect than our more direct British approach. We also have a growing number from West and Southern Africa. Many of them have what is described as a 'fear/power' world-view. They bring a welcome awareness of the Christian's spiritual battle, and our authority in prayer.

Having these differing world-views in the church creates a potential for misunderstanding and offence, but at the same time, a great potential to enrich and strengthen us all. We recently gathered parents and children's ministry leaders for a training event on the theme of 'Third-Culture Kids' (Global Connections, 2023). The input was really helpful, but the question and response time was even more illuminating. Some parents from Hong Kong shared their concerns about how their children would cope adapting to life in a British school. A Nigerian couple responded, encouraging them to pray and train their kids to stand firm on Scripture and in their identity in Christ. Their 'fear/power' perspective was a great challenge to the honour/shame-oriented parents and those of us from a guilt/innocence world-view.

I am convinced that if we are to see intercultural churches thrive here in the UK, church leaders will need to work at developing our 'cultural intelligence' (Earley and Mosakowski, 2004), and become skilled in cross-cultural communication. Business leaders have been aware of the importance of this for a generation now. It's time for the church to catch up. Thankfully, there are a growing number of training courses specifically designed to equip church leaders.

Leadership and power

Hindsight is a wonderful thing, and as I look back on how we planted our initial 'intercultural church', there are a number of things I would do differently today. For one thing, although our core team was not exclusively white British, for much of the time we were a group of 'host culture' Christians, trying to run church for a group of immigrants. I am more aware now of the cultural differences I outlined above, and also of the importance of sharing power and decision-making across cultures. Yucan Chiu, the founding director of the Ethnos Network and a vice president at Redeemer City to City (Ethnos Network, 2025; Redeemer City to City, 2025), speaks of the importance of intercultural churches needing to 'de-centre' their leadership. By this, he means giving other cultures within a church a voice in the key decision-making and power structures of church life. Inevitably this can feel a risky step. It will mean embracing change and upsetting the established centres of power within the church community. It also requires the humility of leaders to recognize that some of our deeply held convictions might be more cultural than biblical.

Although our journey in this area has been slow (we're about 12 years into the process of becoming intercultural), I'm glad we have not rushed the transition. We have had much to learn along the way, and our congregation has had to adapt to many changes. We now have members of the church board, the eldership, the senior leadership team and staff team from each of the main cultural groups within the church. They are recognized as leaders in their own right, not simply as cultural representatives. We also have an 'Intercultural Team', which is more intentionally representative and serves to advise and challenge the ministries and teams across the whole of church life.

Compelled by a vision

Rick Warren wrote: 'A great commitment to the Great Commandment and the Great Commission will grow a great church' (Warren, 2002). If your church is located in a diverse neighbourhood, then I would add that such a commitment will also lead you to grow an intercultural church. It was through obedience to Christ and a love for people that the early church moved out beyond its ethnic and cultural environment and the first intercultural churches emerged. Our move into the centre of Derby 22 years ago was in response to God's prompting to reach out to the nations coming to live among us with the love and good news of Jesus. We soon discovered that we needed to rethink church if we are to fulfil that commission to make disciples 'of all nations'. Church needed to become a place where people could find family and raise their own families, regardless of their cultural background.

I recently attended a dynamic church planted by a group of Tamil believers. It was interesting for me to experience what it's like to be in the cultural minority. They were very welcoming, but I still felt like an outsider. If we are to be effective in reaching the diverse communities around us in modern Britain, we will need churches where people won't feel like outsiders; where they will see people like themselves at the front of the meeting, where songs are sung that at least sound familiar, and where there is access to translation for those who need it.

Many of those who have made their home in the UK in the last generation arrived with a dynamic Christian faith of their own. Sadly, many did not find a welcome in the established British churches, and so started their own. If we can find a way forward to express a united witness in our communities, and to be the one, diverse family that Jesus has called us to be, then our towns and cities will begin to take notice, and our message of reconciliation and hope will be much more compelling.

Bibliography

Cinnamon Network: Equipping churches for Social Action, 2025, https://cinnamonnetwork.co.uk/ (accessed 26.2.25).

Community Church Derby, renamed Reach in 2019, https://www.reachonline.org/ (accessed 26.2.25).

Earley, P. C. and Mosakowski, E., 2004, 'Cultural Intelligence', *Harvard Business Review*, Vol. 82, No. 10, pp. 139–46.

Ethnos Network, 2025, https://www.ethnos.network/ (accessed 26.2.25).

Georges, J., 2023, *The 3D Gospel: Ministry in Guilt, Shame, and Fear Cultures*, Time Press.

Global Connections, 2023, *TCK Resources*, https://globalconnections.org.uk/resources/tck-resources (accessed 26.2.25).

Intercultural Churches, 2025, https://interculturalchurches.org/ (accessed 26.2.25).

Joshua Project, 2024, 'People groups of the world', https://joshuaproject.net/ (accessed 26.2.25.

M4 Intercultural, 2025, https://m4intercultural.org/ (accessed 26.2.25).

Makai, P., 1970, 'God is so good', Songs2Serve, https://songs2serve.eu/songs/god-is-so-good (accessed 26.2.25).

Moon, W. J., and Simon, W. B., 2021, *Effective Intercultural Evangelism: Good News in a Diverse World*, Westmont: InterVarsity Press.

Redeemer City to City, 2025, https://redeemercitytocity.com/ (accessed 26.2.25).

Upbeat Communities, 2005, https://www.upbeatcommunities.org/ (accessed 26.2.25).

Warren, R., 2002, *The Purpose-Driven Life*, Grand Rapids, MI: Zondervan.

Welcome Churches, 2015, https://welcomechurches.org/ (accessed 26.2.25).

10

The New Northern Irish

NATHANIEL JENNINGS

Introduction

If you stand on top of Black Mountain on a clear day, you see the city of Belfast spilling out before you to the east, north and south. Rows of red-brick terraced houses. Old and new centres of business and academia rising at its heart. Slightly to the east of the centre, the giant yellow Harland and Wolff cranes christened 'Samson' and 'Goliath'. Old docklands under their shadows. At one time the busiest in the world and then discarded and becoming a wasteland, but now being regenerated as the Titanic Quarter with brand new, glittering glass-and-steel apartments, colleges, museums, film studios and car showrooms. If you zoom down into the narrow terrace-house-lined streets, you will see flags and murals marking conflicting identities, loyalties, versions of history and aspirations for the future. They are reminders of a violent past and fragile present peace. And so, so many church steeples. If you lift your eyes again, you will see the lush, green hills beyond the city. Farmhouses, villages, a patchwork of fields bordered by hand-built, stone walls, dotted with sheep, decorated by wildflowers and shaded by ancient trees. Familiarity can cause you to forget what a stunningly beautiful land Northern Ireland is.

You are never far from the sea here. Belfast is built along the Lagan River, which endlessly flows into Belfast Lough, the gateway to the Irish Sea and the world. Belfast Lough, beautifully reflecting the ever-changing sky and salty with the tears of its sons and daughters who for centuries have been carried away across it on vessels headed to far-off lands, where they dreamt of finding a more prosperous, peaceful and hope-filled life for themselves and their children.

When I first visited Belfast in 2004, I was very conscious that I looked like an outsider. My Jamaican heritage meant that I did not see many others that shared my complexion. But to assume that this land was populated by a homogeneous people with a homogeneous culture would be to be deceived.

The Island of Ireland

Northern Ireland was created in 1922 by the partitioning of the island of Ireland. The six most north-eastern of the island's 32 counties remained part of the United Kingdom, while the other 26 formed the Irish Free State, today the Republic of Ireland. For the majority in Northern Ireland, this was celebrated as securing their desired future of remaining a part of the British union of nations, but for a significant minority, it was a time to mourn a separation from the rest of the island and its people, who they felt had been liberated by Irish independence while leaving them in a land that continued to be occupied. Northern Ireland has long been a contested land. A theatre of conquest, colonialization and rebellion. But also, a place of welcome and refuge, with people of different cultures and world-views accommodating and honouring each other and peacefully sharing resources and space.

Over the centuries, it has experienced waves of immigrating people settling on the land, including Celts from continental Europe, Vikings, Normans, Anglo-Saxons and, in the seventeenth century, thousands of Scottish settlers under the protection of English rule (Jones et al., 2025). There are also many lesser-known instances of people immigrating to what is today Northern Ireland. In the late seventeenth century, a small community of Huguenots fleeing religious persecution in France settled in Lisburn, working in the linen industry. In the late nineteenth century, Jews facing persecution in the Russian empire fled the present-day Baltic states, some making their homes in Belfast. When Northern Ireland came into being, there was already an Italian community from Frosinone province near Rome. They primarily worked in the catering trade, opening ice cream cafés and fish and chip shops. Their ice cream saloons proved particularly popular and, in 1922, there were over 30 Italian ice cream saloons across Belfast, with dozens more across the region (Crangle, 2021).

There was further Jewish immigration from Germany during the 1930s and 40s, some refugees setting up businesses that provided work for local people. Chaim Herzog, President of Israel from 1983 to 1993, was born in Belfast, and there is still a synagogue in the north of the city. Following the Soviet Union's crushing of an anti-communist uprising in

1956, around 900 Hungarian refugees found refuge in Northern Ireland before later permanently settling in Canada. In the 1960s, several thousand Chinese immigrants settled in Northern Ireland, many setting up and working in Chinese restaurants. Between 1979 and 1980, a number of Vietnamese 'boat people' were settled in the Craigavon area in the aftermath of the Vietnam War (McCullough, 2014).

However, Northern Ireland's relative lack of economic opportunities and then the sectarian conflict spiralling out of control into what is known as 'the Troubles' meant that it was not seen by many as a desirable place to migrate to. The Troubles were an eruption of tensions between the pro-British, primarily Protestant majority (Unionist/Loyalist) and the anti-British, primarily Catholic (Nationalist/Republican) communities. The former wanted Northern Ireland to remain a part of the United Kingdom, and the latter wanted it to become a part of a United Ireland. The British military, Northern Irish security forces and Loyalist and Irish Republic paramilitary groups engaged in armed conflict, though the majority of causalities were civilian. The Troubles started in the late 1960s, continuing for 30 years. Between 1969 and 2003, there were over 36,900 shooting incidents and over 16,200 bombings or attempted bombings. 3,254 people were killed, and there were 50,000 casualties (CAIN Archive, 2024). With a population of around 1.5 million, this meant everyone in Northern Ireland experienced the conflict and likely personally knew someone injured or killed.

Any discussion about multicultural society and intercultural church and Northern Ireland has to include the awareness of the legacy of the Troubles and the way it has shaped individuals and communities. This includes the trauma people live with, the unresolved tensions that still exist between communities, the experience and normalization of violence, and the suspicion and fear of others who are different. It would be naive to think that all this would not influence the way newcomers from outside Northern Ireland might be received.

During the Troubles, a prominent theme of the Northern Irish story was one of emigration. The violence and resulting devastating effects on the economy meant many decided to seek a better life elsewhere. Between 1971 and 1981, the population of Northern Ireland shrank by 300,000. This was not a new experience. During the Great Famine (1845 to 1849), over a million people starved to death across Ireland, and tens of thousands emigrated from the part of the island that is today Northern Ireland. Over the decades, England, USA, Canada, Australia, New Zealand, South Africa and other countries received hundreds of thousands of Northern Irish people (O'Neill, 2024).

The 2021 Oscar winning film *Belfast* was set at the beginning of the Troubles and portrays this very powerfully through the experience of one family. In the final scene, we watch the family boarding a bus to the ferry to leave Belfast, making the agonizing decision to leave the city for the sake of their small son's future, no longer wanting him to witness the horrors taking place around them. 'Granny' (played by Dame Judi Dench) watches her son, daughter-in-law and wee grandson leave her and all that is familiar behind, setting off with just a couple of suitcases for somewhere where they know no one and own nothing, hoping and praying that the people there would be kind to them and offer them the opportunity to build a better life. 'Go, go now, don't look back, I love you,' says Granny, and then turns and goes back into her now empty and silent house (*Belfast*, 2021).

On 10 April 1998, the Good Friday agreement, approved by public votes in Northern Ireland and the Republic of Ireland, was signed. The signatories included all the major parties in Northern Ireland as well as the British and Irish governments. It also involved a commitment by the main paramilitary organizations to demilitarization and the establishment of local power sharing through a devolved Northern Ireland government (BBC, 2023). To many it seemed a miracle that, after years of prayers for peace, former sworn enemies had now agreed to work together for the common good of all of Northern Ireland's people. Though there have been many setbacks, and the peace and power sharing institutions remain fragile, it has resulted in an era of stability and economic prosperity.

This has transformed Northern Ireland from a place many sought to leave to one that is attracting people from other parts of the world. The result has been that, since the Good Friday Agreement, immigration has accelerated and Northern Ireland has become increasingly culturally and ethnically diverse. In 2001, 8.06% of the population was born outside Northern Ireland; in 2021 it was 13.50% (NISRA, 2004; 2022). A variety of push and pull factors have brought people to Northern Ireland. The majority have come to Northern Ireland to either work or study. In the 2021–22 academic year, out of almost 70,000 postgrad students in Northern Ireland, about 15,000 were international students, contributing about £1 billion to the economy (Meredith and Wilson, 2023). Significant numbers of people have also come from Eastern Europe, India, the Philippines, Nigeria and Brazil in particular, to support the health services and business sector. More recently, there has been an increase in people seeking sanctuary in Northern Ireland from parts of the world where they have faced war and political instability, such as Syria, Iran, Sudan, Ukraine and Hong Kong.

The New Northern Irish

The 'New Northern Irish' have come to Northern Ireland for a myriad of reasons, from a variety of backgrounds, and each person's journey and experience is unique. My own experience, and that of many I have spoken to, has overwhelmingly been a reception that is characteristic of Northern Ireland's culture of warmth and welcome. However, many have struggled to get beyond a surface-level welcome, longing to move from feeling like guests to members of the household, from being the recipients of friendliness to having true friends. Unfortunately, many have also experienced instances of outright racism in a variety of forms. In general, newcomers have found more affluent and nationalist areas more welcoming than unionist areas, particularly the less economically prosperous ones. But the message sensed from the majority of the media, those in governance, those providing services and people generally, is that all are welcome here, and that they feel that Northern Ireland is becoming a richer and more vibrant place through the increased cultural diversity.

The attitudes and responses to newcomers among the longer-settled communities has, of course, been mixed, and the attitudes among those found in the church (those identifying as evangelicals at least) have to an extent reflected this. Reactions from fear and prejudice to indifference and to an enthusiastic embracing of the New Northern Irish have all been communicated and embodied. Many have seen the arrival of people from different parts of the world as an exciting opportunity to become involved in showing and sharing the good news of Jesus with the nations and have responded by being involved in and offering a range of services to welcome and bless newcomers. Some churches have moved even beyond this to see the newcomers as gifts to enrich and enlarge their own understanding and worship of the Lord.

There are, of course, also a variety of attitudes and postures among those who have settled in Northern Ireland, particularly those who are Christians. For some, the primary focus is on trying to rebuild devastated lives, having fled livelihoods, homes, family, friends and all that gave them a sense of value and belonging. For others, they may not have fled warzones but have been drawn here primarily by the very natural human aspirations to have a more comfortable and secure life for themselves and their families. For others, there is a real sense that whatever has led them to calling Northern Ireland home, they are here for a God-ordained purpose: to seek the peace and prosperity of the cities and towns the Lord has carried them to (Jer. 29.7, NIV). They seek to live as witnesses to the goodness and grace of God, not just to others from their own cultural or national backgrounds, but to people of all backgrounds in the communities where they live. They have gifts, experiences and perspectives that the Lord wishes to use to build up and expand his church here. When God's people embrace brothers and sisters from the global church who are passionate about embodying and proclaiming the good news of Jesus wherever he leads them, the Lord works in beautiful ways to manifest blessings for his people and makes them an intriguing witness to the communities in which he has placed them. It is wonderful to report that this is happening here in Northern Ireland.

Intercultural Ministries Ireland

In 2021, I was tasked by MAP (the Northern Ireland branch of Global Connections) and the Northern Ireland Evangelical Alliance to do research into and engage with Christian leaders from the global church who are living and ministering in Northern Ireland. Through this I got to know a wonderful group of Christian men and women from Brazil, South Africa, Nigeria, India, Nepal, Ukraine, Hong Kong and China whom the Lord has called to serve him here and through whom the Lord is building his church. With the backing of para-church organizations MAP, the Evangelical Alliance, OMF, Latin Link, ECM, Lausanne Europe and Intercultural Churches, and involving local leaders as well as this multicultural group of church and ministry leaders, in 2023 Intercultural Ministries Ireland (IMI) was established (IMI, 2024). IMI seeks to serve and enrich the church in Northern Ireland, and across the island of Ireland, through four areas of focus:

- *networking and engagement* – seeking to build meaningful connections between local, diaspora and intercultural churches
- *research and reflection* – seeking to collect up-to-date data on the rapidly changing cultural/ethnic make-up of the church in Ireland and being committed to a biblical reflection on contextualized Christian worship and witness in this changing context
- *resourcing and equipping* – seeking to develop and signpost to resources and training that will help churches to grow as intercultural communities in their localities
- *empowering and listening* – seeking to join, create and facilitate broader conversations on issues relating to church and society, and

to bring global and culturally diverse Christian voices into these conversations.

Data and statics are important, but stories are more engaging and powerful. So, I want to take the next part of this chapter to tell the stories of three church leaders who are a part of IMI and the way in which the Lord has called and used them here for his purposes. These are just three concisely told stories, but they give us glimpses of the way the Lord is at work in new and exciting ways through our New Northern Irish brothers and sisters.

Stories of New Northern Irish

A South African missionary in Northern Ireland

Johann Vizagie grew up in South Africa but put his faith in Jesus as a young man in London. The Lord then led him to Dublin, where he was involved in establishing a multicultural church as part of the Every Nation church network, which today has churches in 82 countries (Every Nation, 2025). Then about 15 years ago, Johann and his wife Andrea began to feel a call to 'go north'. Still more specifically, they then felt led to establish a worshipping community in the heart of Belfast that would bring together people from all backgrounds, including Catholic and Protestant, Unionist and Nationalist. To be a place of reconciliation and healing in a divided city.

Every Nation Church Belfast was established in 2013 and today is a vibrant, diverse and missional community, which meets in a school chapel in the centre of Belfast. Johann remembers seeking to reach out and share friendship and faith with local people and, as is common in Northern Ireland, people were trying to figure out which 'side' he was from. Johann would respond by explaining to them that he was not originally from here and therefore did not belong to any side; he was just serving and proclaiming Jesus, as found in the Bible. As a result he found that, whereas many established evangelical churches, because of cultural and political baggage, struggled to engage with people from Catholic and Nationalist backgrounds, their church was growing with people from both sides of the community joining. Two members of the church are John from the Loyalist Shankhill Road and Andy from the Nationalist Falls Road. Both were involved in opposing paramilitary organizations in the past but have found deep friendship as brothers in

Christ and members of Every Nation Church. The barriers of worldly hostility between them have been destroyed by Jesus' work on the Cross, just as the New Testament said would happen where the gospel was preached and lived out (Eph. 2.14).

A Brazilian missionary in Northern Ireland

In the year 2000, Neto Andrade came to faith in Jesus in his native Brazil. Neto, with his now wife Michelle, immediately became involved in local evangelism and started asking the Lord if he wished for them to go further afield in his service. The Lord began to speak to them about the UK, and 10 years later they visited Northern Ireland. Through conversations with a Brazilian mission worker already here and a local pastor, they received confirmation that they were to leave sunny Brazil and move to Belfast. They joined City Church, where Neto became involved in serving and sharing the gospel.

Fast forward to 2024, and having been welcomed warmly and his gifts appreciated, Neto is now the lead pastor of the church. On a Sunday morning, about half the congregation consists of people born in Northern Ireland and the other half of people who have moved here from about 13 different countries. The New Northern Irish are involved in serving in all areas of church life, from the Nigerian lady on the board of trustees to the Thai Christian leading worship.

In the last six years, a bilingual, Portuguese/English expression of church has also emerged through the church and Neto's ministry, meeting weekly on Saturday evenings. It is made up of Brazilians and folk from other Portuguese-speaking nations, as well as a number of locals with Portuguese connections. Excitingly, it continues to grow through people coming to faith, and as I spoke to Neto about his story, he was preparing to baptize seven new members the following weekend.

Filipino workers in Northern Ireland

Danni Quilario and her husband Benji arrived in Northern Ireland from the Philippines 20 years ago, Danni to work as a nurse and Benji as a mechanic. As Christians, sharing the good news of Jesus was a way of life for them, wherever in the world the Lord took them. Before long, Danni was leading a Bible study for 30 Filipino nurses in the Ulster Hospital. Soon they were asking Danni and Benji to lead them in worship and Bible teaching on Sundays, and so the Jesus Generation Church was born.

For the first few years, they were a nomadic community using rooms in the hospital, hotels and other venues as they prayed for a permanent space of their own. Then their paths crossed with members of a Brethren Assembly whose congregation was small and ageing. They had a building on the high street of a small town called Newtownards, which they wanted to be continued to be used by God's people. In 2014, Jesus Generation Church moved in.

Danni and Benji had tried local churches when they first arrived in Northern Ireland. They remember one church they attended where the service was over in an hour, and everyone raced out of the door and home to be with their own friends and family. Danni and Benji were left feeling lonely and wondering what they would do the rest of this day, which they longed to spend with other brothers and sisters in Christ. They also increasingly felt that the Lord was calling them to shepherd the flock he was giving them, and together to create their own community of welcome and worship.

This past summer, I was invited to the church's 18th anniversary. On a chilly Sunday morning, I passed loyalist estates, with slogans and emblems on walls and flying from lamp posts reminding all of the ongoing divisions that persist in Northern Ireland. I entered a simple building full of life, colour and joy. Intercultural and intergenerational. Filipino children making a joyful noise; an elderly local white woman leading us in a beautiful unscripted prayer thanking the Lord for establishing this vibrant community of believers in her town; a new Nigerian family invited on the stage to perform a Yoruba worship song; the youthful worship band leading us in joyful and passionate praise mainly in English but with Tagalog lines woven in. Afterwards, everybody was invited to a feast in the back hall that included a whole roasted hog! And this was not just for that special Sunday; a freshly cooked lunch is always provided for all attendees. Many of the families spend the whole day together at the church. Danni says the children cry in the evening when they are told they have to go home.

The riots in Belfast

If I was writing this chapter before 5 August 2024, this would be an optimistic and hope-filled place to end. However, that Saturday the anti-immigration riots broke out in Belfast. The rioting carried on for days, and indiscriminate attacks against foreign-looking people went on for weeks (Marshall, 2024). Muslim-owned shops were burnt, refugees stabbed, a Filipino care worker's home attacked; there were arson attacks on multicultural churches, and even those seeking to support and serve newcomers to Northern Ireland were threatened.

A couple of months after the riots had died down, I was picked up from Belfast City Airport by a Sudanese taxi driver. With a big smile he struck up a conversation immediately. He said that he had been living here for 17 years. He asked me how I had found life in Northern Ireland. I replied that I had loved it until about 2 months ago – now I was not sure. He shared that this was exactly how he was feeling. It had been a place he had felt welcome and where he and his family had loved living, but something had changed. He now had racist abuse and even eggs hurled at him as he walked down the street he lived on. He did not know what to say to his teenage kids for whom this was the only home they had ever known.

It was heartbreaking to hear an Iranian brother, who had recently moved here, share how wonderful the months before the riots had been for him as he had felt safe, settled and hopeful for the future for the first time in years. However, now once again he was feeling afraid and that he might not be welcome or safe here.

Whether we are new here like this brother, or like me have lived in Northern Ireland for years and now speak with a Northern Irish accent and share their warm and wicked sense of humour, because of the tone of skin we were born with, our sense of belonging has been seriously shaken. My white friends here are surprised to hear how I have been impacted. Many respond by saying that they do not even think of me as not being from here. But while on one hand this is nice to hear, it also highlights their blind spot. Though I may sound like them, and to all purposes have the same right as them to claim I am Northern Irish, because of my skin colour, I experience the world differently to them. That is not their fault, but in an intercultural church where we seek to share each other's joy and pain, we need to be aware of how different people will be experiencing life very differently because of their backgrounds and identities.

Having had time to reflect on and process what happened in the summer of 2024, and though it has cast a shadow over some of our experiences of this beautiful land, it has made me even more sure of how much the Northern Ireland church needs to understand and embody Jesus' intercultural kingdom. The deep darkness of night makes you crave the light of the coming dawn all the more. The good news of Jesus means we have a message and a way of living that can counter the way of fear, prejudice, exclusion, division and violence, which, past and present, has so stained this land.

In a land where the evangelical church is relatively strong and continues to put great value on the proclamation and defence of the gospel, there is a need to reflect deeply on what is meant by this. Is it a narrow gospel that gets us a ticket to heaven if we live a good life? Or is it the declaring and living out of the good news of Jesus in all its fullness? This is the gospel proclaimed and explained in Ephesians 2: how Jesus, through his blood, spilt in agony on the Cross, has made a way for each of us to be individually reconciled to God, but more than this, has destroyed the walls of hate between peoples. As Ephesians 2.19 says: 'Consequently, you are no longer foreigners and strangers, but fellow citizens with God's people and also members of the same household.' Through his death and resurrection, Jesus reconciled people of every tribe, tongue and nation with each other, establishing a new creation, his church. It is our job to live this out, displaying the power and beauty of the gospel.

This good news is not just something to be shouted at people in the streets, shoved into someone's hands in the form of a tract or even outsourced to celebrity or professional Christians who preach it at one-off special events or courses to which you invite your friends. It is good news that is shown and shared by getting to know people who are very different from us – by being willing to have our lives disrupted (and greatly enriched) when we open up our lives and homes. Only in this way do strangers become friends and family. It is through moving towards and taking an interest in others, and offering and receiving hospitality that we fulfil our Christian calling to be involved in the making of disciples of all nations. As Paul wrote to the Thessalonians: 'Because we loved you so much, we were delighted to share with you not only the gospel of God but our lives as well' (1 Thess. 2.8). It is also through our openness to receiving and learning from our Christian brothers and sisters from different backgrounds that the Lord continues to form and grow us as his disciples.

We realize and witness to the wonderful, good news of what God has done through Christ when we form intercultural Christ-centred communities, where people do not just live alongside each other in silos where suspicions, fears and prejudice go unchallenged, but rather in deep relationships of humility, vulnerability and mutual honouring. In these kinds of Christian communities, everyone is transformed, individually and collectively, into who it is the Lord desires us to be. In these communities, we celebrate diversity and strive for unity in submission to our one shared Lord and king. This is the present and future hope we offer our warring and fragmenting world. This is the ministry of reconciliation we are to devote our lives to as Christians.

The bigotry and racism that has raised its head in Northern Ireland poses a challenge to the established church here. How they respond will reveal a lot about them, and already has. Some Christians have shockingly shown sympathy for the racist events (riots) in the summer of 2024 that were in such blatant contradiction of everything the Bible teaches about the way God's people are to treat the strangers, the homeless, the weak and the marginalized around them. Others were disappointingly silent, perhaps unsure of what their response should be or not having fully appreciated the pain their brothers and sisters of different ethnic backgrounds are experiencing. Encouragingly, many did courageously and clearly condemn it, and more importantly reached out to those feeling anxious and the potential targets of abuse with practical help and assurance that, in their eyes, they are welcome and valued members of society.

We can see in Northern Ireland's troubled history how much identity and allegiance have been subjects of contention. Those of us who were not raised here are often surprised by how much worldly identities and allegiances seem to be interwoven with faith. For churches seeking to be Christ-centred, kingdom-reflecting, intercultural communities where there are no non-gospel barriers put up to hinder people of all backgrounds finding Jesus and being embraced by his people, issues of identity, allegiance and loyalty are going to have to be radically challenged in light of the Bible's teachings. We all need to be continually asking ourselves, as disciples of king Jesus, where our value and identity ultimately lie and to which kingdom and people we give our ultimate allegiance and loyalty.

The Christian message sanctifies and liberates every human culture. All cultures contain good things because they are created by people created in God's image, and unhealthy and harmful things because these same people are sinners. The all-sufficient Christian message shines a light and exposes the dark and harmful things in any given culture and illuminates the beautiful things that contribute to human flourishing. It also deals with the guilt, shame, fears and longings for community, purpose and meaning that every heart carries. Sections of Northern Ireland society feel deeply insecure because of the rapid changes in society, which they feel are eroding a world they were familiar with and where they had greater power and influence. Having already been forged in an environment of the conflict against feared 'others', this plays out in suspicion, fear and aggressive attitudes and actions towards those whom they perceive as representing threats. This holds hearts and minds in the bondage of hatred and fear and leads to endless struggle against perceived enemies from outside; this outlook ultimately locks their own communities in a state of mind and being that prevents its flourishing.

What good and liberating news it is to them when they really realize what it means to live as sons and daughters of the king of kings and part of an eternal kingdom that is going to be victorious over and outlive every worldly kingdom. This means that they no longer need to live in constant anxiety of losing worldly control and power, which they will ultimately lose anyway, and instead live with the assurance, meaning and purpose of living for the eternal kingdom and king, who brings peace to every human heart, including their own. It frees the follower of the king of heaven and earth to fearlessly embrace those who are different and whom they long to see giving Jesus the glory he alone deserves and to call brothers and sisters in him. Then their struggle will be for the glory of this king and the building of his kingdom, and in light of this, all secondary identities and allegiances will fall into their proper place.

However, even if all this is understood and accepted as part of the outworking of the good news of Jesus, it does not mean that Christ-honouring intercultural communities will automatically emerge. For a church to develop an intercultural approach and posture, the leadership has to a have an uncompromising commitment to it and be intentional in seeking to bring it about. Their congregations will need to be constantly reminded, in light of the gospel, who they are and what their calling is, and discipled to live it out, individually and in community.

Finally, for the New Northern Irish, the challenge is to remember to whom we also belong and what our calling is. Whatever the circumstance around us, we are not to have a spirit of fear but of power and love (2 Tim. 1.7). We are here because God has appointed and anointed the times and places we will spend our days in accordance with his good purposes (Acts 17.26). In season and out of season, we are to give the reason for the hope we have in Jesus with gentleness and respect (1 Peter 3.15).

We are told to bless even those who seek to harm us, for they too desperately need Jesus. This posture will mark us out as true disciples of Jesus. Even if we are looked down upon, mistreated and misunderstood, it only means that we are walking a Christ-like path, for Jesus experienced the same. May uncertain and unsettling circumstances only drive us closer to Jesus himself. May our experience of our earthly walk with the Lord be that of the apostle Paul to whom the Lord said: 'My grace is sufficient for you, for my power is made perfect in weakness' (2 Cor. 12.9). Paul responded saying: 'Therefore I will boast all the more gladly about my weaknesses, so that Christ's power may rest on me' (2 Cor.

12.9). Let us keep our eyes fixed on Jesus, the author and perfecter of our faith (Heb. 12.2), for if we do, we know that our future on this earth and forever is with him.

Bibliography

Belfast, 2021, Amazon Prime, directed by Kenneth Branagh, Northern Ireland: TKBC and Northern Ireland Screen.

BBC, 2023, 'Good Friday Agreement: What is it?', 3 April, https://www.bbc.com/news/uk-northern-ireland-61968177 (accessed 26.2.25).

CAIN Archive, 2024, 'Background Information on Northern Ireland Society – Security and Defence', CAIN Web Service, last modified 15 August 2024, https://cain.ulster.ac.uk/ni/security.htm (accessed 26.2.25).

Crangle, J., 2021, 'Immigrants, Diversity and Race Relations in Twentieth-Century Northern Ireland', *Creative Centenaries*, https://www.creativecentenaries.org/blog/immigrants-diversity-and-race-relations-in-twentieth-century-northern-ireland (accessed 26.2.25).

Every Nation, 2025, 'Every Nation. Every Campus', https://www.everynation.org/ (accessed 26.2.25).

IMI (Intercultural Ministries Ireland), 2024, 'Our Vision', https://www.interculturalireland.org/ (accessed 26.2.25).

Jones, E., Bottigheimer, K. S., Smyth, J., Coulter, C., and Aughey, A. H., 2025, 'Northern Ireland', *Britannica*, https://www.britannica.com/place/Northern-Ireland (accessed 26.2.25).

MAP, 2024, 'The Northern Ireland network for world mission', *Global Connections*, https://globalconnections.org.uk/map (accessed 26.2.25).

Marshall, D., 2024, 'Belfast violence: What happened at the weekend?', *BBC*, https://www.bbc.co.uk/news/articles/c9wjjr7wq120 (accessed 26.2.25).

McCullough, J., 2014, 'Northern Ireland's Vietnamese boat people, 35 years on', *BBC*, 5 March 2014, https://www.bbc.co.uk/news/uk-northern-ireland-26434981 (accessed 26.2.25).

Meredith, R. and Wilson, R., 2023, 'Northern Ireland international student boom adds £1bn to economy – report', *BBC*, 16 May 2023, https://www.bbc.co.uk/news/uk-northern-ireland-65602563 (accessed 26.2.25).

NISRA, 2004, '2001 Census – Migration, Travel to Work and Workplace Population', https://www.nisra.gov.uk/publications/2001-census-migration-travel-work-and-workplace-population (accessed 26.2.25).

NISRA, 2022, 'Census 2021 main statistics demography tables – country of birth', https://www.nisra.gov.uk/publications/census-2021-main-statistics-demography-tables-country-of-birth (accessed 26.2.25).

O'Neill, A., 2024, 'Population of Northern Ireland from 1821 to 2011', *Statista*, https://www.statista.com/statistics/1015418/population-northern-ireland-1821-2021/ (accessed 26.2.25).

Further Reading

Jennings, N., 2024, 'How can we reconcile racial injustice as a church?', *Evangelical Alliance*, 1 October, https://www.eauk.org/news-and-views/how-can-we-reconcile-racial-injustice-as-a-church (accessed 26.2.2025).

Kwiyani, H., 2020, *Multicultural Kingdom: Ethnic Diversity, Mission and the Church*, London: SCM Press.

Marzouk, S., 2019, *Intercultural Church: A Biblical Vision for the Age of Migration*, Minneapolis, MN: Fortress Press.

McKittrick, D. and McVea, D., 2012, *Making Sense of the Troubles: A History of the Northern Ireland Conflict*, London: Viking.

Olofinjana, I., 2024, 'Contextual Mission Theology and Migration Theologies', *israelolofinjana*, 1 October, https://israelolofinjana.wordpress.com/2024/10/01/contextual-mission-theology-and-migration-theologies-reverse-missiology-diaspora-missiology-and-reciprocal-missiology/ (accessed 26.2.25).

Olofinjana, I., 2024, 'God's intercultural kingdom in the island of Ireland', *Evangelical Alliance*, 10 May, https://www.eauk.org/news-and-views/gods-intercultural-kingdom-in-the-island-of-ireland (accessed 26.2.25).

O'Toole, F., 2021, *We Don't Know Ourselves: A Personal History of Ireland since 1958*, London: Head of Zeus.

Park, N., 2015, *Ministry to Migrants and Asylum Seekers: A Guide for Evangelical Churches*, Dublin: Evangelical Alliance Ireland.

Reiss, M. J. and White, J., 2013, *An Aims-based Curriculum: The Significance of Human Flourishing for Schools*, London: IOE Press.

Various contributors, 2013, *For God and His Glory Alone: A Contribution Relating Some Biblical Principles to the Situation in Northern Ireland*, Belfast: Contemporary Christianity.

PART 3

Intercultural Justice: Racial Justice and Reconciliation

11

Just Leadership: Developing Radical Empathy to Break Systemic Strongholds

KATE COLEMAN

> *This chapter is taken from Kate Coleman's book* Metamorph: Transforming your Life and Leadership *(2024). Permission granted by Kate Coleman.*

The tragic killing of George Floyd in Minneapolis, Minnesota, on 25 May 2020, shocked the millions who witnessed it through the media and those who learned about it indirectly. The implications of what had been caught on camera were so appalling that it triggered massive protests across the US, the UK and the rest of the world. Some referred to it as a pivotal moment of racial reckoning (Quarcoo and Husaković, 2021), while a number of Christian groups recognized it as nothing short of a *kairos* moment: God's opportune time for tackling racial injustices being perpetuated within workplaces, ministry spaces and beyond.

For me and many other Christians of colour, reaction to Floyd's death and its aftermath exposed the painful realities of a church fraught with the same racially and culturally charged tensions on display in media outlets. It also brought to light the stark lack of genuinely diverse Christian congregations in Europe, the UK and the US. I use diverse to mean having *mutual respect and appreciation* for people who are different.

Some Christian leaders were surprised to learn for the first time that congregational worship was, in Martin Luther King Jr's words, still 'the most segregated hour of the week' (King, 1958, p. 119), including in churches that considered themselves multi-ethnic or intercultural.

So, it came as no surprise when organizations, institutions and churches alike, nationally and internationally, Christian and non-Christian, found themselves faced with the same challenge of what it means to lead effectively in a world divided by race. The George Floyd moment seemed to serve as a 'great awakening', prompting many to commit to doing all they could to tackle racial inequality. In fact, by the end of May 2020, just days after Floyd's death, 55 CEOs of global corporations, along with leaders of smaller entities, publicly pledged change through statements and detailed action plans posted on social media.

Making the 'Invisible' Visible

While some corporations were quick to respond, similar recognition and a commitment to act were notably slower to come from churches, denominations and Christian organizations in the UK, Europe and the US. Justin Welby, the Archbishop of Canterbury in the UK, openly referenced the 'hostile environment' endured by people of colour within the Church of England. His language was unequivocal: 'When we look at our own church, we are still deeply institutionally racist. Let's be clear about that' (Sherwood, 2020). Ben Lindsay, founder and CEO of Power The Fight, highlighted the deep-seated racial disparities within UK church leadership in his timely publication *We Need to Talk About Race* (2019), in which he describes the 'Guinness effect' – a term used in the Black community to denote white-dominated leadership over a predominantly Black congregation or workforce.

In his insightful paper 'Europe 2021: A Missiological Report', Jim Memory examines the health and future of mission work in Europe. He makes a critical observation: 'The future of the church in Europe may well depend on the emergence of a truly European Intercultural Christianity' (Memory, 2021). However, Memory identifies significant obstacles to achieving this vision, noting that many native European churches have either been unwilling or unsure how to assist diaspora churches (Memory's preferred term for ethnic or migrant churches). He later adds, 'In some parts of Europe, church leaders have simply not woken up to the potential of collaborating with diaspora churches. To do that, European church leaders may need to face up to their unconscious racism and colonial attitudes' (Memory, 2021, p. 47).

On 15 June 2020, Rick Warren, the renowned author of *The Purpose Driven Life* and founding pastor of Saddleback Church in the US, made a poignant statement on his social media: 'Racism is not some minor issue to God. It's at the heart of the gospel' (Warren, 2020). Following this, Saddleback Church outlined steps they were taking to confront the root causes of racial inequality. However, the very next day, on 16 June, *Christianity Today* published an article revealing that only 62% of US churches acknowledged that churches had a responsibility to denounce racism in the wake of George Floyd's death. The same *Christianity Today* article also reported that a disheartening 20% of US pastors (one in five!) believed the church had no role in responding to the country's history of racism (Roach, 2020). So, although there were some Christians who recognized the church's role in combating racial injustice, it became increasingly clear that many churches were willingly minimizing the pain experienced by people of colour and exacerbating their anguish by failing to address or even acknowledge racism adequately.

And for those leaders who understood the church's role in addressing racial injustice, it soon became clear that they didn't necessarily know how to respond. Many who felt guilty as they became aware of the full extent of the challenge took to responding with default commitments and platitudes to 'think and pray' about the issue. Those who sincerely wished to do better often focused on individual efforts, while overlooking the need to challenge and change the underlying theologies and structures in their churches and wider society that perpetuated the injustices and disparities in the first place.

Consequently, the wave of eloquent statements and promises made by churches, workplaces and organizations in the aftermath of George Floyd often lacked follow-through in terms of measurably tangible results. There was so little consistency that the following wry remark fast became commonplace: 'When all was said and done, there was a lot more said than done!'

Evading Racism

While Christians have ample reason to excel in matters of justice and have responded accordingly in some areas, the response to racism within many Christian communities has been disappointingly lacklustre. In the realm of public discourse, where various forms of discrimination are increasingly being highlighted, the issue of racial injustice has frequently been the most evaded and least addressed, even in the post-George Floyd era. Groups and organizations, including those with Christian affiliations, have often acted on diversity and inclusion measures while conspicuously sidestepping issues related to racism and racial inequality. This has led some (including me) to surmise that they either consider racism the most daunting 'ism' of all or the least relevant by far. All the while, anti-Black sentiment continues to insidiously intersect with and exacerbate the challenges faced by every other socially marginalized group or 'protected characteristic' in society. In a section entitled 'How to Talk About Race When – eek! – it is so Hard!', author Kelly McDonald addresses the difficulties surrounding race discussions, especially for many white people. She points out,

> Unlike other issues at work that you have to resolve and work through, this is about people. For most White people, the subject of race is incredibly uncomfortable to talk about because we have no skills in this area. We weren't taught how to do it. In fact, most of us were probably taught not to discuss race. (McDonald, 2021, p. 67)

Unfortunately, the reluctance to engage in conversations about race historically also extends to church and ministry settings where racial tensions have either been ignored or rationalized with spiritual and theological justifications, and silence over racial matters has, in some cases, been elevated to a spiritual virtue. The aftermath of George Floyd's death made it clear that racial barriers are not simply confined to Western Europe or the US. Part of the reason the protests were worldwide is precisely because race-related barriers are a global issue (Lopez, 2018). *The Guardian* columnist Ahmed Olayinka Sule underlines this:

> In today's Brazil, Black people are still treated as second-class citizens; while in India, students of African origin are persecuted. In South Africa, a majority Black country, 72% of the country's private farmland is owned by white people, who make up 9% of the population. During the apartheid era there was a clear racial hierarchy with whites at the top, Indians and 'Coloureds' in the middle, and Black people at the bottom. (Sule, 2019)

Out of Sight, Out of Mind

As I mentioned earlier, much like the rest of the world, the initial response of white church leaders in the UK to the killing of George Floyd was painfully and frustratingly slow. There were, I believe, several underlying reasons for this.

First, many leaders, while appalled, perceived the incident as an individual and isolated event and therefore as personal rather than systemic racism. Second, there was a prevailing belief that racism, as highlighted by the incident, was a problem confined to the US and not relevant to the UK. Third, many churches in the UK were convinced they were wonderfully happy families because racial issues were not openly discussed. Fourth, churches lacking racial diversity did not see racism as their issue because their congregations were homogeneous – the people around them looked, believed, sounded and acted like them. Therefore, they didn't consider themselves overtly exposed to the challenges of racial diversity. Yet, as I have often said, this lack of exposure doesn't necessarily equate to an absence of racial biases or prejudices. Anyone who reads the national media or watches the daily news is already forming opinions and developing a mindset about 'race' that is seldom informed by biblical principles or shaped by biblical values, leading inevitably to unbiblical attitudes, behaviours, and responses whenever the occasion arises. Finally, like many white people in the UK, there are church leaders who struggle to believe racism is an issue for them because they don't feel *they* have a personal problem with it as it doesn't manifest in US-style issues.

Although it's true that the British media doesn't frequently report racially motivated violence, overt racial discrimination like the 'n-word' is rarely used any more, and police brutality isn't generally reinforced with firearms, this does not imply an absence of racism in the UK. The shooting of Chris Kaba – a 24-year-old, unarmed soon-to-be father – by a police officer in London on 5 September 2022 starkly illustrates this point. This tragic event occurred over two years after George Floyd's death and serves as a reminder that generalizations about the absence of racial issues can be misleading, especially considering Mr Kaba had been followed by a police car without lights or sirens and was not a suspect when he was shot and killed. A simple internet search reveals numerous other heartbreaking examples of racial injustice in the UK.

Britain's history of slavery also might feel distant in comparison to America's, primarily because the brutality of the plantations did not take place in Britain itself but in the West Indies and other British colonies. This geographical distance often masks the true extent of Britain's pervasive and extensive involvement in and profiting from slavery.

So, for many, the last few years have been partly about getting to grips with the realities of a racism that, for them, has simply been 'out of sight, out of mind'.

Systemic Discrimination in the Early Church

In Acts Chapter 6, frustrations associated with 'overlooked' systemic discrimination, not unlike racism, erupted in the early church. The chapter introduces us to five distinct groups: the Greek-speaking believers (the 'Hellenistic Jews'), the Hebrew-speaking believers ('Hebraic Jews'), the apostles (who were also predominantly Hebrew-speaking), the broader church community, and the seven individuals appointed to address the significant fallout.

The Hellenistic Jews were 'foreign' diaspora Jews who had grown up in Greek-speaking regions outside of Israel. They had assimilated Greek culture, including language and dress. Conversely, the Hebraic Jews were native to Israel, speaking Hebrew and Aramaic, and adhered closely to traditional Jewish customs, including the way they dressed. Despite being followers of Jesus, they still harboured deep-seated cultural biases regarding the Hellenists. The Hebraic Jews often viewed their approach to Judaism and, subsequently, their Christian faith as a more 'pure' or authentic expression. This sense of superiority and entitlement, ingrained in their majority culture, inevitably spilled over into discriminatory practices within the early church.

Various translations of Acts 6.1 highlight the issue at hand: The Hellenist widows were being 'overlooked' (NIV), 'discriminated against' (NIV), or 'neglected' (NKJV). In other words, the situation was sufficiently dire, systemic, and negative that the Hellenists were unhappy enough to raise strong objections and make their voices heard regarding what was being witnessed and experienced by their community.

The way discrimination spilled over in this situation is noteworthy because, in Jewish law, widows without male relatives to support them were particularly vulnerable. The church's initiative to provide for these widows led them to pioneer an early form of social welfare. Yet it was precisely as the church was trying to do something right that they discovered that something was very wrong ... systemic discrimination, not unlike racism, was alive and well in the church.

Caste Aside

Racism affects different so-called 'races' in different ways. There is anti-Black racism, anti-Asian racism (which affects East and South Asians differently), anti-Arab racism (which often combines with Islamophobia), and multiple other types of racism. Each racism is also usually accompanied by varying degrees of xenophobia. Ellen E. Jones, journalist, broadcaster, and author of *Screen Deep: How Film and TV Can Solve Racism and Save the World*, helpfully clarifies a common misunderstanding:

> In colloquial English we use the same inadequate word – 'racism' – to describe two distinct, but connected, phenomena. 1) Racism is interpersonal prejudice or bigotry based on skin colour or other racially coded physical traits. But 2) Racism is also the pervasive and deeply embedded disadvantage that people of colour experience as a holdover from European colonialism and transatlantic slavery, and the way in which it is produced, condoned and perpetuated by a multiplicity of social systems and structures. This is often referred to as 'structural racism' or 'systemic racism' but, just as often, simply as 'racism'. (Jones, 2022, p. 7)

To effectively combat all forms of racism, we must recognize that the idea of 'race' itself operates similarly to a caste system, binding and compelling even those oppressed by it to sometimes perpetuate the cycle of oppressive practices by competing for scarce and questionable 'rewards'. The system bears a striking resemblance to the apartheid regime in South Africa mentioned earlier, where the distinction of skin colour – both literal and symbolic – defines the boundaries of separation.

I sometimes get asked, 'What makes racism different from simple ethnocentrism?' It is this racial hierarchy that partly distinguishes the two. Ethnocentrism is a prejudice in thought or action that ranks ethnic and cultural groups against one another, but it is mutable and transferable, whereas racism acts as a ranking of inherited human value and usage and positions the perceived 'superior' race at the top and the 'inferior' one at the bottom. Just as caste systems rely on the stigmatization of those deemed inherently inferior based on their birth, racism does the same. I often have to remind people that racism is never primarily about personal feelings or morality. It is always about *power* – which groups get to make the decisions and which do not; *resources* – which group gets to acquire, control and distribute them; and *legitimacy* – which groups are considered worthy of being heard, respected, deemed competent and worthy of authority, and why. The distorted image of whites as superior is so globally pervasive that even if Black people are prejudiced or ethnocentric against whites, they don't usually have the social power to act on those feelings in ways that can impact the futures of white people. The reverse, however, is simply not the case.

Similar to the caste system, racism is a process by which systems and policies, actions and attitudes create unequal and inequitable opportunities and outcomes for people based on their so-called 'race'. As such, it has been a tool for oppression with socio-economic motives, as exemplified during the transatlantic slave trade and even today continues through the global arrangements marked by neocolonialism. Historically, it has usually been Black or darker-skinned people who have been relegated to the lowest rung of this racial hierarchy. There are multiple and complex reasons for this. However, the sale of almost ten million Africans to Arabia and the Indian subcontinent by Arab slave traders between 650 CE and the 1800s and the transportation of at least twelve million Africans across the Atlantic by European slave traders between the sixteenth and nineteenth century have undoubtedly contributed to a lasting global legacy that continues to affect Black and darker-skinned people even today.

Before the development of racialized hierarchies, slavery was practised widely across a variety of civilizations but was rarely linked to notions of inherent racial inferiority. Instead, it was often viewed ethnocentrically or as the unfortunate consequence of being on the losing side of battle and ancient warfare.

Today, Black and darker-skinned people 'inherit' a perceived racial inferiority and thus experience a range of disparate outcomes in virtually every sector of every society around the globe. This racial bias is evident in the continued use of pejorative terms for Black people in virtually every geographic context imaginable. Ahmed Olayinka Sule notes the following examples, which readers are advised include offensive language for the purposes of criticism:

> The Arabic word *abeed*, which means 'slave,' is still used to describe Black people in countries from Algeria to Yemen. In the US, they are called 'nigger,' in Brazil they are termed *macaco*; in South Africa, they are nicknamed *kaffir*; in India, *bandar*; in China *hakgwai*. (Sule, 2019)

The Race for Truth

The irony of all this is that despite its prevalence, the modern category of 'race' is grounded in neither biology nor any reputable science. Biologically speaking, all people living today belong to one species, *Homo sapiens*, and this species has evolved together without branching off into different human species. Likewise, the concept of 'race' is not a biblical construct. The Bible acknowledges only one human race and addresses issues of diversity, not by starting with the differences in the human family but with the oneness of humanity created in the image of God. One of the first things we learn about God's intentions for humanity is that we are created to be like him and, in some way, to reflect who God is and what God is like. Genesis 1.26 states, 'Let us make humankind in our image, according to our likeness' (NRSV). This directive establishes God, not humanity, as the ultimate reference point for all reality. To put it another way, both diversity and distinctiveness are not only part of God's design, but they are also characteristics of God himself, and it is God who 'sets the bar' for their meaning and value.

At the very beginning of the biblical narrative, we discover God as a collective 'we' rather than a solitary 'me'. In theological terms, this is expressed through the doctrine of the Trinity, where three distinct persons – coequal and coeternal – exemplify perfect unity amid diversity. However, we should note that God values unity in diversity characterized by equality just as much in the human family too, including cultural and ethnic differences. This fact is reflected throughout the Bible in texts such as Revelation 7.9: 'Then I looked, and there before me was a great multitude that no one could count, from every nation, tribe, people and language, standing before the throne and before the Lamb.' Exodus 12.38 describes the exodus of God's people from Egypt as a 'mixed multitude' (ESV), so their identity wasn't grounded in the concept of 'race' as understood today. Instead, their distinctiveness throughout their developmental journey was their worship of the one true God.

The modern notion of 'race' emerged in the late sixteenth century as a social construct and attempt to categorize people into different 'types' based on their physical and cultural traits. By the mid-eighteenth century, this misguided notion had been conveniently solidified by white Europeans, particularly the British, into a means of justifying the cultural and economic domination of other groups through mechanisms like slavery, indentured servitude, and oppression. While the term 'race' lacks biological or scientific validity, the ideology of race wields significant and often destructive power. Worse still, it has acquired a seemingly tangible and common-sense-like quality. As a result, systems of racial hierarchy have thoroughly co-opted our consciousness, language, and behaviour and continue to be knowingly and unknowingly perpetuated today, even among Christians worldwide, from Africa to India and Europe to China.

It is therefore more important than ever for Christians to reject the concept of racial hierarchies and to proactively oppose all attempts to reassert them all over the world.

A Diversifying World Needs a Diversifying Church

While 'race' is a human construct, increasing diversity is a growing reality. The twenty-first century, in particular, has been characterized by a significant increase in global diversity. However, contrary to popular opinion, the most culturally diverse nations are not in Western Europe or the Americas but in Africa. At the time of writing, Uganda, Liberia, Chad, Cameroon and Togo are among the top ten most culturally diverse countries in the world, as confirmed by the multiple methods used to measure them (Wisevoter, 2024). According to the World Population Review, Canada is the only Western country in the top 20 most culturally diverse countries (World Population Review, 2024), with both the US and the UK ranking significantly lower.

This surge in diversity has been driven by political, social, environmental and economic factors that have led to displacement, forced migration and large-scale movements of people across borders. The extent of this global mixing is expected to increase significantly in the coming years, but the US and Western Europe will experience a relatively small amount of this, despite the inflammatory rhetoric suggesting otherwise.

These rapid demographic changes and advances in communication have led to unprecedented levels of interaction among different ideologies, philosophies and religions. People are increasingly encountering diverse perspectives in their own homes, workplaces and educational establishments in ways that were previously unheard of. We are living at a time in history where vastly different world-views – with all their associated opinions, distinctives, values, and beliefs – not only coexist but also sometimes clash ... violently.

In the UK, projections already indicate that by 2061, over 35% of the population will be of non-white English or Irish descent, a significant increase from 13% in 2011 (Taylor, 2019). This demographic will include individuals identified as 'Black', 'Asian', 'UK minority or 'Global Majority', depending on the terminology adopted. In the United States, people of colour are expected to constitute around 54% of the population by around the same time. Europe is also expected to be a whole shade darker. Notably, UK, European and US churches are witnessing these demographic shifts much faster, partly because people of colour are far more likely to be involved in faith communities. This should come as no surprise, given the centre of gravity of Christianity has shifted decisively from the Global North to the Global South and from the West to the East. Christianity is growing substantially within these regions and among these people groups all over the world.

As we look to the future, whatever the context, it will inevitably become more diverse and thus more complex over time. This escalating diversity and complexity will require Christian leaders to employ biblical wisdom in leading and guiding their churches, workplaces and wider society through the massive cultural transitions that will accompany them.

Even if 'race' is not an issue in the classic sense, every society, including those plagued by colourism, will need to engage in some kind of soul-searching, as each community likely harbours some form of insider/outsider dynamic informed by racial legacies (Ellen E. Jones helpfully describes colourism as follows: 'White supremacy ... often functions as a hierarchy, with whiteness at its apex. Within that hierarchy people of colour with lighter skin, straighter hair or other European-proximate features can be privileged in relation to people with darker skin tones or less European features' (Jones, 2024, p. 15). Many churches and Christian organizations are still coming to terms with the reality that racism functions in every society, community and church context – albeit in slightly different ways. This means we all have our own version of a racialized world, and the way it shows up in your church or organization is likely to reflect how it shows up in your wider society and community. In reality, as people come to Christ, they inevitably bring with them attitudes, habits and practices all in need of a metamorphic transformation. Given our history of valuing some bodies over others – men over women, rich over poor, Christian over Jewish, and white over Black and brown – it's no surprise that these biases are reflected in our churches. The UK home-grown variety of racism may look different to varieties found elsewhere, but just because it is often wrapped up in a politer package doesn't make it any less destructive, systemic, or soul-destroying! All this raises the question of what will be required of leaders and leadership in diversifying contexts, a question that will become increasingly critical.

Just ... Just Leadership

Leadership is increasingly defined by its capacity to influence rather than by titles, and hinges more on trust than on a hierarchical position. In diversifying and racialized landscapes, trust is often scarce due to historical misuses of spirituality, pseudoscience and bias (conscious or not) in ways that uphold existing power structures. In low-trust environments, recognizing and achieving breakthroughs can be particularly tricky. So, the concept of 'just leadership' is even more critical.

When we think about 'justice', it is often in the context of retribution or punishment aimed at those who cause harm or make people suffer. The common cry for 'justice' usually means seeking one's rights, often from a specific individual or legal system. However, the biblical concept of justice is far deeper and wider, and punishment is not even its primary concern. In the Old Testament, the Hebrew word for justice, *misphat*, is frequently paired with *tsedeqa*, translated as 'righteousness'. Together, these terms often appear as 'justice and righteousness' and encompass the ideas of corrective/restorative justice (i.e. putting things right) and distributive justice or impartiality and fairness (i.e. doing things right). An example of this is Isaiah 1.17: 'Learn to do right; seek justice. Defend the oppressed. Take up the cause of the fatherless; plead the case of the widow.'

In the New Testament, these concepts are encapsulated in the Greek word *dikaiosune*, which encompasses both aspects of correction and fairness. It is clear from this that God's focus is not primarily punishment but on fostering right relationships, actions and order. This holistic view of justice emphasizes the importance of fairness and restoration in leadership, particularly in contexts where trust needs to be rebuilt and historical injustices addressed. As leaders, embracing this broader, more restorative notion of justice is key to navigating and leading effectively in diverse and complex environments. It is often why churches and Christian organizations that show little interest in corrective practices are regarded with suspicion by marginalized communities.

The kind of 'justice' the Bible has in view has no limit or boundaries and applies in private as well as in public life. It also encompasses personal, interpersonal and systemic aspects of our relationships. Essentially, justice is relevant wherever God has interests, which means absolutely everywhere!

Removing the Ceiling of Blindness

There are no easy ways to rid the world of the evils of race-related thinking and oppression, but it will demand nothing less than a metanoic change of mind and a metamorphic display of transformation. Both suggest that the church not only has a part to play but also an opportunity to lead this change.

Yet, our pivotal role cannot be realized if we fail to confront the truth of our own historical involvement in the creation and perpetuation of racial categories and oppression in the first place. 2 Corinthians 3.18

provides the crucial reminder: 'And we all, who with unveiled faces contemplate the Lord's glory, are being transformed into his image with ever-increasing glory, which comes from the Lord, who is the Spirit.' This verse suggests that the transformation we seek for our churches, Christian organizations and daily lives is a profound journey that requires divine intervention. But we must first be willing to remove the veil that blinds us to our own biases and shortcomings, especially when it comes to race-related thinking, and earnestly seek God's transformative power.

We can, of course, try to bury our heads in the sand and pretend that everything in our churches and organizations is wonderful, but there is no getting around the fact that it is always and only 'the truth that sets us free'! Conversely, self-deception is very costly, and denial of the truth only keeps us stagnating in unresolved issues for even longer. The metamorphic transformation we long for and that takes us from 'glory to glory' is only possible when metanoia is embraced as an ongoing daily practice of unlearning and relearning and not merely a one-off event.

There is a misconception among Christians that merely sharing the same space, beliefs and practices, and attending the same church along with those who differ from us, actually changes things. It rarely does. There really is no substitute for intentionality when it comes to catalysing metamorphic change. Just because we live, work and even worship alongside diverse others doesn't mean we have learned how to relate effectively, navigate faith, or even worship authentically together.

Recent years have demonstrated how painful it can be for people to work or worship together across the barriers of 'race', ethnicity and culture without understanding what is really at stake. In her article 'Why Developing Intercultural Management Skills Is Essential in Today's Complex World', independent global executive coach and intercultural leadership consultant Myriam Callegarin spells it out:

> Most people interact with others across cultures without being aware of the communication breakdowns and the invisible conflicts they unintentionally create. They are unaware of the unwritten rules and the invisible codes that are valid in the other culture. Most interactions are careless and clueless, not due to bad intentions, but rather because of a lack of knowledge and self-reflection. (Callegarin, 2018)

We seldom notice that the low engagement of particular communities within our institutions, organizations, churches, and even our neighbourhoods and networks has less to do with their disinterest in our vision, mission, community or Jesus and more to do with our lack of awareness and cultural sensitivity. The need for racial sensitivity and cultural competence has never been more pressing than it is today.

Ironically, Christians are the custodians of the unique narrative, practices and resources so crucial for both effective communication and community building in racially and culturally diverse spaces. Yet, all too often, it is Christians who are the most hesitant to engage and the least willing to change.

The Desperate Need for Radical Empathy

I believe that a lack of empathy lies at the core of this failure. Likewise, it is radical empathy that lies at the core of our much-needed metamorphic transformation, just as it always has. Empathy is embodied in the scriptural principle found in Romans 12.15, which encourages believers to 'Rejoice with those who rejoice; mourn with those who mourn' and in 1 Corinthians 12.26, which states, 'If one part suffers, every part suffers with it.' This captures the essence of what it means to be part of genuine community. The New Testament and church history provide compelling evidence that it is strong communities that ignite potent and effective mission. We desperately need leaders who are capable of leading in radically empathetic ways.

In her insightful book *Radical Empathy*, political scientist and entrepreneur Terri E. Givens offers a transformative perspective. She defines empathy as:

> The ability to see the world from another person's perspective, in order to understand their feelings and life experiences. 'Radical empathy' takes this a step further, encouraging each of us not only to understand the feelings of others, but also to be motivated to create the change that will allow all of us to benefit from economic prosperity and develop the social relationships that are beneficial to our emotional wellbeing. (Givens, 2021, p. 1)

In my work, I often draw parallels between 'radical empathy' and the concept of 'incarnational practice'. Although incarnation is a concept found in various religions, such as Buddhism and Hinduism, it acquires a unique dimension in Christianity and is exemplified by Jesus Christ. Incarnation in the Christian context involves a deep commitment to fully understanding and sharing in the experiences of others. It means standing in their shoes, hearing with their ears, and seeing through their eyes. Jesus not only epitomized this approach but also went beyond simply imagining the pain of others to actually experiencing and transforming that pain. Philippians 2.5–7 exhorts believers to emulate this attitude:

> In your relationships with one another, have the same mindset as Christ Jesus: Who, being in very nature God, did not consider equality with God something to be used to his own advantage; rather, he made himself nothing by taking the very nature of a servant, being made in human likeness.

Radical empathy and incarnational practice remind us to go beyond exploring how *we* feel about *their* struggles to actually *experiencing* how *they* feel about their struggles too.

Effectively addressing racial challenges requires an understanding of the lived experiences of marginalized groups. Engaging with what they see, hear and feel in their everyday lives can be the revelation that enables organizations, businesses, churches and individuals to reassess and modify their actions and approaches toward them. However, empathy rooted in a profound belief in the power of connection is crucial for today's leadership practices for reasons that extend beyond effectively engaging with marginalized groups. Julia Middleton, founder of Common Purpose, acknowledges, 'If for no other reason than that today's world is full of trauma, primary and secondary, empathy feels ever more essential to leading' (Middleton, 2003, p. 174).

It's important to recognize that the discipline of 'incarnational practice' is not necessarily a reciprocal exercise. Historically, people of colour have been expected to understand and adapt to the perspectives of white experiences for the sake of their well-being, economic advancement, and even physical survival. They are constantly expected to see through white eyes, hear with white ears, and modify their actions to suit white sensibilities. Sharing her own personal experience in her book *Our Unforming*, Cindy S. Lee explains,

> As an Asian American growing up in the United States, I am trained to put the white experience at the center. As I learned history and literature, the white experience was the center. As I watched TV and movies, the white experience was the center. As I work in predominately white institutions, the white experience is the center. (Lee, 2022, p. 266)

As a result, white people, and white Christians in particular, will need to get used to making a conscious effort to engage with perspectives outside their own racial experiences. This can happen through deliberate exploration or indirectly through relationships, such as marriage, friendships, growing up, or simply becoming immersed in multicultural environments. Such experiences can significantly broaden a person's perspective and reveal aspects of life they may not have previously considered.

Indeed, the discipline of radical empathy or engaging in incarnational practice is necessary for any majority group who normatively wields power. I practise it when I am in marginalized Global South environments. The challenge of justice, as exemplified by Jesus, involves actively choosing to understand and empathize with the experiences of the minority or less powerful groups we encounter. Emulating this approach requires stepping out of our own comfort zones to embrace and learn from perspectives that differ from our own, hopefully fostering a deeper sense of empathy in our interactions and decision-making as we do. Jesus also exemplifies this, reminding us that actions are the primary way we express empathy rather than just through words, thoughts and prayers.

Joseph: A Metamorphic Awakening

Several years had passed since I had last seen Joseph, and I found our last interaction particularly challenging. I had felt compelled to distance myself from his organization for the sake of my own well-being. Joseph was a dynamic leader and sincere believer but had unfortunately mishandled the rising racial tensions among his leaders and church members. His approach of stifling debate and labelling dissenters as 'woke' only exacerbated the situation. It was only a matter of time before it would all erupt, and erupt it did. The situation reached boiling point, and leaders and members alike began to vote with their feet by leaving and resigning.

However, when I met Joseph again, I could see the change in him. Amid this turmoil, something remarkable had happened – Joseph had a notable shift in disposition, a new humility, and an openness to change. Joseph had clearly been working on his 'stuff' since our last interaction and had undergone a profound transformation.

He spoke of mentoring a young Black man, a relationship in which he found himself becoming something of a father figure. Through this experience, Joseph noticed the biases and judgements the young man faced in his interactions with others. He saw how people regarded the young man when they were out together, how they often assumed the worst if he was boisterous and having fun, and how they judged the nature of the relationship without asking or waiting to be informed.

Joseph's eyes were now open to realities he had previously ignored or even denied. And now that he had seen, he couldn't unsee. Joseph admitted that much of the learning in this mentoring journey was happening on his part, a humbling revelation that marked his journey toward greater awareness and empathy. I expressed how heartening it was to see the work God was doing in his life. As we hugged, I encouraged him to continue this path of growth and understanding. Joseph's response was one of gratitude, tinged with relief. He hugged me again, and this time his smile reached his eyes. 'I thought you would judge me,' he said. 'Thank you.'

Just Leadership in the Early Church

Recognizing what we might be missing in our understanding and perception of racism is invaluable. Adopting incarnational practice or a radically empathetic approach humbles us and reminds us that no one has it all, and no one knows it all, including in matters pertaining to God.

In the Christian context, every gathering for prayer, worship, Bible study or fellowship in our workplaces or churches presents us with both discipleship opportunities and prophetic moments. The early church only gradually came to understand this, and in Acts 6.1–7, we meet them at one of many *kairos* moments in the biblical text and in their own version of a diversifying yet racialized environment. It is here we discover how their discipleship opportunity and prophetic moment became a key turning point for both strengthening and maturing their community, as well as fuelling and accelerating the growth of the early church itself. Essentially, it is only leadership infused with justice and radical empathy that can facilitate this process. The following reveals some of the critical leadership principles that emerge from their story.

Raise Awareness

It is noteworthy that in Acts 6, it was the Hellenists, not the Hebrews, who noticed the persistent pattern of discrimination. And even as hard feelings and resentment began to arise, it was the Hellenists who had to make their voices heard. This pattern reveals a common reality: those who are least affected by structural discrimination are often the most unaware of its existence. This phenomenon is what some describe as the 'curse of privilege'. Father Richard Rohr said in an interview:

> We largely do not recognize the structural access we enjoy, the trust we think we deserve, the assumption that we always belong and do not have to earn our belonging. All this we take for granted as normal. Only the outsider can spot these attitudes in us. (Rohr, 2016)

This lack of awareness was evident during the racial justice protests following George Floyd's death. Many church leaders in the UK who were not directly impacted by the racial injustices being protested expressed surprise and confusion about the extent of the issues. They had no idea how bad things were for people of colour, even within their own congregations. In fact, many church leaders contacted people within their congregations to find out if the media reports were accurate or exaggerated. Some found themselves on the receiving end of very broken and angry church members and revelations about the presence of racial injustices within their own church communities. One wise church leader I know asked the right question when he said, 'How did I not know?'

Christians of colour have long had to wrestle with the historical reality of who God has been for white Christianity and with the fact that the faith of white people has often been complicit with white patriarchy, slavery, colonization, and the genocide of indigenous communities. Many white Christians have yet to fully acknowledge or wrestle with that history or to ask themselves the question, 'How could this have happened?'

It seems that the Hebrew-speaking believers in Acts 6 were also initially unaware of what was happening in their midst. Even the apostles, Hebrew-speaking believers themselves, were ignorant of the dynamics until the moment the Hellenists brought it to their attention. They could, of course, have dealt with it in much the same way as some church leaders continue to do to this day: 'Oh, the Hellenists are imagining it. They always "play the Hellenist card". I think it's a foreign thing. I can't see what they're going on about, can you? Don't they know we love them? This is not a "gospel" priority. Let's ignore it, and maybe it'll go away.' But that's precisely the problem – these things don't go away. They go underground, smoulder, create resentment, distrust and deep-seated conflict. They damage the credibility of our witness and compromise the sense of genuine community we're seeking to model as followers of Jesus.

Prioritize Impact over Intention

While it may not have been intentional, the actions of the Hebrew-speaking believers in the early church had introduced the ugly ethnocentric, xenophobic and elitist behaviours so prevalent in their wider society into their own church behaviours and structures. This is why it is so important to distinguish between intention and impact.

Much of what needs addressing in our churches and organizations goes beyond the realm of what people *feel* about each other. While I rarely question the sincerity of people's love or good intentions, there is good reason why God asserts, 'The heart is deceitful above all things' (Jer. 17.9). Sin is not just what we *commit*; it is also what we *omit*, and although the Bible recognizes *personal sin* and individual actions, it also acknowledges *social sin* and structural oppression. The Bible consistently highlights the plight of certain groups who are regularly denied power, resources, respect and authority. These groups are disproportionately vulnerable to injustice and disproportionately victims of injustice. Some scholars refer to them as the 'quartet of the vulnerable'. They include widows, orphans, immigrants and the poor. These groups are systemically excluded from economic opportunities and social justice, as well as persistently exploited and marginalized both physically and materially.

Theologian Nicholas Wolterstorff, who popularized the term 'quartet of the vulnerable' (2008), points out that God is constantly reminding his own people, as well as the surrounding nations, that widows' lives matter, orphans' lives matter, immigrants' lives matter, and poor people's lives matter, because unfortunately, sometimes both Israel and the nations behaved as if those lives didn't matter at all.

We may *feel* that we aren't personally sinning against others intentionally, but if we are doing things (committing) or failing to do things (omitting) in ways that effectively reinforce or maintain social structures that preferentially impact one group of people over another, we are still 'implicated subjects' and it is still sin. Much of what both white people and people of colour have learned about each other is rooted in a systemic racialization that keeps reproducing itself at a level most of us are unaware of. Some refer to this underlying dynamic as 'unconscious bias', a term that highlights how these ingrained beliefs and attitudes can influence our thoughts and actions without our conscious awareness.

Therefore, in Acts 6, the discriminatory challenges can be seen as embedded in structures, not just in individuals, and we must recognize the themes of power, resources and legitimacy mentioned earlier in this chapter. Just like the Early Church in Acts 6, many churches and organizations that have good intentions don't necessarily recognize these dynamics at play until the boiling point is reached.

Merely intending to do the right thing is not the same as *actually* doing the right thing (righteousness), and an intention to put things right is not the same as *actually* putting things right (justice). Metamorphic transformation always has an outward manifestation; if there is no evidence of this, we cannot assume any actual internal change has occurred.

Thankfully, in an effort to address the difference between intention and impact, more and more church and organizational leaders are choosing the route we find in Acts 6. Some describe this as the practice of 'allyship'; I prefer the term 'radical solidarity'. Because, although I appreciate the willingness of others to enter into what I may be feeling and experiencing (radical empathy), I'd much rather they did something concrete that prevented me from having to feel and experience it in the first place!

From Radical Empathy to Radical Solidarity

The difference between *feeling* like taking action and *taking action* on what we're feeling is reflected in the difference between incarnational practice and structural repentance. Radical empathy or incarnational practice is a necessary beginning that gets us oriented and motivated, but without the restorative steps of radical solidarity, what we have is aspiration rather than transformation.

The apostles in this story apply radical solidarity. They belong to the dominant group, but once the matter is brought to their attention, they respond by using their influence and their privilege to rectify the discrimination. They move beyond unproductive feelings, relinquish claims to control, refuse to prioritize the interests of their own group, and act in concert with the desires and needs of the marginalized group. Their actions affirm that 'Hellenist lives matter' – not to the exclusion of Hebrew lives but in recognition that in this specific instance, it is the Hellenists who are experiencing injustice and vulnerability.

When the dominant group works on diversity and justice issues, it's crucial to move beyond feelings of guilt, shame or fear. Although these emotions are important to acknowledge and reflect upon, they can become a huge distraction to actually getting anything done and creating necessary change. The way to acknowledge and move beyond feelings of guilt, shame, and fear is through structural repentance, similar to what follows.

The apostles call the entire church to participate in the process of repentance. Unlike an apology, as already intimated, repentance is not just a one-off event but a continuous and ongoing process. They demonstrate that followers of Jesus aren't called to pretend everything is okay or to even avoid feeling bad at all costs. Discipling moments, with all their pain and discomfort, are designed to return us to God's ways and the pursuit of his purposes. This is how the apostle Paul speaks about it in 2 Corinthians 7.11: 'See what this godly sorrow has produced in you: what earnestness, what eagerness to clear yourselves, what indignation, what alarm, what longing, what concern, what readiness to see justice done.'

Those who are radically empathetic initiate and engage in acts of biblical repentance that are both personal and structural because they are eager to take actual steps to put things right. This empathy leading to solidarity is the essence of 'just leadership'. I once overheard a church leader remark,

> Romans 12.15 instructs us to 'weep with those who weep' not 'justify why we aren't weeping' or 'correct those who weep'. To weep with, we need to feel the pain. To feel the pain, we need to understand. To understand, we need to be informed. To be informed, we need to listen [read/watch/learn].

The responsibility for our re-education about racism and its impacts should not fall on the shoulders of those who experience it. Expecting our minority-ethnic friends or colleagues to provide all the answers or insights into racism places an unfair burden on them. What's more, they may or may not know the answers! No one is born with this knowledge, even if they have to live with its reality.

Listening is only one part of the journey toward understanding. Do your own work, as this will also enable you to stay aware of the evolving narratives around race and racism and will free your friends or employees of colour to focus on their own well-being (and sanity!) and to volunteer rather than feel obliged to offer their contributions.

It's only as we listen, read, watch, and learn that we become better equipped to use our influence to change things where needed, especially if we are senior decision-makers and members of dominant groups. Unless radical empathy finds expression in radical solidarity, it is of little use to anyone.

References

Callegarin, Myriam, 2018, 'Why developing intercultural management skills is essential in today's complex world', *CUOA Business School*, February, https://www.cuoaspace.it/2018/02/why-developing-intercultural-management-skills-is-essential-in-todays-complex-world.html (accessed 27.2.25).

Givens, Terri E., 2021, *Radical Empathy: Finding a Path to Bridging Racial Divides* [Kindle e-book], University of Bristol, England: Policy Press.

Jones, Ellen E., 2022, *Screen Deep: How Film and TV Can Solve Racism and Save the World*, London: Faber & Faber.

King, Martin Luther, Jr, 1958, *Stride Toward Freedom: The Montgomery Story*, New York, NY: Harper & Brothers.

Lee, Cindy S., 2022, *Our Unforming: De-Westernizing Spiritual Formation*, Minneapolis, MN: Fortress Press.

Libreri, Samantha, 2018, '"Let us share the land" – land ownership dominates South African election debate', *RTE*, 19 March, https://www.rte.ie/radio/radio1/clips/21526760/ (accessed 27.2.25).

Lindsay, Ben, 2019, *We Need to Talk About Race: Understanding the Black Experience in White Majority Churches*, London: SPCK.

Lopez, German, 2018, 'There are huge racial disparities in how US police use force', *Vox*, https://www.vox.com/identities/2016/8/13/17938186/police-shootings-killings-racism-racial-disparities (accessed 12.3.2025).

McDonald, Kelly, 2021, *It's Time to Talk about Race at Work: Every Leader's Guide to Making Progress on Diversity, Equity, and Inclusion*, Hoboken, NJ: John Wiley.

Memory, Jim, 2021, 'Europe 2021: A Missiological Report', https://www.ecmi.org/de/europe-2021-a-missiological-report (accessed 27.2.25).

Middleton, Julia, 2003, *If That's Leading, I'm In: Women Redefining Leadership*, Julia Middleton.

Quarcoo, Ashley and Husaković, Medina, 2021, 'Racial Reckoning in the United States: Expanding and Innovating on the Global Transitional Justice Experience', Carnegie Endowment for International Peace Working Paper, https://carnegieendowment.org/research/2021/10/racial-reckoning-in-the-united-states-expanding-and-innovating-on-the-global-transitional-justice-experience?lang=en (accessed 27.2.25).

Roach, 2020, 'Most US Pastors Speak Out in Response to George Floyd's Death', *Christianity Today*, Vol. 64, No. 6, 16 June 2020, https://www.christianitytoday.com/2020/06/pastors-george-floyd-racism-church-barna-research/ (accessed 12.3.2025).

Rohr, Richard, 2016, 'Richard Rohr on White Privilege', interviewed by Reverend Romal J. Tune, *Sojourners*, 19 January, https://sojo.net/articles/richard-rohr-white-privilege (accessed 27.2.25).

Sherwood, Harriet, 2020, 'Justin Welby says he is "sorry and ashamed" over church's racism', *The Guardian*, 11 February https://www.theguardian.com/world/2020/feb/11/justin-welby-tells-synod-he-is-sorry-and-ashamed-over-churchs-racism (accessed 27.2.25).

Sule, Ahmed Olayinka Sule, 2019, 'Racism Harms Black People Most. It's Time to Recognise "Anti-Blackness"', *The Guardian*, 9 August, https://www.theguardian.com/commentisfree/2019/aug/09/black-people-racism-anti-blackness-discrimination-minorities (accessed 27.2.25).

Taylor, Ros, 2019, 'What the UK population will look like by 2061 under hard, soft or no-Brexit scenarios', *LSE Brexit Blog*, 1 July, https://blogs.lse.ac.uk/brexit/2019/07/01/what-the-uk-population-will-look-like-by-2061-under-hard-soft-or-no-brexit-scenarios/ (accessed 27.2.25).

Warren, Rick, 2020, 15 June, *Facebook*, https://www.facebook.com/pastorrickwarren/photos/a.41414%209010902/10158492478790903/?type=3 (accessed 27.2.25).

Wisevoter, 2024, 'Most Racially Diverse Countries', *Wisevoter*, https://wisevoter.com/country-rankings/most-racially-diverse-countries/ (accessed 27.2.25).

World Population Review, 2024, 'Most Diverse Countries 2024', *World Population Review*, https://worldpopulationreview.com/country-rankings/most-diverse-countries/ (accessed 27.2.25).

Wolterstorff, Nicholas, 2008, 'Why the Quartet of the Vulnerable?' in *Justice: Rights and Wrongs*, Princeton, NJ: Princeton University Press.

Further Reading

Banks, Kira Hudson and Harvey, Richard, 2020, 'Is Your Company Actually Fighting Racism, or Just Talking About It?', *Harvard Business Review*, 11 June, https://hbr.org/2020/06/is-your-company-actually-fighting-racism-or-just-talking-about-it (accessed 27.2.25).

Baylor University News, 2020, 'Racially Diverse Congregations in the U.S. Have Nearly Tripled in the Past 20 Years, Baylor University Study Finds', *Baylor University News*, 11 November, https://news.web.baylor.edu/news/story/2020/racially-diverse-congregations-us-have-nearly-tripled-past-20-years-baylor (accessed 27.2.25).

Bazelon, Coleman, Vargas, Alberto, Janakiraman, Rohan, and Olson, Mary M., 2023, *Quantification of Reparations for Transatlantic Chattel Slavery*, https://www.brattle.com/wp-content/uploads/2023/07/Quantification-of-Reparations-for-Transatlantic-Chattel-Slavery.pdf (accessed 27.2.25).

Eddo-Lodge, Reni, 2017, *Why I'm No Longer Talking to White People About Race*, New York, NY: Bloomsbury Publishing.

Elkins, Caroline, 2022, *Legacy of Violence: A History of the British Empire* [Kindle e-book], New York: NY: Random House.

Equality and Human Rights Commission, 2020, 'Race Discrimination', https://

www.equalityhumanrights.com/equality/equality-act-2010/your-rights-under-equality-act-2010/race-discrimination/ (accessed 27.2.25).

Ghosh, Rudroneel, 2018, 'Bridge The Gap: Attacks on Africans in India highlight a glaring lack of people-to-people connect', *The Times of India*, 24 November, https://timesofindia.indiatimes.com/blogs/talkingturkey/bridge-the-gap-attacks-on-africans-in-india-highlight-a-glaring-lack-of-people-to-people-connect/ (accessed 27.2.25).

Ignatiev, Noel, 2008, *How the Irish Became White*, New York, NY: Routledge Classics.

Lewis, Thomas, 2024, 'Transatlantic Slave Trade', *Encyclopaedia Britannica*, 14 September, https://www.britannica.com/topic/transatlantic-slave-trade (accessed 27.2.25).

Markovitz, Gayle and Sault, Samantha, 2020, 'What companies are doing to fight systemic racism', World Economic Forum, 24 June, https://www.weforum.org/agenda/2020/06/companies-fighting-systemic-racism-business-community-black-lives-matter/ (accessed 27.2.25).

Masters, Robert Augustus, 2010, *Spiritual Bypassing: When Spirituality Disconnects Us from What Really Matters*, Berkeley, CA: North Atlantic Books.

Morin, Rich, 2013, 'The most (and least) culturally diverse countries in the world', Pew Research Center, 18 July, https://www.pewresearch.org/short-reads/2013/07/18/the-most-and-least-culturally-diverse-countries-in-the-world/ (accessed 27.2.25).

New African, 2018, 'Recalling Africa's harrowing tale of its first slavers – The Arabs – as UK Slave Trade Abolition is commemorated', *New African*, 27 March, https://newafricanmagazine.com/16616/ (accessed 27.2.25).

Ortman, Jennifer M., and Guarneri, Christine E., 'United States Population Projections: 2000 to 2050', United States Census Bureau, https://www.census.gov/content/dam/Census/library/working-papers/2009/demo/us-pop-proj-2000-2050/analytical-document09.pdf (accessed 27.2.25).

Passel, Jeffrey S. and Cohn, D'Vera, 2008, 'U.S. Population Projections: 2005–2050', Pew Research Center, https://www.pewresearch.org/hispanic/2008/02/11/us-population-projections-2005-2050/ (accessed 30.05.2024).

Saini, Angela, 2019, *Superior: The Return of Race Science*, New York, NY: HarperCollins.

PRRI, 2021, '2020 PRRI Census of American Religion: County-Level Data on Religious Identity and Diversity', PRRI, https://www.prri.org/research/2020-census-of-american-religion/ (accessed 27.2.25).

University of Edinburgh, 2024, 'What is Xenophobia?', *University of Edinburgh*, https://reportandsupport.ed.ac.uk/pages/what-is-xenophobia (accessed 30.05.2024).

Walls, Andrew, 2000, 'The Expansion of Christianity: An Interview with Andrew Walls', *Religion Online*, https://www.religion-online.org/article/the-expansion-of-christianity-an-interview-with-andrew-walls/ (accessed 27.2.25).

12

Intercultural Life Together: Racial Justice as Love Lived Out in Worship, Fellowship and Mission

SHARON PRENTIS

Introductory Reflections

A few years ago, I came across the thought-provoking phrase 'A Just Church'. The bold statement was used to describe a community that prioritized justice, equity and responsibility as being fundamental to its mission and practice. The term caught my attention because it provoked questions that have remained with me ever since: quite simply, is there any other kind of church than one where justice is a core feature? As disciples of Christ, isn't it something we should do? In Hebrew Scripture, the words for righteousness, right behaviour and charitable acts (*tzedakah*) and justice (*mishpat*) are similar in meaning and are almost interchangeable when referring to God (Laino, 2022). The biblical emphasis is on the active pursuit of both. From the Sermon on the Mount (Matt. 5.10), Jesus teaches that living righteously will inevitably challenge the prevailing norms and expectations since kingdom life is radically different (King, 2022). Deeply embedded in Judeo-Christian practices is the belief that justice is an essential part of God's character granted to humanity (Laino, 2022).

For this reason, the call for justice, rooted in God finds expression in repentance and lament that precede acts of mercy. In the Bible, grief and lament have two main purposes: first, as a form of protest and appeal that bears witness to the wickedness and gross injustice that should not be tolerated. And second, as a way for God's people to articulate their sorrow, anger, confusion and disappointment at the destruction caused by their sin. Lament gives space to the questions 'why' and 'how' this could happen and seeks earnestly for a response from God (Prentis, 2020, pp. 40–1).

I lived in an urban area where social and economic challenges were the everyday experience. For me, because of the proximity of these realities, there was no separation of justice as framed by the biblical text. Church was the collective noun for a group of disciples who work together for God's kingdom of justice and righteousness. In that context, a just church is one where the reality of the suffering, crucified and risen Christ is the embodied reality of the experiences of its members. Describing the vitality of life together, Dietrich Bonhoeffer uses the analogy of a chain, with each Christian member as an indispensable link to one another, bearing burdens, desiring the freedom of the other person, living a life of costly love, and taking up the Cross for the sake of others (1954, p. 108). At the same time, the answer to my question might seem obvious (a resounding yes); nevertheless, different approaches to racial healing inevitably must consider justice and the pain of the fracture between people. If this were not the case, the struggle to be a church that reflects every tribe, tongue and cultural group would have been achieved long ago. After years of being in leadership and supporting the development of intercultural church, it became clear that the implementation of racial justice varies across different contexts, requiring a more nuanced understanding. The nature of its membership is shaped by historical, cultural, and social dynamics that affect how individuals and communities experience and advocate for justice.

My experience of work in partnership with diverse communities has deepened my interest in how intercultural churches live out God's righteousness and justice in ways that embody the experiences of life and faith of their members. Through my work, I have observed that, for some, racial diversity is often equated with achieving racial justice. For some, the fact that people of diverse cultural heritages are included in the congregation is seen as sufficient evidence of equity and no further work of discernment about what that means is required. At best, where there is some acknowledgement and ensuing discussion, there is minimal exploration of how this aspect of communal life is lived out in terms of personal discipleship, church fellowship, polity and mission. This chapter suggests that for an intercultural community racial justice is integral to what it means to do life together. Bearing one another's burdens (see Gal. 6.2) is a strong motif, as is the divine mandate to go out into the world with the golden rule of loving others as you love yourself. An understanding of what justice means in an intercultural context is vital for it to be both meaningful and transformative. I propose that an intercultural approach to justice is rooted in love and lived out in worship, fellowship and mission. If we view ourselves as interconnected, with mutual responsibilities for one another's well-being, then our practice of justice becomes a key aspect of spiritual formation and communal cohesion. I contend that racial justice in an intercultural context distinctly inhabits these perspectives.

Likewise, it should follow that concerns of injustice that affect the few will affect those we are in communion with, becoming the focus of prayer and service. The associated work of justice never ceases. The Spirit of God calls every follower of Jesus into a radical understanding of justice, where we are accountable to God and each other in this journey of faith (Douglas, 2015, p. 93). Such a radical consideration goes beyond a superficial understanding of difference. While love and justice may be different, their intersection lead to transformative outcomes for individuals and communities. When love is present, the best interest of the other is in mind.

Restorative relationships and systemic change are essential components of a just society and even more so in an intercultural setting where they are evidence of the kingdom. An often-quoted biblical text that refers to justice is Amos 5.24: 'But let justice roll on like a river, righteousness like a never-failing stream.' The implication is that engaging in justice is not a singular event but a continuous endeavour that seeks the good of others. The God of justice calls us to unceasing effort and vigilance. The imagery in Amos is often called upon concerning racial justice because it suggests that justice cannot be stagnant, instead rolling on like rivers, and the call to act righteously is an ongoing commitment to issues of fairness and equity. The pursuit necessitates sustenance from within a community. Living by the kingdom of heaven involves more than just the outward application of laws; it calls for an inward transformation that reflects God's character of love, mercy and fairness. Much like the direction of a flowing river, the work is to address systemic injustice, ensuring marginalized voices are heard.

Injustice Defined

To reflect on justice means to understand what it is not. A formal definition defines injustice as, 'the violation of another's rights often manifesting as unfair or discriminatory treatment that undermines an individual or group's dignity and equality leading to legal, social, or economic disparities' (Merriam-Webster, 2024). Racial justice then is the conscientious effort to listen to the voices that are frequently ignored, creating opportunities for their involvement in community life, while also addressing the historical inequities that have shaped their experiences.

For the Christian, to do justice means living beyond a purely legal definition, out of the kingdom's values and speaking against things contrary to them, undermining all the kingdom stands for. Even when a faith community addresses these issues, it must come from a perspective of integrity – acknowledging and removing the logs in our own eyes (see Matt. 7.3–5). This self-examination is crucial for authentic grace-filled relationships that lead to faithful witness. To encounter another with grace represents a continuous journey, not merely an endpoint that is evidenced by love. As Mae Elise Cannon writes, 'Grace is not the end of the story! Grace shows itself in love an active force and an acute responsiveness to the needs of those around us' (2009, p. 19).

Justice, then, as it relates to ethnicity and culture, means being attentive to the fact that people experience discrimination based on skin colour and how the broader processes of ethnicization and cultural stereotyping play out within the church context. It is their voices added to those who usually dominate that create a richer tapestry of perspectives that lead to a better understanding of God. Contextual theologies emerged in response to the marginalization of certain voices from mainstream theological discourse. By offering a platform where those experiences can be articulated and understood, relationships are forged across diverse groups. Inevitably, personal stories of the harsh realities of injustice will speak about who the God of justice is and what living righteously entails; however, how this is lived out depends on a community's understanding of what justice truly means. For some, it involves maintaining an ongoing awareness of the context in which the body of Christ exists and remaining vigilant toward the biases, prejudices and racism that influence relationships. As Cornel West comments, the profound power of love fosters social renewal and justice because it is relational in its very nature. He further contends that the prophetic voice from Black people has always challenged societal norms and continues to challenge injustices because of their experience (2014, p. 24). Historically, xenophobia and racism have led to significant disparities in health, education, employment and within the church community. Individuals from different ethnic and racial backgrounds have faced systemic barriers which have had a significant impact (Bhopal, 2007; Gillborn, 2008).

From a British perspective, Harvey Kwiyani observes that the examination of race relations within the Christian community is relatively recent and has been galvanized by events such as the tragic murder of

George Floyd. The tendency had been to assume that churches did not need to interrogate the phenomenon of multiculturalism at any depth. Before 2020, few if any books addressed issues of intercultural aspects of mission and ecclesiology. However, that is changing, and going beyond a superficial understanding will become necessary as globalization increases and more people from around the world settle in the UK (Kwiyani, 2020, pp. 42–4). The relative newness of multicultural Christianity has meant that certain subjects, such as how different ethnic groups relate to one another, and race are being discussed more widely. Nevertheless, the assumption is that subjects such as intercultural relations in congregations once broached do not need to be revisited.

Furthermore, there is even more of a reluctance to address topics like racism and colonialism due to a perspective that there is no need to dwell in the past, as Christianity is functioning effectively in the present. There is an underpinning feeling that once the topic of race has been discussed, Christians no longer need to revisit the subject area. Such is the delicacy around intercultural relationships. There are sensitivities about navigating the subject, which is often reduced to a superficial understanding of historical legacy of the transatlantic trade in enslaved Africans, and the postcolonial narrative continues to shape current relationships between those racialized as Black, Asian or white. The result is a reluctance to talk about the ongoing impact and experiences of siblings in Christ. It is those stories from the past that help us to understand the present. If racism is to be confronted, the fallacy that fails to recognize that the past has ongoing repercussions for the present must be brought to light and historical wrongs openly discussed in order to move forward. Recognizing the inherent social biases and tendencies towards treating individuals differently based on cultural, ethnic, regional or linguistic backgrounds is crucial to engaging in the work of racial justice and reconciliation (Breckenridge, 1995).

Justice

Throughout Scripture, justice is defined, acted on and prophetically spoken to individuals who act contrary to Godly principles. Scriptures reveal God's character as just and righteous, denouncing wrongdoing while prioritizing those who are marginalized and oppressed. God's justice, in its truest form, aims to restore the inherent dignity of every individual. I am convinced that this mission of love begins with repudiation of racism, repentance and rejection from the guilt of failure that masquerades as fragility and relational distance. It is by embracing those who bear the weight of suffering – the marginalized and oppressed – that the God of liberation is made known (Douglas, 2015, p. 197). Psalm 11.7 affirms, 'For the Lord is righteous, he loves justice; the upright will see his face.' Therefore, we are called to act in the face of injustice according to God's word giving precedence to those most at need.

In an intercultural church setting, embracing a theology of justice is essential for several reasons. Being part of a diverse community provides opportunities to learn about other cultures, understand the realities of different experiences, and be a source of education about broader global issues through immediate relationships with colleagues, friends and neighbours. By collectively engaging with unfamiliar or contentious issues, the church becomes a place where justice is discussed and acted upon, advancing mediation, reflection, and action. God's justice, in its truest form, aims to restore the inherent dignity of every individual. This mission often begins with those who bear the weight of suffering – the marginalized and oppressed. The core aspect of living a moral life in God prioritizes righteousness in believers' lives. This understanding is particularly emphasized in Isaiah Chapter 1, where God passionately calls attention to the need for followers to practise forgiveness, seek justice and engage in moral actions. Kelly Brown Douglas eloquently articulates God's solidarity with those who are marginalized, emphasizing a concept she calls 'the preferential option for freedom'. This approach roots justice in the experiences of the least among us, suggesting that true justice flows upwards from those on the margins (Douglas, 2015, p. 197).

The interconnected nature of justice, love, and the experiences of marginalized individuals is fundamental to the church's role and mission. The connection between them is an embodiment of Christ's teachings to advocate for the oppressed and recognize the image of God in whom we are made. As the church responds to the marginalized, it not only fulfils its calling to reflect the heart of God but is being formed as an interdependent community. At the core of a Christ-centred community, Douglas suggests, is the understanding that God has a unique connection with those who are oppressed, and it calls for a commitment to advocate for their liberation. This idea is deeply rooted in the belief that true justice is not a gift bestowed by the privileged, but comes from the ground up, starting with those who have been historically the most alienated and disenfranchised.

Racial Justice as Worship

In worship, the vision of God and God's creation is brought back into focus. Worship is both an act of devotion and a witness to the world, especially for worship leaders who need to focus on the nature of worship and its impact. Sandra Maria Van Opstal emphasizes that authentic worship in the context of mission must be inclusive and representative of all cultures within the body of Christ (2016, p. 78).

The moral obligation to help the oppressed, stand up for the vulnerable, advocate for foreigners, orphans and widows, is to reject forms of social and institutional wrongdoing. Such experiences, though not exclusive to Black and brown people, are more acutely experienced because of compounding factors, the chief of which are those arising from racial bias. Such actions embody what it means to truly worship God, as this form of ethical behaviour is intrinsically linked to the pursuit and enactment of justice. Therefore, genuine worship can be viewed as a call to action, prompting believers to align their lives with the principles of justice and righteousness that God advocates. True worship is demonstrated not through empty rituals, but through a heartfelt commitment to ethical living that seeks to uplift and support those in need. God's solidarity with those who are marginalized roots justice in the experiences of the least among us, suggesting that true justice flows upwards from these foundational voices rather than prescribed by the powerful and those in privileged positions.

Authentic worship is not only a matter of individual spirituality; it is a collective act that reflects a commitment to justice and the flourishing of all humanity. Worship serves as a powerful testimony to faith that extends beyond individual interactions to encompass communal relationships (Piper, 2008, pp. 15–20). What God requires is that justice thrives in the body of Christ – the church; this means that moral obligations take precedence over mere ritualistic practices. From God's viewpoint, no matter how meticulously people adhere to rituals and ceremonies, if these acts done for the sake of worship are conducted without an underlying commitment to justice and righteous behaviour, they fall short of divine acceptance. Several verses in the Bible illustrate God's preference. In Isaiah 1.11–17, the prophet Isaiah critiques the empty rituals of the people, urging them to do good: 'The multitude of your sacrifices – what are they to me? Stop bringing meaningless offerings! … Learn to do right; seek justice. Defend the oppressed.' Likewise, in Micah 6.6–8, the prophet stresses that God desires justice, mercy and humility over ritualistic offerings.

Worship, as an offering to God, encompasses not simply the act of gathering but also the profound expression of cultural identity among diverse congregations. Authentic worship thrives when it integrates the cultural elements of the worshippers, making it a genuine reflection of who they are in Christ. This is particularly significant in an intercultural church context, where worship becomes an act of collective identity each member brings to the sacred space. The diversity in worship styles – whether through music, language, or rituals – becomes a testament to the unity of the body of Christ, demonstrating that the church transcends cultural boundaries. Paul reminds us that in Christ, there is neither Jew nor Gentile (Gal. 3.28), emphasizing that true worship is not only an offering but a witness to the unity that reflects the manifold nature of God's creation. This confluence of identities in worship challenges us to view cultural expressions not as barriers but as bridges, fostering a richer experience of community and faith. An interconnected, diverse community inevitably creates and offers diverse worship and an atmosphere that honours both the Creator and the community.

Worship leader Sandra Maria Van Opstal contends that followers of Jesus Christ who genuinely value mutuality and community are called to empty themselves, relinquish power and share a seat at the table. This invitation involves taking meaningful risks. She acknowledges that there is often an aversion to risk-taking, primarily fuelled by pride, fear and doubt. Recognizing these barriers is essential, as many view sharing power as a low priority (Van Opstal, 2016, p. 80). To avoid 'exoticism', where identities, worship practices and mission strategies are reduced to curiosities rather than recognizing the complexity of God's creation, the need to scrutinize actions in the light of God's justice and righteousness within an intercultural framework is a requirement. Engaging with a theological understanding of these concepts and their significance in our communities is crucial. Ignoring these essential components risks prioritizing performative aspects of diversity, such as varied music and cultural expressions, over the fundamental accountability we owe to one another as a gift we keep giving each other (Ortberg, 1997).

The cultivation of authentic participation in worship is to understand that tokenism is not an option. Worship is not solely about singing songs in various languages; it is about inclusive participation where all voices are heard and valued throughout the process – from selecting songs to sharing theological insights with the congregation (Van Opstal, 2016, p. 91). Justice-oriented worship emphasizes mutuality among worshippers. Coming together is also a celebration of one another acknowledging the various backgrounds, travails and experiences in a collective gift of praise to God. Everyone's voice is valued. A modern example occurred when intercultural churches were present during challenging times. For instance, during the Covid-19 pandemic, many congregations joined forces to meet the needs of their communities, particularly those hardest hit because of health and socio-economic inequalities, which disproportionately affected them (JLI, 2022; Platt, 2021).

Racial Justice as Interdependent Disciples

Arising from worship to God is the congregation being sent out to live and work to God's praise and glory. Subsequently, living out racial justice in church involves the essential quality of interdependence among believers. A congregation then is more than an affiliation of acquaintances, but a deep connection between people inspired by the sharing of personal stories, prayer and the commitment to mutuality. When listening to narratives of experience, the congregation is called to suspend its presumptions and navigate issues of marginalization and rejection alongside fellow Christians.

One way to traverse cultural boundaries is through the sharing of personal stories. Storytelling is not just a creative endeavour but allows the sharing of another's lived reality. In recounting her pastoral experiences in an intercultural context, Christine A. Smith highlights that issues of power and perception around who is in the church cannot be ignored. As congregations change, intentionality is required to be available to discuss, learn about one another and explore questions (Smith, 2017, p. 102). Truth-telling means a willingness to be open and go beyond superficial engagement to share personal histories and encourage compassion. As Smith points out, 'To reach the place of being in one accord, individuals must be prepared to be honest about their thoughts. Have open conversations about people's individual questions, hopes, dreams, fears and hesitancies. Truths must be spoken in love.' Megan McKenna, a theologian who explores storytelling as a medium for understanding biblical justice and community advocacy, sees it as a 'spiritual act that has the power to bring justice to the oppressed and light to the darkness' (1992, p. 102).

It follows that discipleship should involve: the practice of justice by diverse congregations; demonstrating cultural sensitivity and a commitment to the teachings of Christ; and living rightly with one another – especially when that other has a significantly different life experience from our own.

God's justice is to restore the inherent dignity of every individual. This mission often begins with those who bear the weight of suffering – the marginalized and oppressed.

Douglas underscores that justice embodies the very order demanded by love. This love is deeply intertwined with the crucifixion itself, where the love of God calls us to stand unwaveringly in solidarity with those who suffer (Douglas, 2015, p. 202).

Walter Brueggemann further explores the plight of those in the crucified community. He refers to them as the minority community – those who find themselves marginalized, disenfranchised and stripped of power. Brueggemann draws attention to the overlooked narratives of the oppressed, including enslaved individuals and midwives, asserting that this minority community has a unique capacity to advocate for justice and compassion in ways that challenge the prevailing oppressive structures (2001, p. 22). In considering the cultivation of compassion, we are prompted to reflect on its role as a powerful alternative to the oppressive impositions often seen in society. Compassion requires a conscious effort to understand what it truly means to lack freedom within the divine context, thus fostering a deeper commitment to justice and compassion. The prophetic imagination invites us to recognize that authentic freedom in God cannot exist apart from pursuing justice and compassion (Brueggemann, 2001, p. 9). Within this interplay, we can begin to envision a world rooted in empathy and equity, where love drives the efforts toward a just church. Discipleship that focuses on Jesus' teachings on serving others furthers the bonds of interdependence by helping us move towards each other with costly, loving compassion and care.

Fellowship and the Practice of Racial Justice

The vitality of a community hinges on the richness and quality of its relationships. A community's identity emerges from a shared sense of purpose. While uniformity – where everyone feels pressure to conform – offers a comforting illusion of unity, it can breed problems when individuals are stifled into sameness. In the letters of Paul, we witness various church communities, each endeavouring to embrace the transformative principles of the kingdom by following Christ.

Embracing a theology of justice that recognizes that the sin of racism dehumanizes and disfigures the image of God in an intercultural church community requires a commitment to fellowship – a desire to close the gaps that divide us. To engage in a close encounter with another highlights our interdependence and reliance on each other. A theology rooted in the realities of the oppressed challenges us to embrace our differences and cultivate the diverse community that reflects God's kingdom (Isasi-Díaz, 1993, p. 77).

Following the example of Jesus Christ, who integrated religious and political spheres, the church is called to uphold values rooted in justice, equality and radical hospitality. By embodying the teachings of the Beatitudes and striving for change and liberation, the church can create a transformative environment where those facing injustice find solace and support. The principles of the Beatitudes guide believers to revolutionize norms, resist individualism and consumerism, and champion a kingdom-focused way of living. Rejecting the tendency towards fracture and separation that runs through our lives, theologian Catherine Keller contends that, 'In a world where everything is interconnected, the challenge is not merely to receive the blessings but to recognise that each act of love and justice is a thread in the tapestry of creation' (203, p. 189).

Authentic fellowship requires us to be aware of people's wounds and pains and create a safe healing space. In exploring the stories of Black and Asian Christians in Birmingham, Mukti Barton highlights the profound impact of institutional racism and the importance of understanding these narratives as part of the broader story of the church. She suggests that recognizing and engaging with these complex relationships can provoke meaningful discussions about resistance and identity (Barton, 2005, p. 45). Consequently, a deep appreciation of identity as God-given can serve as forms of resistance and assertions of identity, contributing to a richer collective narrative. Barton poignantly references the prophet Jeremiah, who warns against the dangers of ignoring injustice, stating that 'everyone is greedy for unjust gain' and that those who claim 'peace' often contribute to a lack of true peace (Jer. 8.10–11). She advocates for storytelling as a means of healing, suggesting that sharing our experiences opens the door to understanding and restoration (Barton, 2005, p. 11). This act of revealing wounds is courageous, reflecting our willingness to confront our vulnerabilities.

Just as Scripture warns against showing partiality and discrimination based on outward appearances, the church must adopt a fair and equitable approach towards all its members, irrespective of their background or status. Practising justice within the discipleship framework involves fostering a culture of inclusivity, humility and compassion while actively challenging biases, assumptions and power dynamics that may hinder the pursuit of righteousness and mercy in an intercultural church's diverse and dynamic context. The message in 1 Peter 4.16 highlights the believers' response to maintaining an ethical stance, advocating for a response that does not involve retaliation, even in the face of significant provocation and mistreatment. It emphasizes the importance of glorifying God through one's conduct and being confident in the greater purpose of bearing witness to God's kingdom.

When confronted with attacks, misunderstandings or offences, the call is to demonstrate a different behaviour and response to provocation. As Cleveland contends, encouraging the move beyond divisive categorizations to embrace a spirit of generosity and love, means fostering a mindset that sees individuals not as 'them' versus 'us' but as part of a shared human experience (2013, p. 60). This involves questioning our default assumptions and dismantling erroneous perceptions that our experiences though different are somehow equitable. I may not know what it is like to be rejected because I have a regional accent, but I do know what it is to be rejected for another reason. The principle of justice thrives when it is nurtured by a community that recognizes that not everyone has been dealt with fairly.

Racial Justice as Mission and Service

The missional orientation of a church is always outward towards those seeking hope. Witnessing the gospel's transformative power has a profound impact when lived out as a reflection of the change in human hearts. Mission then is not merely an activity of the church but an expression of God's intention for the world (Gittens, 2016, p. 27). Being attentive to others means appreciating the distinctiveness of their experience, including that of inequality. For Walter Brueggemann, biblical justice is rooted in the character of God and is central to God's redemptive mission in the world (2001, p. 99). The cross as the ultimate metaphor of prophetic criticism means Christians are not bystanders. Since the church's missional nature reflects God's reign in every area of life, challenging injustice and witnessing God's love and truth is intrinsic.

To act justly means to seek fairness and equity; to love mercy is to extend compassion and forgiveness; and to walk humbly is to approach others with humility and respect. Christians witness to the need for righteousness by standing in solidarity with those who experience oppression, especially in contested areas, showing evidence of Christ's love and compassion. The ability to empathize aligns with the biblical teaching to identify with and comfort those who mourn and weep (see

Romans 12.15). More than building alliances, loving others to the point of selflessness is a characteristic that challenges the all-too-pervasive culture of individualism.

Profound connections lead to a strong sense of community. Where individuals exercise grace, an environment that supports justice, forgiveness and reconciliation can flourish by our acting justly, loving mercy and walking humbly. Making sure that people are treated the right way is living out our faith. Our mission is to reflect on our shared identity in Christ, which shows our concern and calls us to reconcile and embrace our differences (Cleveland, 2013, p. 114).

We foster a community built on compassion, forgiveness and mutual respect through deep and meaningful relationships guided by honesty and intentionality. Following the examples set by Jesus and embracing solitude as a path to true fellowship, we cultivate a culture of love, mercy and justice that transforms individuals and communities, fostering unity, peace and harmony. From a Christian perspective, justice and living justly are not necessarily synonymous. According to the Bible, living justly means adhering to this divine definition. To live justly is to embody and enact the principles God has set forth. How we choose to glorify God in every area of our lives is as vital as the power of our witness, and it says something profoundly about the level of relationships and the depth of love we experience between individuals within a fellowship. The attentiveness of an intercultural congregation to the things that affect any one of its members is particularly relevant because it speaks of the depth of relationships and the willingness to stand alongside one another. It is shown by how people behave towards one another and their responses to the challenges and difficulties experienced inside and outside a fellowship.

Justice is intrinsically linked to the outworking of the gospel, compelling believers to aid those in need, such as widows and orphans. As noted by theologian Walter Brueggemann, the role of the prophet is to bring us back to confront and challenge the denial of reality, particularly the limitations of those in power, through symbols such as the exodus and the kingdom of God, where righteousness and justice meet, revealing the character of God to the world (2001). This mission challenges normative assumptions entrenched in a racially stratified society, calling the church to embody a different reality that advocates for justice and equity. By engaging in such acts, the church evidences its commitment to justice and echoes the heartbeat of God's kingdom – a realm where the marginalized encounter hope and restoration. Therein lies a paradox in this mission. On one hand, it requires confronting existing societal structures that perpetuate injustice, which can be a daunting task. On the other hand, it simultaneously holds the promise of transformation, reflecting the kingdom's values in a world often marked by division. As the church lives out this calling, it becomes an agent of change, embodying the gospel's radical invitation to justice, love and communal flourishing.

In the context of intercultural engagement, missiologist Anthony Gittens draws on Geert Hofstede's framework to highlight community power dynamics. Gittens distinguishes between high and low power distance cultures, where power distribution significantly affects relationships. In high power distance contexts, authority is accepted hierarchically, often leading to entitlement and privilege among leaders. In contrast, power is more evenly distributed in low power distance contexts, and inclusivity is valued. Gittens emphasizes that a spirituality rooted in the empty tomb and the Cross calls for non-violent, sacrificial service toward the most marginalized in society. The humility of Christ's redeeming work and the entitlement and privileges that make up the dynamics in different communities is why the pursuit of justice is ongoing (Gittens, 2016, pp. 216–17).

No Justice, No Peace?

In May 2020, like thousands of people, I was drawn to attend peaceful gatherings where people stood together to display their shock and dismay at the murder of George Floyd. Amid the cries of 'No justice, no peace!', there was a palpable sense that things had to change and that, as a society, we could no longer ignore the social reality of discrimination. We knew that Black and brown people had experienced the worst ravages of the pandemic and had the worst health and social outcomes. The relationship between race and disadvantage was evident for all to see. For many of us, it was a statement of truth some of us were living, for we had all become painfully aware of injustice. There can be no sense of peace while people live in fear. I had participated in a group organized by churches determined to show unity as Christians and take a stance against institutional injustice. We prayed about the pain due to the historical struggles for racial justice, the church's institutional role and the importance of repentance, healing and the restoration of relationships.

The power of collective action was unmistakable in the unity displayed during the protests. Churches came together in solidarity and humility. Personal narratives from protestors highlighted experiences of racial injustice and reflections on peace and justice, inspiring hope for a better future. All those present articulated the ultimate vision of God's justice and righteousness. Furthermore, the commitment to work towards this vision with hope and determination was made clear.

For many denominations, the events marked a seminal point in their own history. For over 30 years, the Church of England had apologized for marginalizing minority voices. However, it was only during the heightened focus on racial injustice that significant conversations about addressing the lack of inclusion of Minoritized/Global Majority Heritage Christians occurred. The church's historical entanglements were brought to light in the report *From Lament to Action* (Church of England, 2021, p. 10), which revealed that over 30 years of reports and 160 recommendations toward equity had not been acted on. The length of time and number of recommendations underscored the church's failures and its struggle to evolve. The public outcry following George Floyd's murder amplified the frustrations of those within the church who felt disheartened by the incremental pace of change, leading to urgent calls for a sincere commitment to actionable reform.

Amid these discussions, some sought to understand how church practices might unwittingly sustain inequalities. Many denominations view interculturalism as a pathway to rectify inequities. However, the label of 'intercultural' is frequently applied without a critical examination of power dynamics and notions of righteousness in a diverse setting, calling for a more engaged and thoughtful approach.

After examining the relationship between racial justice, worship, righteousness and the mission of the church, we now turn our attention towards a heavenly vision. The intercultural experience not only shapes our understanding of justice within our communities now but reflects the future hope.

Moving Towards the Heavenly Vision of Righteousness and Justice

By being explicit and encouraging the gift of diversity, the intercultural community of faith exercises justice and righteousness among its relationships as a witness to the kingdom of God. While justice is acknowledged as an essential aspect of the kingdom and character of God, its practice within multicultural churches, although an integral part of church life, often goes unspoken regarding the challenges and difficulties encountered in enacting it. It tends to be treated as a taken-for-granted aspect of life together, fulfilled by diverse literature, liturgies, worship methods and various faces in worship. Yet, it requires a willingness to reflect on who we are in the light of Scripture and Christian teachings. By aligning our efforts with the narratives of the oppressed, we participate in a transformative movement that uplifts all, witnessing to a God who walks alongside the suffering and seeks to liberate them from the chains of oppression. This deep spiritual commitment not only empowers marginalized individuals but also enriches and transforms our understanding of justice, love and community as we work toward a more equitable society.

An intercultural church is inherently just when its discipleship, fellowship and mission have an integral understanding of what God's justice means for healing relationships across racialized groups. The Church cannot address the sin of racism if it has not confronted it within its walls. As stated in James 2.1, 'My brothers and sisters, believers in our glorious Lord Jesus Christ must not show favouritism.' Confronting favouritism and discrimination within the church is essential to its mission. In the past decade, the 'multiculturalism industry' has rapidly developed, proposing solutions to the problem of how different groups of people can coexist, which range from increasing cultural competence to understanding differences and combating racism. While these approaches undoubtedly play a role, the underlying issue often goes back to one fundamental problem: the fear of 'the other'. As Willie Jennings acutely observes, there is a growing conversation regarding the possibilities of a truly cosmopolitan citizenship that imagines cultural transactions that signal the emergence of people whose sense of agency and belonging breaks open geopolitical and nationalist confines (2010, p. 10).

One of the most pervasive issues of brokenness in our world today – racism – requires a conscious effort to engage with another to create interdependence. It is by stepping out of our own circles of comfort and familiarity to listen with humility, starting with the deconstruction of power around leadership and leaning towards what biblical scholar Tat-siong Benny Liew calls 'status inversion' (2011, p. 133). Christ desires that we are one as he and the Father are one (John 17.21). This unity is not superficial but deeply rooted in love, mutual respect and shared purpose. It is a unity that transcends cultural, ethnic and racial barriers, reflecting the diversity and oneness of the body of Christ as described in 1 Corinthians 12.12–14.

Navigating the complex landscape of human interactions and affinity groups requires wisdom, humility and grace. Adopting another's perspective is to practise what it means to go into oneself to identify the unconscious biases, those automatic assumptions and stereotypes that stem from cultural and social influences that undermine mutual flourishing. By grappling with these realities and reflecting on the timeless teachings of humility and justice, we can strive towards creating a more compassionate and equitable community within and beyond the church walls. The book of Isaiah challenges those who think religious piety could be a private affair done through individual acts. If the body of Christ is to become a space where all people are welcomed, honoured, and feel they belong, then justice and righteousness must be significant characteristics of the intercultural community. Challenging the structures that limit the capacity of people to flourish as God intended has to become a central focus. In Jeremiah 27, the exiles were encouraged to seek the city's peace, to find peace. As we collectively strive for justice so everyone can flourish, peace will be integral to the outcome we seek together.

To effectively address divisions and conflicts, the church must be willing to engage in authentic conversations, intending to highlight those difficult areas of historic pain, fragility and guilt to bridge divides and build relationships based on mutual respect and understanding. When limited perspectives on discipleship, fellowship and mission occur, an incomplete witness of the kingdom ensues. The inability or unwillingness to explore how the justice and righteousness of God impact human experience leaves a vacuum open to assumptions that perpetuate injustices. Micah 6.8 urges us to 'act justly, love mercy, and walk humbly with our God'. Love and grace call for congregants to engage in difficult conversations, advocating for justice, and embodying the love and equity that God desires for people.

The duty of kinship is to affirm one another's value – to see and treat one another not as defined by social norms and expectations. Having people of diverse heritages is a gift that provides the opportunity to demonstrate the power of the kingdom of God. The offer of unconditional acceptance woven through the collective expression of difference is profoundly relational, with the power to move beyond performative interculturalism to righteous justice living. The notion that racial justice equates to a diverse congregation fails to acknowledge the ongoing work required to see justice done by challenging the pressure to assimilation, the tendency to concede to inclusion on limited terms, and the prevalence of debilitating rather than enabling power dynamics. By living out these principles, the church not only addresses the sin of racism but also embodies the very essence of the kingdom of God. In this kingdom, every tribe, tongue and nation are united in worship and fellowship (Rev. 7.9). The struggle to realize such a vision raises the issue of how a church speaks prophetically to a society marked by division, where injustice stubbornly persists, and the sin of racism continues to affect everyone. It is essential to remain attentive to the pain, trauma and wrongdoing stemming from our historical legacy of division and the ongoing impacts on human relationships. A racially just and intercultural church is a testament to the power of the gospel's good news that righteousness and healing are possible.

Bibliography

Barton, Mukti, 2005, *Rejection, Resistance and Resurrection: Speaking out on racism in the Church*, London: Darton, Longman & Todd.

Bhopal, R., 2007, 'Ethnic and Racial Health Inequalities in the UK: An Overview', *Journal of Public Health*, Vol. 29, No. 1.

Bonhoeffer, Dietrich, 1954, *Life Together: The Classic Exploration of Christian Community*, trans. John W. Doberstein, New York: Harper & Row.

Breckenridge, James F. and Breckenridge, L., 1995, *What Color Is Your God? Multicultural Education in the Church*, Illinois: Victor Books.

Brueggemann, Walter, 2001, *The Prophetic Imagination*, 2nd edn, Minneapolis, MN: Fortress Press.

Cannon, Mae Elise, 2009, *Social Justice Handbook: Small Steps to a Better World*, Downers Grove, IL: InterVarsity Press.

Church of England, 2021, *From Lament to Action: The Report of the Archbishops' Anti-Racism Taskforce*, London: Church of England.

Cleveland, Christena, 2013, *Disunity in Christ: Uncovering the Hidden Forces That Keep Us Apart*, Downers Grove, IL: InterVarsity Press.

Douglas, Kelly Brown, 2015, *Stand Your Ground: Black Bodies and the Justice of God*, New York: Orbis Books.

Isasi-Díaz, Ada María, 1993, *En la Lucha: A Hispanic Woman's Perspective on the Intersection of Feminism and Theology*, New York: Orbis Books.

Gillborn, D, 2008, *Racism and Education: Coincidence or Conspiracy?*, London: Routledge.

Gittens, Anthony J., 2016, *Living Mission Interculturally*, London: SCM Press.

Jennings, Willie James, 2010, *The Christian Imagination: Theology and the Origins of Race*, New Haven, CT: Yale University Press.

Joint Learning Initiative on Faith and Local Communities (JLI), 2022, *Lessons Learned: Faith-Based COVID-19 Response*, https://files.anglicanalliance.org/wp-content/uploads/2022/03/17105543/Lessons-Learned-COVID-19-and-Faith.pdf (accessed 3.3.2025).

Keller, Catherine, 2003, *On the Mystery: Discerning God in Process*, Minneapolis, MN: Fortress Press.

King, Gordon, 2022, 'Righteousness, Justice and the Darkness of Our Times', *Good Faith Media*, 11 May, https://goodfaithmedia.org/righteousness-justice-and-the-darkness-of-our-times/ (accessed 3.3.2025).

Kwiyani, Harvey C., 2020, *Multicultural Kingdom: Ethnic Diversity, Mission and the Church*, London: SCM Press.

Laino, Henrique K., 2022, 'The Jewish, Catholic, and Protestant Definitions of Justice and the Liberation Theology', *Liberty University*, https://digitalcommons.liberty.edu/cgi/viewcontent.cgi?article=1382&context=hsgconference (accessed 3.3.2025).

Liew, Tat-siong Benny, 2011, 'Redressing Bodies in Corinth: Racial/Ethnic Politics and Religious Differences in the Context of Empire' in Stanley, Christopher D., ed., *The Colonized Apostle: Paul through Postcolonial Eyes*, Minneapolis, MN: Fortress Press, p. 133.

McKenna, Megan, 1992, *The Word Made Flesh: A Guide to Appreciating the Flesh in the Spiritual Life*, Maryknoll, NY: Orbis Books.

Merriam-Webster, definition of 'injustice', https://www.merriam-webster.com/dictionary/injustice (accessed 25.2.2025).

Ortberg, John, 1997, *The Life You've Always Wanted: Spiritual Disciplines for Ordinary People*, Grand Rapids, MI: Zondervan.

Piper, John, 2008, *Worship Matters: Leading Others to Encounter the Greatness of God*, Wheaton, IL: Crossway.

Platt, Lucinda, 2021, 'COVID-19 and Ethnic Inequalities in England', *LSE Public Policy Review*, Vol. 1(4), No. 4, pp. 1–14.

Prentis, Sharon, 2020, 'The Need for Lament', *ANVIL: Journal of Theology and Mission*, Faultlines in Mission: Reflections on Race and Colonialism, Vol. 36, Issue 3, pp. 39–43.

Smith, C. A., 2017, 'Laying a foundation for a true and viable intercultural church' in Kim, G.S. and Aldridge Clinton, J., eds, *Intercultural Ministry: Hope for a Changing World*, Valley Forge, PA: Judson Press, pp. 97–110.

Van Opstal, Sandra Maria, 2016, *The Next Worship: Glorifying God in a Diverse World*, Downers Grove, IL: InterVarsity Press.

West, Cornel, 2014, *Black Prophetic Fire*, Christa Buschendorf, ed., Boston, MA: Beacon Press.

13

Intercultural Holiness and Justice: Challenge, Cross, Community and Celebration

MOHAN SEEVARATNAM

Introduction

When my wife Sarah and I were first married, we lived in Peckham, south-east London, which is also where one of my favourite British comedy shows is set, namely *Only Fools and Horses*. We were part of a church in Peckham and at one point, we had a family from Sierra Leone stay with us. The father, Dennis, had gone abroad to work for a couple of months, and Nancy, the mother, and her two-year-old son, little Dennis, came to live with us. Occasionally, Sarah and I would babysit for little Dennis, and I distinctly remember us taking little Dennis to the supermarket a few times. On the journey down the aisles of the supermarket, there would be me, as someone of South Asian heritage, and my wife Sarah, who is white British, going around with this two-year-old child of African Sierra Leonean ethnicity. This caused great bewilderment and perplexity among the other shoppers, as we could see their eyes going backwards and forwards and up and down, trying to work out how such a family unit could be genetically possible.

The reason I tell this story is that I firmly believe, when it comes to the area of race, culture and ethnicity, we as the church of Jesus Christ should be making the world sit up and look intently at us, as they should be seeing something different about us. However, sadly we have to say that as the church, we have often failed to live out anything significantly different from the world around us.

As God's holy people, we are called to be set apart from the world, and to live and think differently. A repeated refrain in the Bible is that God calls us as his people to 'Be holy because I, the Lord your God, am holy' (Lev. 11.44; 19.2; 20.7, 26; 1 Peter 1.16). So what does it mean to live in a world where Jesus said 'nation (*ethnic group*) shall rise against nation' (Matt. 24.7), to be a church of unity and cultural diversity? What does holiness mean when it comes to intercultural living? So often as the church we have limited holiness to sexual ethics and a few other things perhaps – and yet we know that, for us as Christians, to walk in holiness is about the totality of life. We are to keep sabbath rest because the sabbath is holy. Holiness affects how we use our finances and possessions; it affects how we treat and honour our parents; and it also affects how we relate to people of different cultures and ethnicities.

With regards to our own culture, we are to recognize it as God's gift, but we are also to die to it as part of dying to self. With regards to our view of other cultures, we must learn to see these through Christ's eyes. In Leviticus 19, as part of the practical outworking of holiness for the people of Israel, God tells them this: 'When a foreigner resides among you in your land, do not ill-treat them. The foreigner residing among you must be treated as your native-born. Love them as yourself, for you were foreigners in Egypt. I am the Lord your God' (Lev. 19.33–34). Sadly, not only did Israel fail in this aspect of holiness; so has every other nation in the world, both past and present.

In our call to be God's holy people, we must recognize that there is both a responsibility on our part as well as a sanctifying gift on God's part: 'Consecrate yourselves and be holy, because I am the Lord your God. Keep my decrees and follow them. I am the Lord, who makes you holy' (Lev. 20.7–8). Holiness for us requires the intentional setting apart of our lives for God and obedience to his commands, as well as receiving the gift and status of holiness that God wants to impart to us.

So what might 'intercultural holiness and justice' look like for us as God's people in the twenty-first century? I have divided the topic into looking at the following four aspects – the Challenge, the Cross-Centred Solution, the Community and the Celebration.

The Challenge

Through our reading of Scripture, we see that neither faith in God, nor holding a significant leadership position within the biblical worshipping community prevents us from being ethnocentric and culturally prejudiced. Here are some examples:

- Jonah – A reluctant Jewish prophet, Jonah did not want to follow God's call on his life to preach to the people of Nineveh (Jonah

1.1–3); then when the Ninevites repented, Jonah was displeased at God's grace and compassion shown to this other people group (Jonah 3.10—4.4).

- Miriam and Aaron – In Numbers 12, opposition arises within Moses' family because of the ethnicity of Moses' new wife, as she was a Cushite. Cush was an ancient kingdom that today would include southern Egypt, Eritrea, Ethiopia and parts of Sudan. Here is where a Black African civilization has flourished for over 6,000 years, so it is highly probable that Moses married a Black African woman. Miriam and Aaron were Moses' sister and brother, and both of them played significant roles in the salvation and deliverance history of Israel. Miriam was closely involved with Moses' protection at birth and entrusted him into Pharaoh's daughter's care (Ex. 2.1–10). She was also said to be a prophetess and, as a co-leader of worship, she sang a song of praise together with Moses following Israel's deliverance across the Red Sea (Ex. 15.19–21). Aaron, on the other hand was Moses' spokesperson (Ex. 4.14–16), and the one through whom the privileged high priestly line would flow (Ex. 28.1). Yet despite having these privileged positions in the faith community, Miriam and Aaron here seem to show prejudice and discrimination, and object to Moses' inter-ethnic marriage. As the story unfolds, one sees God's approval of this marriage and his rebuke and judgement of Miriam, as he afflicts her with leprosy.
- Peter – In Acts 2, at Pentecost, Peter preached a spiritually fruitful message to Jews from many different nations and 3,000 people were added to the church that day. Yet it seems that even for the apostle Peter, the biblical truths about God's love for the nations had not entered his heart, and he still shared the same cultural prejudices of his fellow Jews in his attitude towards Gentiles. Therefore, Peter needed to have a special vision from God to teach him otherwise. In Acts 10, Peter has a vision and goes to the house of Cornelius, a Gentile; there it seems Peter has a spiritual awakening, as he acknowledges: 'I now realize how true it is that God does not show favouritism but accepts people from every nation who fear him and do what is right' (Acts 10.34–35). Sadly, despite this spiritual revelation, a number of years later, the apostle Paul had to challenge Peter about not eating with Gentiles. Peter succumbed to nationalistic peer pressure from the Jewish circumcision group, and Peter's actions also led Barnabas astray (Gal. 2.11–14).

You see, for Jonah, Miriam, Aaron and Peter, there was a spiritual disconnect between the Scriptures they read, and quoted and sang about, and the reality of how they treated cultural and ethnic other. Correspondingly for us, is there a mismatch between the biblical truths and the heavenly vision we proclaim where we speak of a glorious church made up of people from every language, nation, tribe and tongue and the reality of how we relate and interact with people who are culturally different to us?

We also know that prejudice and discrimination are not just confined to the area of race, culture and ethnicity, but also affect gender, class, disability, sexuality and so on; and it is easy to apply the apostle James' teaching on wealth discrimination to other areas of life (James 2.1–6). The apostle James pointedly reminds us how discrimination and prejudicial treatment dishonours others:

The apostle James has this to say:

> My brothers and sisters, believers in our glorious Lord Jesus Christ must not show favouritism. Suppose a man comes into your meeting wearing a gold ring and fine clothes, and a poor man in filthy old clothes also comes in. If you show special attention to the man wearing fine clothes and say, 'Here's a good seat for you,' but say to the poor man, 'You stand there' or 'Sit on the floor by my feet,' have you not discriminated among yourselves and become judges with evil thoughts?
>
> Listen, my dear brothers and sisters: has not God chosen those who are poor in the eyes of the world to be rich in faith and to inherit the kingdom he promised those who love him? But you have dishonoured the poor. (James 2.1–6)

One wonders who over the years are the people we have dishonoured by our discriminatory looks, attitudes and ignoring? The reality is that we all have aspects of prejudice in our hearts – it may be Islamophobia or anti-Semitism; it may be people speaking in a certain accent, or dressing a certain way; or it may be colour prejudice. The first place we must address the issues of prejudice, discrimination, favouritism and bias is within our own sinful hearts; then, as we do that, we are better placed to speak into some of the structural and institutional injustices of our society and of our nation.

As a person of colour who has experienced prejudice and discrimination, it is a deep and painful thing – because our ethnicity, whatever that may be, is part of our core identity. It is part of our humanity, which we take into heaven. Therefore, when the dignity of our ethnicity is violated, it leaves deep wounds. So for me, some of the painful things would have been the calling of 'Paki' at school, or when playing cricket in a team I had temporarily joined, someone holding their nose and pointing to me, when I was standing next to people fielding. Then there would be going to a pub in Devon or Norfolk and standing patiently waiting at the bar to be served, and being totally ignored on a number of occasions. I have also had the experience of being sidelined and overlooked when it comes to job applications, both as a minister and a doctor.

My stories are less painful and aggressive compared to some of the people I have met, and yet it is so important in a church family for us to ask and listen to one another's stories, if we are to strengthen our life together and have more than superficial relationships with one another. I am keen to hear from my African Caribbean brothers and sisters, about how they are processing colonialism, slavery, Windrush and other things. I want to hear from my white English brothers and sisters, about how they are processing the rapid cultural changes and dynamics going on in the UK, and the associated challenges and joys.

Friends, the reality is that racial and ethnic bias, prejudice and discrimination are part of our human sinfulness and brokenness, and we have all probably been perpetrators as well as victims of this sinfulness. Yet the wonderful news is that the Cross points us to victory and freedom in this area, which brings us to our second point.

The Cross-centred Solution

When it comes to the building of intercultural church communities, Ephesians 2 is a key text that proclaims the cultural divisions that the Cross of Christ has overcome for the church – Jew and Gentile reconciled through Christ:

> Therefore, remember that formerly you who are Gentiles by birth and called 'uncircumcised' by those who call themselves 'the circumcision' (which is done in the body by human hands) – remember that at that time you were separate from Christ, excluded from citizenship in Israel and foreigners to the covenants of the promise, without hope and without God in the world. But now in Christ Jesus you who once were far away have been brought near by the blood of Christ.
> For he himself is our peace, who has made the two groups one and has destroyed the barrier, the dividing wall of hostility, by setting aside

in his flesh the law with its commands and regulations. His purpose was to create in himself one new humanity out of the two, thus making peace, and in one body to reconcile both of them to God through the Cross, by which he put to death their hostility. He came and preached peace to you who were far away and peace to those who were near. For through him we both have access to the Father by one Spirit. (Eph. 2.11–16)

Within the temple in Jesus' time, there were various barriers in the temple court that separated people from one another, and ultimately from the Holy of Holies. There was the court of the Gentiles, as well as separate worshipping areas for men and women, and for priests and lay people. Furthermore, there was the restricted access area of the Holy of Holies, which the High Priest could only enter once a year. Within the old temple, there was a system that perpetuated a hierarchy of people and all kinds of barriers between different people. For example, between the proper temple itself and the court of the Gentiles, there was a stone wall inscribed in both Greek and Latin: 'No one of another nation to enter within the fence and enclosure round the temple. And whoever is caught will have himself to blame that his death ensues' (Stott, 1989, p. 92).

However, we know that through Jesus' death on the Cross, the curtain in the Holy of Holies was torn in two from top to bottom and we now have immediate access to God through Christ. As a result of Jesus' death for us, we can come freely into the presence of God – we can know him intimately and personally, and call God 'our Father'. However not only that, but Jesus has also destroyed the old temple with its various barriers, and has formed a new temple, his church, where there are to be no barriers and no religious hierarchy. Through the Cross, Jesus has *decisively destroyed* all the divisive barriers that human societies have created.

So when it comes to our new life in Jesus, let us live in the freedom of our vertical reconciliation with God – that our sins have been forgiven and are not counted against us, and we can call God our Father. However, let us also live in the freedom of our horizontal reconciliation with ethnic and cultural other. Let us rejoice in the multi-ethnic church of Jesus Christ, where we can call people who are culturally very different to us 'brother' and 'sister' and treat each other as such. For this is part of the freedom and victory that Jesus has won for us, and that is why Paul can confidently say those famous words in Galatians 3.28: 'There is neither Jew nor Gentile, neither slave nor free, nor is there male and female, for you are all one in Christ Jesus.'

Christ has broken down the barriers; let us not then as his people start putting them up again. The world is divided ethnically, but through the power and victory of what Christ has done on the Cross, we can live a different way, continually resolving to break down ethnic and cultural barriers.

Embracing Christ's holiness for intercultural living

As Christians, when we repent of our sins and put our faith in Jesus' salvation for us, the Bible tells us that we partake in this wonderful sin and righteousness exchange – 'God made him who had no sin to be sin for us, so that in him we might become the righteousness of God' (2 Cor. 5.21). At the Cross, Jesus paid the price for all our sinful prejudice and discrimination of cultural other – the belittling, the mocking, the pride, the superiority and much more. In exchange, we receive the righteousness and holiness of God, so that we can embrace Christ's love for the nations, and with a renewed strength 'love the alien' as ourselves.

It is through the Cross that we can be clothed with the purity and holiness of Christ. Consequently, the divine biblical command 'to be holy as I am holy' is made easier for the believer in Christ in comparison to the Old Testament Israelite. The word 'holy' occurs almost 700 times in the Bible, and no other attribute is joined to the name of God with greater frequency than holiness (Wilkin, 2018, p. 23). The holiness of God conveys the idea of his otherness, his purity, that he is set apart and sacred; amazingly, we can reflect and carry something of that holiness, as his chosen people.

Furthermore, as previously mentioned and as Wilkin tells us, our holiness is both gifted to us on receiving salvation (positional holiness), but also a process we journey on and participate in, which is sometimes referred to as our sanctification (practical holiness) (Wilkin, 2018, p. 26). Concerning positional holiness, Hebrews 10.10 reassuringly tells us that 'we have been made holy through the sacrifice of the body of Jesus Christ once for all'. We are God's *holy* people – this is an assigned attribute to all followers of Christ. In terms of pursuing practical holiness, we can be certain as Christians that this is part of God's will and call for our lives: 'It is God's will that you should be sanctified' and 'God did not call us to be impure, but to live a holy life' (1 Thess. 4.3, 7).

Now as we relate all of this to intercultural holiness, first and foremost, we rejoice that our spiritual position and status is secure among the multi-ethnic redeemed people of God. The eternal salvation that Jesus has won for us, means that our heavenly place is guaranteed among the multitude from every nation, tribe, people and language, when we will worship God wearing our white robes (Rev. 7.7–8). Second, we must recognize that our journey in intercultural holiness requires an intentional desire on our part for transformation in this area, and the pursuit of a Christ like sacrificial love for cultural and ethnic other.

Lastly, as we think about our journey of holiness, let us be encouraged and stand firm on God's determined commitment to this cause:

> Now the Lord is the Spirit, and where the Spirit of the Lord is, there is freedom. And we all, who with unveiled faces contemplate the Lord's glory, are being transformed into his image with ever-increasing glory, which comes from the Lord, who is the Spirit. (2 Cor. 3.17–18)

> His divine power has given us everything we need for a godly life through our knowledge of him who called us by his own glory and goodness. Through these he has given us his very great and precious promises, so that through them you may participate in the divine nature, having escaped the corruption in the world caused by evil desires. (2 Peter 1.3–4)

The Cross as a place of healing and forgiveness

When I was four years old, I had a third-degree burn on my thigh from boiling water. I am told by my mother that I spent about a month in hospital, during which time I ate mainly ice cream, resulting in a somewhat changed body shape. The burn also left me with a permanent scar, which you would not know about when you meet me, as it is hidden. Similarly, for many people who have experienced racial injustice and encountered prejudice and discrimination, there are painful, deep and hidden scars. For such people, Christ and the Cross offer a hope for healing and transformation. However, as Seamands reminds us:

> to bring our wounds to the foot of the cross, we have to walk the road to the cross and choose the way of the cross ... this means choosing the way of acceptance rather than denial, confronting instead of concealing. It also means costly forgiveness over resentment and bearing unjust suffering over retaliation. (Seamands, 2003, p. 13)

In Isaiah 53, the famous messianic prophecy about Jesus, we are told: 'He was despised and rejected by men, a man of sorrows, and familiar with suffering' (Isa. 53.3). It then goes on to say: 'Surely he took up our infirmities and carried our sorrows ... and by his wounds we are healed' (Isa. 53.4a, 5b). For those in our churches who have suffered any racial injustice and experienced deep wounds of prejudice and discrimination, Jesus shares our pain and sorrow, but is also our healer.

It is also at the Cross that we receive divine power to forgive those who have caused hurt and offence to us. Jesus, as he was crucified and suffered the greatest injustice, was still able to pray, 'Father, forgive them, for they do not know what they are doing' (Luke 23.34). Through Jesus, we are given not only an exemplary model, but also supernatural power to forgive those who have caused us much pain; this may be an individual, a people group or a nation. In 1983, there were ethnic riots in Sri Lanka, during which Tamil homes were burnt and looted by violent Sinhalese mobs. At the time, my father's childhood home was also destroyed, resulting in my uncle and family narrowly escaping with their lives and fleeing to Australia. It has taken several years for God to bring me to a place of genuine forgiveness for what happened to my family and the Tamil people, with whom I identify. Furthermore, as I did some more soul searching and reflecting, I also became aware and sorry for the wrongs and injustices that the Tamil people had done to the Sinhalese people.

For those who have been hurt by racial injustice, we must pray for an extra measure of God's grace to extend towards those who have caused their pain. Racism or ethnocentrism is not the unforgiveable sin – and thank God it is not, because none of us would stand innocent before God. As the apostle Paul says, 'We preach Christ crucified ... to those whom God has called, both Jews and Greeks, Christ the power of God and the wisdom of God' (1 Cor. 1.23–24). Consequently, we are thankful for the Cross, which is good news both for the victims of racism and for those who have shown prejudice.

Praise God that he can forgive, redeem and transform racist attitudes in anybody. The apostle Peter began his Christian ministry believing God overly favoured him and his Jewish people (Acts 10.34–35); even after several years of ministry, he needed to be challenged about not eating with Gentile believers (Gal. 2.11–14). However, God changed him, and he became firmly committed to building a diverse, multi-ethnic church. His letters of 1 and 2 Peter are written to both Jewish and Gentile Christians scattered throughout the Roman empire.

Then there is the apostle Paul, who described himself before becoming a Christian as a 'Hebrew of Hebrews' (Phil. 3.5). Before his encounter with Christ on the Damascus road, Paul was all about being Jewish – he was Jewish to the core; and yet God called him to be an apostle to the

Gentiles, and to help build and create intercultural church communities that displayed the power of the Cross and the power of the gospel. Similarly, I think of a contemporary Dutch church leader known to me, who, before he became a Christian, had very far-right views politically, with a hatred of foreigners. Then Jesus began his transforming work in him, and after this, he became the national leader of an intercultural church-planting network

So what about us? Our biblical reflection points us not to write off people, no matter how prejudicial or discriminatory they may be. We are also challenged to pray for the Holy Spirit to reveal our blind spots and our cultural biases, and to ask God's forgiveness and help to see people as Jesus sees them.

Embracing Christ's justice for the nations

With so much injustice going on within nations and across nations, both historically and in the present, it is not difficult to say, 'Where are you, God, in all of this?' Yet the repeated emphasis in the Bible is that God is in control, and that his justice will prevail, if not in this lifetime, then certainly in the one to come. Although seldom preached about, justice is integral to God's character and central to the mission and ministry of Jesus, the Messiah:

> Righteousness and justice are the foundation of your throne. (Ps. 89.14a)

> He is the Rock, his works are perfect, and all his ways are just. A faithful God who does no wrong, upright and just is he. (Deut. 32.4)

> 'Here is my servant, whom I uphold,
>   my chosen one in whom I delight;
> I will put my Spirit on him,
>   and he will bring justice to the nations.
> He will not shout or cry out,
>   or raise his voice in the streets.
> A bruised reed he will not break,
>   and a smouldering wick he will not snuff out.
> In faithfulness he will bring forth justice;
>   he will not falter or be discouraged
> till he establishes justice on earth.
>   In his teaching the islands will put their hope.' (Isa. 42.1–4)

'The Spirit of the Lord is on me,
   because he has anointed me
   to proclaim good news to the poor.
He has sent me to proclaim freedom for the prisoners
   and recovery of sight for the blind,
to set the oppressed free,
   to proclaim the year of the Lord's favour.'
(Luke 4.18–19, quoting Isa. 61.1–2)

A commitment to justice is in the heart of God, and an outworking of the kingdom of God is to do justice and see that justice is done. This most definitely includes addressing racial injustice – where individuals or people groups do not receive fair and just treatment based on their race, culture or ethnicity. Finally, it is important to say that an outworking of our holiness as God's people is inextricably linked to a demonstration and proclamation of justice. One of the repeated things that the Old Testament prophets rebuked the nations of Israel and Judah for was their neglect of justice. What are the aspects of racial justice that we need to speak up about and live out? This could mean advocating for and helping asylum seekers and refugees to get the healthcare, social care and housing that they are entitled to. It could also mean challenging prejudicial or discriminatory comments made both in the public arena and in private conversations.

Community

One of the key outworkings of the Cross in our churches is building communities that demonstrate the breaking down of cultural barriers and divisions. Our churches are not to be merely places of racial tolerance and tacit acceptance of cultural others, while keeping them at arm's length. Rather, within them, there should be a wholehearted commitment to inclusiveness, and cultural honouring and celebration. Furthermore, our call to intercultural holiness and justice as God's people cannot be done in individual isolation but is to be lived out in community both at a local and global level.

Now, the Bible says that 'the earth is the Lord's and everything in it, the world and all who live in it' (Ps. 24.1), and within each and every culture, we see the hand of God's blessing as well as the consequences of the Fall. It is important that the cultures and the people groups we belong to do not become 'idols' that we worship and place proudly above others. The global church currently finds itself in an interesting cultural position. Since the fourth century and Emperor Constantine, Western Christendom has had a profound impact not just on Western culture but also on global history and the global church.

With the rise of secularism, and the growth of the church in the Global Majority world, important changes in attitude and practice are now needed to demonstrate that we are part of 'one, holy, catholic and apostolic church', as stated in the Nicene Creed. This calls for the humble posturing of the Western church, and a willingness to listen and receive from the church in the Global Majority Heritage church. It was telling that in my relatively recent theological training for ordination within the Church of England, I had lectures about sixteenth-century liberal German theologians, but nothing from contemporary Global Majority world theologians.

Furthermore, if the global church is to move towards being more 'interculturally equal', then there will need to be a sacrificial letting go of power and privilege by the Western church, which will not be easy. This will be a challenge not just for the Western church but in our increasingly heterogeneous world, also for all largely homogeneous national churches. In Philippians 2, Jesus gives a great example of not holding on to power and privilege:

> Jesus who, being in very nature God,
>   did not consider equality with God
>   something to be used to his own advantage
> rather, he made himself nothing
>   by taking the very nature of a servant,
>   being made in human likeness.
> And being found in appearance as a man,
>   he humbled himself
>   by becoming obedient to death –
>   even death on a cross! (Phil. 2.6–8)

Jesus was willing to leave the glory and the majesty of heaven, and its culture and comfort, to become like us, to share our humanity and identify with us. A literal meaning of verse 6 says that Jesus did not consider equality with God something to be grasped or held on to. As we seek to build intercultural church communities, are we prepared to leave our cultural comfort zones and our places of familiarity, and be willing to make sacrifices in order to connect with people who are different to us? The apostle Paul tells us:

> Do nothing out of selfish ambition or vain conceit. Rather, in humility value others above yourselves, not looking to your own interests but each of you to the interests of the others.
>
> In your relationships with one another, have the same mindset as Christ Jesus. (Phil. 2.3–5)

Humility says 'my way of doing things and seeing the world' is just one way, but not the only way of doing things and seeing the world. All of us view the world in a unique way, which has been shaped by many factors including our experiences, our personalities, our family upbringing and our cultural environment. Humility calls us to respect a diversity of perspectives, and accordingly adopt a humble posture in relation to others, including 'cultural others'. It calls us to selflessness. If we want to develop good intercultural relationships, we need to value others above ourselves and look to their interests. We should aim to be attentive listeners, who desire to learn from and be transformed by those different from us. Such humble positioning will also lead us to more celebration and honouring of cultural differences.

One of the great joys for me over recent years in my Christian faith has been learning and receiving from cultural and ethnic 'other'. From my Iranian brothers and sisters, I have learnt about Persian New Year (21 March) and its cultural significance, as well as learning about and enjoying various Iranian foods, such as *ghormeh sabzi* (lamb stew), *salad-e shirazi* (a finely diced salad of tomatoes, cucumbers and onions) and *gaz Isfahan* (a nougat made from pistachios and other ingredients). I have also learnt about the cost and sacrifice of being persecuted Christians, as many of my new Persian brothers and sisters have left family in Iran to come to the UK.

In his seminal book *Transforming Mission*, Bosch highlights the necessity for paradigm shifts in mission. Bosch points out that paradigm shifts have come about at critical points in the church's history. The first occurred when the early Christian church was challenged to move beyond the confines of its relatively small Jewish world into a wider context, and it was into Hellenistic culture that Christianity was first introduced. Bosch says this Hellenization was equivalent to universalization and gave the church a more spacious frame of reference (Bosch, 1991, p. 211).

Although writing in 1991, Bosch's words still carry significant weight today, and he goes on to say that each paradigm shift results in the end of one world and the birth of another, resulting in the redefining of much of what people do and think. Furthermore, these paradigm shifts create not only dangers but opportunities, and have had a significant bearing on missionary thought and practice, with a number of imaginative responses. With this in mind, is it not too bold to propose that the church in Britain and the Western world today stands in the midst of a paradigm shift? In response to this, new missional and ecclesiological thoughts and practices are called for; among these I suggest are the development of intercultural, multi-ethnic church communities.

Returning to the early church in Acts, we often idealize what this early Christian community was like. Of course, there was evangelistic boldness and radical fellowship, but there were also cultural tensions and issues of racial justice to deal with. In Acts 6, as the number of disciples grew, we see that there was ethnic tension between the Hellenistic Jews and the Hebraic Jews, with the former group feeling that their widows were being overlooked in the distribution of food (Acts 6.1–7). To address this issue, the apostles chose seven Hellenistic Jews to oversee the situation. Power was given to the 'weaker' group to help deal with the perceived injustice.

Moving on in the book of Acts, as the church grew and expanded into Samaria and beyond, many more Gentiles started joining the church. To help the church with this spiritual harvest, God called Paul to be an apostle to the Gentiles, and started working in Peter's life to break through his cultural prejudices. One way of seeing Paul's rebuke of Peter in Galatians 2 for not eating with Gentiles is as an act of standing up against racial injustice. For Paul, this was religious hypocrisy and it needed to be called out. It is then in the ethnically diverse church of Antioch that the disciples are first called Christians (Acts 11.19–26), and it is this Antioch church community that produces the first multi-ethnic leadership team. This also is an act of racial justice, as minority-ethnic groups are empowered as leaders.

Moving forward, we then come to the Council at Jerusalem in Acts 15. As Gentiles started coming into the church, there was an insistence by some Jewish believers that 'The Gentiles must be circumcised and required to keep the law of Moses' (Acts 15.5b). An apostolic council was convened led by the apostle James, at which testimonies were heard about what God was doing among the Gentiles. At the end of the meeting, James pronounced the following conclusion – 'It is my judgment, therefore, that we should not make it difficult for the Gentiles who are turning to God', and then proceeded to state four things that Gentile believers should avoid. Though not often described as such, the Council of Jerusalem sought to give wisdom and make godly decisions in relation to racial or cultural injustice. There was an insistence from some in the church that following Christ was linked just to one cultural and ethnic group. Those early Jewish believers were wanting to impose their cultural beliefs and values on the Gentile Christians.

While many in the early Christian church were happy for mono-ethnic church communities to continue to be developed, the apostle Paul was committed to an intercultural ethos and vision. He was passionate to see Jew and Gentile living out the love of Christ in community, despite the challenges. It is somewhat significant that Paul was finally arrested and condemned by some Jews in Jerusalem based on a false accusation that he brought an Ephesian Gentile, Trophimus, into the Jewish worshipping area of the temple:

> 'Fellow Israelites, help us! This is the man who teaches everyone everywhere against our people and our law and this place. And besides, he has brought Greeks into the temple and defiled this holy place.' (They had previously seen Trophimus the Ephesian in the city with Paul and assumed that Paul had brought him into the temple.)
>
> The whole city was aroused, and the people came running from all directions. Seizing Paul, they dragged him from the temple, and immediately the gates were shut. (Acts 21.28–30)

Following his arrest, Paul then requested to speak to the crowd, and gave his testimony about how Christ had found and transformed him. All was going well until he said this:

> 'Then the Lord said to me, "Go; I will send you far away to the Gentiles."'
>
> The crowd listened to Paul until he said this. Then they raised their voices and shouted, 'Rid the earth of him! He's not fit to live!' (Acts 22.21–22)

From his arrest in Jerusalem, the remainder of the book of Acts details his journey to Rome and his trial and house arrest there. At the end of the book, Paul makes this final statement that divides the Jewish leaders: 'Therefore I want you to know that God's salvation has been sent to the Gentiles, and they will listen!' (Acts 28.28).

Considered theological reflection on the book of Acts shows how pertinent this book is to the building of intercultural church communities. Those first-century Christians were faced with a number of challenges as they sought to take the gospel out to all nations and live out their faith in diverse cultural contexts. Similar challenges face the twenty-first-century UK church. Our learning from the church in Acts is that, while mistakes were made and injustices occurred, the church did not bury its head in the sand but, by and large, faced its cultural challenges head on. So for us, today, the message seems clear: if we are to live out our calling as God's holy people in the UK, we must embrace the joys and challenges of the intercultural mandate of the gospel. Building church community in a mono-ethnic context is difficult in itself as we are all sinful redeemed people, whom God gathers together. When you add a multi-ethnic and intercultural dimension to it, many would say we are asking for unnecessary trouble, and yet, like the apostle Paul, God is calling his people to give themselves wholeheartedly to this heavenly cause.

Celebration

In the book of Revelation, the apostle John gives us a preview of the worldwide heavenly church, in verses that will be familiar to many of us:

> After this I looked, and there before me was a great multitude that no one could count, from every nation, tribe, people and language, standing before the throne and before the Lamb. They were wearing white robes and were holding palm branches in their hands. And they cried out in a loud voice:
> 'Salvation belongs to our God,
> who sits on the throne,
> and to the Lamb.' (Rev. 7.9–10)

An interesting thought came to me recently as I was reading these verses; the Bible says that in heaven the worldwide church will be holding palm branches, and as palm trees mainly grow in warm Mediterranean and tropical climates, it seems the weather forecast in heaven will be nice and hot. As someone who suffers from SAD (Seasonal Affective Disorder), this really cheered me up!

Moving on towards the end of the book of Revelation, the apostle John speaks about the heavenly Jerusalem:

> I did not see a temple in the city, because the Lord God Almighty and the Lamb are its temple. The city does not need the sun or the moon to shine on it, for the glory of God gives it light, and the Lamb is its

lamp. The nations will walk by its light, and the kings of the earth will bring their splendour into it. On no day will its gates ever be shut, for there will be no night there. The glory and honour of the nations will be brought into it. Nothing impure will ever enter it, nor will anyone who does what is shameful or deceitful, but only those whose names are written in the Lamb's book of life. (Rev. 21.22–27)

As part of the heavenly vision in the new Jerusalem, it says that 'the kings of the earth will bring their splendour into it', and 'the glory and honour of the nations will be brought into it' (Rev. 21.24, 26). These verses convey that something of the world's cultural treasures and goodness will be taken into heaven and, in a somewhat mysterious way, add to and contribute to the glory of heaven. What an amazing thought that within every culture and people group, there are things that are glorious and honourable and suitable enough to be taken into heaven!

If this is the case, then how in our church communities are we celebrating and affirming the glory and honour of the nations? The Pasadena Statement, which was a colloquium on the Homogeneous Unit Principle held through the Lausanne Movement, concludes that the church

> is called to anticipate on earth the life of heaven, and thus to develop both cultural richness and heterogeneous fellowship. In particular, we should seek to express and experience these things at the Lord's Supper, which God intends to be a foretaste of the messianic banquet in his kingdom. (Stott, 1996, pp. 67–8)

One of the refrains within the Lord's Prayer states, 'Your kingdom come, your will be done, on earth as it is in heaven' (Matt. 6.10). Is not part of the missional remit of churches in the UK to reflect something of the multi-ethnic and intercultural dimension of the heavenly kingdom? Our churches need to be a countercultural prophetic sign to the world around us, as well as a prophetic foretaste of the glorious kingdom to come.

Summary

The apostle Paul wrote these words to the Ephesian Christians, which also correspondingly apply to us: 'For He chose us in Him before the creation of the world to be holy and blameless in His sight' (Eph. 1.4). We are God's holy people, made in his image and chosen to reflect something of his holiness and justice to the world. In this chapter, I have given thought to how this might relate to matters of race, culture and ethnicity. For us as twenty-first-century UK Christians, addressing the issues of intercultural holiness and racial justice are not optional extras; if we desire our faith to be authentic, credible and relevant, then we must put in the effort in this area to 'work out our salvation with fear and trembling' (Phil. 2.12b). To live interculturally is a way of life, and the pursuit of intercultural holiness and justice will affect all areas of our lives; as in other areas of our discipleship, this will call us to sacrifice, surrender and obedience, but also, more importantly, to much blessing.

Bibliography

Bosch, David, 1991, *Transforming Mission: Paradigm Shifts in Theology of Mission*, New York: Orbis Books.

Seamands, Stephen, 2003, *Wounds That Heal: Bringing Our Hurts To The Cross*, Downers Grove, IL: InterVarsity Press.

Stott, John R. W., 1989, *The Message of Ephesians: God's New Society*, Leicester: Inter-Varsity Press.

Stott, John R. W., ed., 1996, *Making Christ Known: Historic Mission Documents from the Lausanne Movement 1974–1989*, Carlisle: Paternoster.

Wilkin, Jen, 2018, *In His Image: 10 Ways God Calls Us to Reflect His Character*, Wheaton, IL: Crossway.

14

Intercultural Churches as Catalysts for Racial Justice

DOMINIC DE SOUZA AND
CATHERINE DE SOUZA

Introduction

In a world still deeply affected by the painful realities of racial injustice, intercultural churches stand as living proof of the gospel's power to bring diverse people together. These vibrant communities don't just break down barriers – they also build bridges. They create space for genuine reconciliation and become powerful catalysts for justice. By illustrating the beauty of unity in diversity, they offer a prophetic witness to the church's essential role in healing the wounds of racial division. Through their embrace of cultural inclusivity, they not only confront racial prejudice but also offer a glimpse of God's kingdom in action, inviting others to imagine how unity can be lived out even in a fractured society.

While it is common, even among Christians, to seek fellowship with those who share similar backgrounds, the very existence of a congregation made up of people from diverse racial, cultural and ethnic backgrounds is already a profound sign of the gospel's ability to unify. But true cohesion requires more than coexistence, and though multicultural churches achieve diversity, they often stop short of integration. For example, when we stepped into the senior leadership of a large multiracial church some years ago, we saw that progress had been made in helping the church reflect the city's cultural and racial diversity. Yet we also noticed that ethnic groups mostly kept to themselves during the Sunday and midweek opportunities for fellowship, perhaps feeling more comfortable in their familiar spaces. We began to ask ourselves how we could create an environment where authentic relationships could flourish across the board. We realized that the next step for the church was to develop an intercultural model, something that would shift the focus from simply celebrating diversity to cultivating genuine cross-cultural connection and integration.

To be catalysts for racial justice, church leaders and congregations need to do more than just accepting – or even delighting in – the presence of people from different races and cultures; they must confront systemic injustice, including racial inequality, and build communities where everyone feels they can participate. Real connection requires more than simply being in the same room; it happens when we walk together – listening to one another, learning from each other, and building relationships with one another marked by Christ-like love.

Intercultural churches have a remarkable opportunity to cultivate an environment that reflects God's heart for unity and justice. Their diversity puts them in an optimum place to recognize and address the struggles and injustices often faced by people of colour and other marginalized groups. By amplifying the voices of those who might otherwise be silenced, these churches are able to put the gospel's call to reconciliation into action. They offer a foretaste of God's kingdom here on earth, anticipating the beautiful eschatological scene of Revelation 7.9, where people from every nation, tribe and language come together in worship before God.

The Biblical and Theological Mandate for Racial Justice

Justice is not peripheral to the Bible. From the bold pronouncements of the Old Testament prophets to the radical teachings of Jesus, the call for justice resounds throughout Scripture. Micah 6.8 asks what the Lord requires of us; the answer is: 'To act justly and to love mercy and to walk humbly with your God.' The prophet Isaiah echoes this, urging us to 'loose the chains of injustice' and 'set the oppressed free' (Isaiah 58.6), while Amos 5.24 paints a picture of justice as a relentless river that must keep moving forward.

Jesus' manifesto in Luke 4.18–19 is an emphatic declaration of God's heart for justice. In his earthly ministry, Jesus directly confronted the religious and social structures of his day that created inequality and excluded people. Through actions such as healing lepers, considered unclean, and eating with tax collectors, considered outcasts, Jesus revealed the all-encompassing love of God. His parable of the good Samaritan upended ideas about who one's neighbour really is, while his call to 'love your enemies' (Matthew 5.44) pushed his followers to move beyond the fear and hatred of those who are different. When he commanded us to 'love your neighbour as yourself' (Matthew 22.39), he was inviting us to show compassion and justice to all people, not just those who are similar to us.

The apostle Paul expands on this, telling us that Christ breaks down the barriers that divide – whether racial, social or cultural. He declares in Galatians 3.28, 'There is neither Jew nor Gentile, neither slave nor free, nor is there male and female, for you are all one in Christ Jesus.' Likewise, in Ephesians 2.14–15, Paul describes how Christ dismantles the 'dividing wall of hostility' between Jews and Gentiles, bringing them together as 'one new humanity'. Paul's words, as well as the broader teaching of the Bible, remind us that racial justice is not simply a modern issue; it is rooted in the teachings of Scripture and central to the gospel.

The Bible condemns racial prejudice and challenges us to love beyond any human distinctions. Intercultural churches embody this mandate by breaking down the fear and mistrust we often feel toward those who are different. This isn't about erasing unique identities but rather creating a space where diverse cultures can thrive and work together in unity, fulfilling the mission of God in the world while celebrating the richness of our differences. Indeed, the Great Commission in Matthew 28.19 calls believers to 'go and make disciples of all nations', urging the church to cross cultural boundaries in sharing the gospel. Regrettably, this mission has all too often been reduced to a narrow focus on personal salvation, overlooking the gospel's broader call to justice and reconciliation. While personal transformation is clearly central to the gospel, the gospel's power extends far beyond individual change. The gospel is about reconciliation – reconciling people to God, and reconciling people to one another. This means that when we are reconciled to God through Christ, it should naturally lead us to seek reconciliation with one another – and this includes overcoming barriers of race, culture and ethnicity. Churches that welcome this can more readily demonstrate the fullness of the gospel, showing that the good news is not just about individual redemption but the inbreaking of God's kingdom on earth too – a kingdom that has the ability to renew all of creation.

The doctrine of the Trinity provides a valuable theological framework for understanding the church's potential to harness cultural and racial diversity as a force for good. As a united but multi-ethnic people, the church reflects the very nature of the Triune God. The Trinity explains how God exists as three distinct persons – Father, Son and Holy Spirit – yet is united as one being in perfect equality and love. This unity in diversity provides a model for the church, teaching us that cultural differences are not problems to solve but gifts to embrace that showcase

God's nature and creativity. Just as the Father, Son and Spirit work together as one, Christians from all backgrounds are called to live in this kind of interdependent unity.

This isn't just an abstract idea – it is a vital truth rooted in Scripture and the belief that every person bears God's image (*imago Dei*). Genesis 1.27 reminds us that all people are created in 'the image of God'. This gives each person intrinsic dignity and worth, regardless of race, ethnicity or background, and means that when we act unjustly or show prejudice, we are not just harming another person but actually disrespecting the *imago Dei* in them. This understanding of humanity calls us to see every person as deserving of respect, love, and justice.

The biblical and theological mandate for racial justice has profound implications for confronting the sin of racism. As followers of Christ, we are called to be agents of reconciliation, which includes actively working to heal the wounds caused by prejudice and discrimination, both within the church and in society. God's kingdom is inherently multi-ethnic – a vision that intercultural churches seek to bring to life. But this kingdom isn't simply diverse – it is just. While racial justice isn't the entirety of the gospel message, it isn't incidental to the kingdom that Jesus came to proclaim either. Intercultural churches, enriched by their diversity of cultures, languages and experiences, have a unique opportunity to live this out, showing the world the power of the gospel to heal, reconcile and restore, making God's kingdom tangible here and now.

The Sociological Context of Intercultural Churches

Picture a church where Ethiopian sambusas, Chinese bao buns, and Brazilian empadinhas are served alongside English shepherd's pie, Jamaican jerk chicken and Nigerian jollof rice at a bring-and-share lunch (such a church would be proof that diversity can be delicious!). In an increasingly interconnected world, marked by global migration and cultural hybridity, the vision of a truly diverse church is no longer a distant dream. The emergence of multi-ethnic churches represents an exciting sociological phenomenon; no longer having to be confined to a single culture, today's local church has an incredible possibility to reflect the diversity of heaven right here on earth.

This is not about pursuing diversity for its own sake. Worshipping and serving alongside people from different backgrounds opens a window into God's amazing creativity and helps us see life and faith from fresh perspectives. Though it may mean navigating cultural misunderstandings or adjusting to unfamiliar customs, it is precisely in these tensions that the gospel's power to unify shines brightest. Together, believers can model God's kingdom on earth in all its beautiful complexity.

This is not a new concept. The early Church was born in the culturally rich Roman Empire, and diversity was part of its DNA. At Pentecost (Acts 2), the disciples supernaturally spoke in multiple languages, making it clear that the gospel was for everyone, no matter their culture. The blending of cultures in the Antioch church (Acts 11) challenged social norms and became a template for the church's evangelistic expansion. Similarly, the Jerusalem Council (Acts 15) addressed cultural tensions between Jewish and Gentile believers – a reminder that diversity isn't always easy, but also that union in Christ runs deeper than cultural differences.

But though globalization has brought cultures closer together in the twenty-first century, the rise of intercultural churches is not just a response to modern trends. Across many towns and cities in the UK, monocultural churches still prevail as the norm. Intercultural churches, however, represent a proactive, mission-driven response to the Bible's call to make disciples of all nations, seek unity in Christ, welcome strangers, and look forward to the day when every tribe and tongue will join in worship before the throne of God.

The intercultural church is more than a sociological phenomenon; it is a biblical necessity. These churches are living examples of God's reconciling work in the world. In a diverse society, they testify to the gospel's power to destroy barriers, heal deep divisions, and unite people across differences that often feel impossible to overcome. At a time when our world feels increasingly divided, intercultural churches offer not only a taste of heaven's diversity; they show how the world can move toward real, authentic community, where justice and reconciliation can flourish.

Practical Strategies for Addressing Racial Injustice within the Church

Although the Bible unequivocally calls us to pursue racial justice, the church sadly has a complicated history with this issue – all too often falling short of its holy mandate. Today, many congregations still wrestle with racial and ethnic disparities, cultural insensitivity and the marginalization of minority voices. Even in churches that seem diverse, dominant cultural norms can diminish non-white cultural expressions, leaving those of Global Majority Heritage feeling secondary or excluded.

To tackle these deep-seated issues, we need to take deliberate action on several fronts. Intercultural churches, with their diverse make-up, are particularly well placed to lead this effort by offering a truly inclusive vision of God's kingdom. Below, we outline eight practical strategies, among many, that churches – especially those striving for greater diversity and inclusion – can implement to promote justice, create belonging and establish solidarity across cultural divides. Ultimately, though, it is the Holy Spirit who fuels all of these efforts. The Spirit convicts us of sin, including the pernicious sin of racism, and helps us feel God's compassion for the disenfranchised and downtrodden. Through the Spirit's power, we can learn to see others through Christ's eyes and grow in a love that rises above racial and cultural divides. By taking intentional, Spirit-led steps such as the ones outlined below, churches can confront racism and create inclusive, intercultural communities that reflect the beauty, justice and love of God's kingdom.

Diversifying leadership

One of the major obstacles in advancing racial justice in the church is the lack of diversity in leadership positions. Even in churches that seem multicultural, leadership can be white-dominated, leaving minority voices under-represented in decision-making and governance. In multiracial churches, this imbalance can, ironically, reinforce existing power disparities.

To tackle this issue, churches need to make a conscious effort to diversify their leadership. This can't be left to chance. Multi-ethnic churches, in particular, must seek to avoid replicating the very inequalities that many of their members face in their everyday lives. Accessible pathways need to be created for people from under-represented backgrounds to step into influential roles. While mentoring and leadership development programmes are vital for raising up new leaders from the Global Majority, pastors must also recognize that there may already be qualified individuals from these backgrounds within their congregations who simply lack the opportunity or clear routes to step into leadership. Unconscious bias sometimes shapes leadership selection, so rethinking how leaders are identified and appointed is necessary to ensure an inclusive and fair process.

Churches must focus on raising up leaders from under-represented backgrounds, equipping them with the tools and support they need to move forward. Just as Jesus personally invested in his disciples, church leaders should intentionally invest in emerging leaders from

Global Majority communities. By intentionally developing and releasing leaders who reflect the rich diversity of their congregations, intercultural churches can begin to dismantle power imbalances and form congregations that embody the values of diversity and inclusion.

Embracing inclusive worship

In many multiracial churches across the UK, white Western musical worship styles dominate the landscape, inadvertently pushing other cultural expressions of worship to the margins. This unacknowledged prioritization can send a subtle but significant message that some ways of praising God are more valuable than others. Worship in multicultural settings, however, should be a beautiful – even complex – mosaic that illustrates the remarkable breadth of God's people, as well as the multitude of ways they can express their love and devotion to him. To fully reflect the unity and diversity of the body of Christ, worship must incorporate and honour the cultural expressions represented within the congregation. Worship leaders should prayerfully try to discern the unique sound of their congregation, which will be influenced in many ways by the people groups that God has brought together in that specific church family.

Creating multicultural worship experiences and liturgical practices that reflect the congregation's variety requires a posture of humility, as well as a genuine effort to embrace diverse traditions. Pastors can make worship more inclusive by inviting those from diverse backgrounds to participate or lead in worship; by integrating songs, prayers and liturgical elements from different languages and traditions; by praying regularly in church services for the nations represented in the church family; and by celebrating cultural festivals that highlight the church's diversity. These should not be thought of as novelties but as part of the church's regular practice.

Many multiracial churches set aside one Sunday each year to celebrate the wonderful variety of nationalities within their congregations. These joyful services often incorporate national dress, prayers and worship in multiple languages, and food from around the world. While these celebrations are vibrant and meaningful, we need to be careful they don't become the sole occasion for intercultural expression. If we confine intercultural experiences to a single event, we risk reducing them to a token gesture, overlooking the ongoing need for inclusive and integrated worship throughout the rest of the year. A church's liturgy – encompassing prayer, singing and preaching – should be a consistent reflection of the diversity within the congregation.

Cultivating authentic cross-cultural community

As churches create spaces that enable people from different backgrounds to genuinely get to know one another, they take significant steps toward forming communities where everyone feels they belong. While there is value in homogeneous gatherings, it is also important to nurture cross-cultural relationships beyond the usual silos of culture and ethnicity. These connections rarely happen by chance; church leaders need to motivate members to step outside their comfort zones, put aside stereotypes and engage with those who are different. Small groups, fellowship events or ministries targeted at bringing diverse people together are great ways to facilitate these cross-cultural connections and break down the invisible walls that typically separate us.

When churches invest in cultivating cross-cultural relationships, they help members grow in cultural intelligence – a process of learning, self-reflection and continuous growth that enables them to understand, appreciate and effectively interact with people from different cultural backgrounds. This develops a cultural fluency, enabling churches to navigate cultural dynamics with sensitivity and grace, while also minimizing misunderstandings and tensions that are likely to arise from unspoken assumptions or cultural differences. This also allows churches to more fully live out the so-called 'one another' commands of the New Testament: accepting, loving, serving, encouraging, and bearing one another's burdens, regardless of cultural or ethnic differences.

Facilitating listening and dialogue

Racial justice requires more than theoretical discussions; it calls for a commitment to active listening and meaningful dialogue. Intercultural churches are in a great position to facilitate opportunities for individuals, especially those of Global Majority Heritage, to share their experiences and hopes for change without fear or judgement. When church members feel truly safe and valued, the environment shifts from polite tolerance to genuine understanding. Honest discussions about power, privilege and injustice are never comfortable, but they are vital for any church committed to healing and justice. These conversations are capable of helping those from dominant cultural backgrounds to recognize their own biases and develop the self-awareness necessary to combat the ethnocentrism that often stands in the way of real racial justice.

Leaders have a key role to play here; they should model openness, humility and a willingness to learn from cultures different from their own, recognizing that no single culture can capture the fullness of the gospel, and that a church is stronger, richer and more biblically faithful when diversity is embraced. Practical listening and dialogue initiatives such as forums, surveys and one-on-one conversations can help leaders understand the specific challenges faced by people of colour within their congregations. For instance, after the murder of George Floyd, our church – like a number of others – held a listening forum where Black members courageously shared their personal experiences of pain and injustice. It was a vulnerable but memorable moment, not only providing space for healing but also strengthening the congregation's ability to deal with cultural differences with empathy, care and respect. Strategies like this serve to deepen solidarity among church members and establish a church-wide commitment to peace-making and reconciliation.

Communicating the intercultural vision

It is paramount for leaders to communicate a clear and compelling vision of what it means to be an intercultural church, especially when it comes to inspiring the congregation to pursue racial justice. This vision cannot simply be a statement tucked away on the church website; it has to be woven into the fabric of daily church life, and constantly reinforced through both words and actions. Leaders should take advantage of the many occasions they have to articulate this vision, whether in team meetings, leadership gatherings or during worship services. But it is not just about talking; it is also about showing what it means to be a church that truly values and welcomes diversity.

To make sure the vision is effectively communicated, it starts with getting all leaders, staff and volunteers on the same page. When everyone is clear on the commitment to racial justice and inclusion, the message can be consistent throughout the church family. Preaching and teaching also play a key role; diversity, inclusion and racial justice should be themes that come up regularly in sermons, Bible studies and Sunday school lessons, as well as in other church activities. Equally important is visual communication; the diversity reflected on the church's website, social media and digital and printed materials sends a strong message that racial justice is not just an ideal but a foundational value.

By consistently reinforcing the commitment to intercultural engagement in these ways, leaders can provide both clarity and direction, sending a clear signal that intercultural unity is not an afterthought but a non-negotiable part of the church's identity and future.

Public engagement and advocating for justice

In tackling the scourge of racial injustice, churches must recognize their God-given responsibility to speak up. To equip congregations for this important task, churches can access digital training or bring in experts to lead training workshops on topics such as systemic racism and unconscious bias, or establish outreach programmes that support marginalized communities. Such initiatives not only raise awareness but empower members to engage more meaningfully in the pursuit of justice. By combining these efforts with open dialogue and collaboration among different cultural groups, churches can gain a better understanding of the root causes of inequality and develop effective ways to respond.

The Church has a vital role to play in advocating for broader societal change. This is part of its witness to the gospel and includes tackling systemic racism and working for justice in areas such as education, housing, healthcare and criminal justice. By engaging in these efforts, intercultural churches can offer a valuable faith-based perspective, showing how the gospel's message of reconciliation speaks powerfully to these challenges. Church leaders would also do well to participate in discussions about the intersections of race, injustice and the gospel, engaging critically and theologically with contemporary frameworks on racial justice such as Critical Race Theory (CRT). While CRT provides valuable insights into systemic inequality, it is imperative to make sure that the gospel remains central to these discussions. Rooting justice in Scripture enables the church to offer a biblical, Spirit-directed voice to personal, societal and academic discussions about racial justice, ensuring that the gospel guides these conversations, rather than being shaped by them.

Recognizing the spiritual warfare dimension

Racial justice is not just a social issue; it is a spiritual one. For the church to make a lasting impact, it must recognize that racial injustice goes beyond societal structures and has spiritual roots. This understanding is particularly important for intercultural churches, who must understand that dealing with racism is not just about activism; it also requires spiritual engagement. Once this is grasped, disciplines like intercessory prayer and fasting are seen as formidable tools for addressing the deeper issues at the root of division, oppression and racism. The practice of spiritual warfare also plays a crucial role in this fight, as it invites God's help to overcome spiritual strongholds and align the church's efforts with his will for justice. As Paul reminds us in Ephesians 6.12: 'Our struggle is not against flesh and blood, but against the rulers, against the authorities, against the powers of this dark world and against the spiritual forces of evil in the heavenly realms.'

In the intercultural church we pastored, we often gathered together to pray specifically about racial injustice, whether during Sunday services or special prayer meetings. These efforts were not merely symbolic; they acknowledged the spiritual forces that perpetuate division, and prayer became a powerful tool for seeking God's wisdom, power and courage to challenge injustice. Through persistent prayer and spiritual warfare, churches can access God's strength and direction as they strive for justice. Of course, when people come together in prayer, it not only invites God's transformative power but also unites their hearts too.

Implementing ongoing self-evaluation

Church leaders should regularly reflect on their own cultural assumptions, biases and blind spots. This ongoing self-reflection helps them stay open to adapting their leadership styles, ensuring that their approach is inclusive and honours the broad cultural spectrum within their congregations. Regular self-evaluation is essential for church leadership teams to stay accountable to their commitment to diversity, inclusion and equity. Establishing mechanisms for this evaluation allows leaders to track their growth and identify areas for improvement. Some key questions to guide this process include:

- Is our leadership truly representative of the diverse make-up of our congregation, not just in appearance but also in influence and decision-making?
- Do our hiring practices and volunteer opportunities prioritize diversity at every level of the church?
- Are our programmes and ministries, such as small groups, creating real opportunities for intercultural relationships and dialogue?
- Is the language and media we use in our preaching, teaching, writing and visual communication inclusive, accessible and representative of our congregation's diversity?
- Do we need to broaden our musical worship to include a wider range of voices, languages and styles?
- Are we consistently celebrating and honouring the diverse cultures within our congregation in meaningful ways?

- Do we have clear avenues to address any experiences of bias, discrimination or cultural conflict within the church?
- Are we regularly listening to feedback from under-represented groups about how included and valued they feel?
- Are we equipping our congregation to understand and address issues such as systemic racism and cultural sensitivity as part of their discipleship journey?
- Are we tracking our progress in becoming a more inclusive and just church, and making adjustments when needed?
- Do our outreach efforts reflect an understanding of the diverse cultural needs of the community we serve?
- Are we regularly praying about racial justice and seeking God's guidance in how to respond to the needs of marginalized people?

This process of self-assessment is not about simply ticking boxes; it's about engendering a cultural shift where everyone feels seen, heard and empowered to fully participate as an integral part of the body of Christ. By thoughtfully and prayerfully addressing questions like these, church leaders can create a dynamic and equitable environment that reflects the radiance of God's kingdom, leading to the mutual flourishing of all.

Navigating Challenges, Seeing Opportunities

The intercultural vision is a worthy and godly pursuit, but it is not without its challenges. When people from different cultural backgrounds come together in one place – even with the shared goal of worshipping God – differences in worship practices, leadership styles and communication can create misunderstandings and tension. Simply being an intercultural church doesn't automatically lead to racial harmony. Deep-seated power dynamics, systemic biases and the complexities of developing genuine cross-cultural understanding can all slow progress.

For those starting the journey toward becoming intercultural, it is important to understand that resistance to change – whether subtle or overt – often stems from discomfort with challenging long-held racial hierarchies or a desire to maintain the status quo. For those who benefit from being part of the dominant culture, moving toward an intercultural vision may provoke fears of losing power. Some may need support in recognizing their own privilege, while others may resist letting go of cultural norms that have long been prioritized. For example, in one congregation we served, as the church began to take on a more intercultural identity, we began to hear concerns about 'the changes'. Upon closer examination, it became clear that this unease was not about the development of new programmes or practices, but rather about seeing Black and brown individuals in more visible leadership roles. Such resistance highlights the need for patient education, clear vision and compassionate pastoral care.

Though the challenges may seem overwhelming at times, we must not lose sight of the fact that they present unique opportunities for development. Addressing these issues encourages church members to examine their own cultural assumptions, helping them grow in humility and self-awareness. It opens up space for the church to confront racial injustice, encouraging everyone to listen, learn and consider perspectives they may not have engaged with before.

Leading in an intercultural context requires wisdom, patience and resilience. While the journey may involve misunderstandings, criticism or even outright opposition, the rewards of seeing individuals and communities move toward reconciliation, shed old biases and celebrate God's beautiful diversity are worth the struggle. The path to racial justice is not simple and requires navigating cultural differences, power imbalances and differing viewpoints. But it is precisely in wrestling with these challenges that the true potential of intercultural churches as catalysts for racial justice is revealed. Resistance may arise, but leaders must remain unwavering, relying on the Holy Spirit to guide them in the mission of justice and reconciliation.

Conclusion

Intercultural churches offer a powerful, prophetic witness to the church's ability to overcome even the most entrenched divisions. They demonstrate what becomes possible when diverse communities come together with mutual respect, love and a shared commitment to Christ. Though racism damages relationships and stifles community, intercultural churches embody God's vision for unity and equity. They work to tear down the barriers that have long divided the body of Christ and the wider world, creating a space where all people are treated with dignity, no matter their race or ethnicity.

Intercultural churches give us a glimpse of God's multi-ethnic kingdom, where justice is not merely an aspiration but a lived reality. They provide a foretaste of the unity, peace and righteousness that will one day characterize God's eternal reign. They allow the radical hospitality of God – who, through Jesus, invites all people to be part of his family – to shape their mission, building communities where strangers are welcomed, needs are met and relationships flourish across cultural and social divides.

In a time of increasing polarization, we believe the witness of intercultural churches is needed more than ever. Their display of radical love, mutual respect and a commitment to justice offers a compelling counter-narrative to the inequality and separation that surround us. Through their example, we are reminded of the church's calling to be agents of reconciliation.

Racial justice safeguards the unity we share in Christ, ensuring that no one is overlooked and every voice is heard. But it is a journey, not a destination – and the road involves confronting uncomfortable truths, listening with empathy and reimagining what community can look like. Intercultural churches possess the power to challenge racial injustice and spark systemic change, not just within their walls but throughout wider society. As catalysts for racial justice, they are called to engage in conversations in the public square, speak truth to power, stand with the oppressed and advocate for lasting transformation.

In a world desperate for healing, intercultural churches offer a striking preview of what God's kingdom will be – a place where people from every nation come together in worship and justice flows freely. This vision is a call to action, inviting us to embody the gospel's revolutionary power and build church communities that reflect the beauty and justice of God's diverse and united kingdom.

15

Antiracist Mission in Postcolonial Britain

USHA REIFSNIDER

Introduction

There is a certain level of trust and honesty that I have been afforded by being given the honour to bring my perspective on this important topic. There is a privilege that we as the body of Christ can discuss with honesty with the understanding that we all have perspectives. I decided to unmute the awkwardness around the terms 'antiracist', 'mission' and 'postcolonial'. By 'unmute', I mean to open the discussion beyond the polarized stances. Depending on who is speaking about whom and whether they are within a dominant or subordinate status, which in itself may vary by degrees or change entirely, these terms are being contested, deconstructed and perhaps even demolished.

This chapter is written from my perspective and experiences. As the author, I am currently in the dominant position. However, my unmuted voice and interactions are as a woman of colour from a Hindu background. I hope to offer the reader an opportunity to engage with the issues surrounding the practical realities of conscious and subconscious interpretations of the three terms 'antiracist', 'mission' and 'postcolonial', both as individual terms and as the phrase that labels this chapter.

The reader must measure their capacity of the risks in putting aside shame and guilt and delicacy to call into question the current prevalent patterns and their own location within those perspectives. We ought to contemplate an outlook that holds the past carefully and honestly from marginalized and centralized positions in ways that might need to influence alternative understandings for a broader hope for the future.

In order for me to even begin this chapter, I will put in place my own understanding of the terms 'antiracist', 'mission' and 'postcolonial', but not necessarily in that order. I choose to begin with the term 'antiracist'. The relevance of this term is much debated beyond the church, in ways that also impact the church.

In the current political/religious climate of the Western world, issues of race are deeply significant for me within my multiple geographical locations among mostly English-speaking Europeans and North Americans. While I am racially situated as a South Asian, brown Caucasian and second-generation migrant, my husband is a white American and recent migrant to Britain. Our children, though mixed race, are in a category I will refer to as 'racially ambiguous'. They grew up as 'missionary kids' among a strong 'white American evangelical missionary culture' overseas. We migrated to the US during their late primary and secondary school years. After university, they both married white Caucasians. They continue to reside within the southern United States, while my husband and I have recently relocated to Britain.

Antiracist discourse is never far from real-life experiences within my family, most especially during recent national elections on both sides of the Atlantic where the issues of nationalism, religion, race and migration are highly significant.

Furthermore, my roles of leadership within Western European and American Christian Evangelical institutions as a British Gujarati convert to Christianity, cultural anthropologist and theologian bring me into spaces where my racial, cultural, postcolonial lenses are relatively rare. The readership of this book is most likely to be within the range of Western Christianity, so I will begin with commonly quoted verses that seem to undergird all discussions of discrimination and are often applied to exonerate all Christians of racial, class and gender bias.

Rereading Galatians 3.26–28: Implications for Antiracist Mission

> So, in Christ Jesus you are all children of God through faith, for all of you who were baptized into Christ have clothed yourselves with Christ. There is neither Jew nor Gentile, neither slave nor free, nor is there male and female, for you are all one in Christ Jesus. (Gal. 3.26–28 NIV)

This Scripture is often quoted as a mantra, as proof of our own position in terms of how we believe we live our lives. The application of these verses is a continuous challenge to be 'antiracist'. It is more than a suggestion to choose to live with the belief that all of humankind is created in the image of God. It is our responsibility to continuously dismantle the ongoing divisions generated by humanity.

I would argue for another interpretation of this Scripture as proffered by Gigi Khanyezi:

> Is it possible that the author of this Scripture is not suggesting that differences cease to exist? Rather, the author is positioning the dominant versus subordinate groups. Greeks oppressed the Jews; men oppressed the women, the free oppressed the slave. Perhaps the author of this chapter is suggesting a dismantling of power dynamics once we are in Christ. (Reifsnider, 2024, p. 284)

In almost four decades of international cross-cultural mission in every inhabited continent, I have not come across Majority World Christians who do not have some level of personal awareness and experience of the conceptual framework of race that is part and parcel of working with the church, even when the discriminatory practices have produced for them benefits in terms of paternalism, political correctness or personal promotion. Actions are often based on well-meaning decisions made by European/American dominant structures to balance a perpetually swinging pendulum of power dynamics.

On the one hand we can quote Scriptures of equality, justice and unending forgiveness. I doubt that racism will ever be completely erased from the cultures we live in. However, it is only the extreme cases of racism that are ever brought to the surface and those are by media. The reality is that we live every single day surrounded by racial inequalities, injustices and ongoing unforgiveness. It actually takes conscious ongoing effort to commit to continuous proactive anti-racism. This is why, as followers of Jesus, we must consciously commit to antiracism as a way of life as demonstrated by Jesus. Our interpretations of the actions of Jesus can be manipulated. We know little of Jesus' everyday life. However, we know of his interactions with the Samaritan woman at the well and his parable of the good Samaritan.

We turn to the letters written by the apostles as first-generation Christ followers. The book of Acts unpacks the cultural challenges and shifts and the difficult decisions that had to be made. We are perhaps subconsciously taught that these disputes were settled once and for all and thus settled for us. However, habitual cultural sin is not easily resolved. Culture is not static, and neither is the spread of the gospel.

Peter's vision opens the door of the gospel to the Gentiles, and then continues to take the message of the gospel forward to every tribe, tongue and nation. Peter's previously completely normal racialized belief structures and rituals are negated by a direct instruction from the

Holy Spirit to share the gospel with Gentiles. Despite this clear direction, in Galatians 2.12, Peter is found compromising his own instruction as he reverts to his discriminatory behaviour of separating himself from Gentiles and setting the example for the other Jewish Christ followers to do the same. The seriousness of the influence of leaders cannot be understated. Had Peter not been made aware of his relapse into prejudiced behaviour through the argument with Paul, he might not have spoken out at the Jerusalem council in Acts 15 against the need for Gentiles to be bound to Jewish laws in order to belong to the community of Christ followers. Racial and cultural divisions might have continued to become part of the normal practice of the early church. This demonstrates the need for ongoing accountability and repentance that goes beyond a one-time confession or repentance of racist words and actions. Impact and intent indeed have two very different trajectories.

In today's contexts, the cultures and terminology of World Christianity are still often located within the English language. Regardless of the fact that since the 1980s the majority of the world's Christians are not white, nor living in the West, the dominant cultural voice (especially in leadership), whether echoing in the mega cities of Asia, Africa or Latin America, is that of the West.

When people of colour dare to mention their experiences, especially among fellow Christians (even among those from the Majority World!), we most often find we are not believed. The proof of not being racist is stated in awareness of positive experiences of enjoying the variety of foreign food and culture. These examples are cited as evidence of equality with which they believe themselves to conduct all interactions with all people. This is especially notable when majority Western Christians, English speakers of every ethnicity, are careful to add a person of colour to their leadership team, but do not readily encourage them to speak up. Sometimes it is because they have been on mission trips where they, alongside multi-ethnic Christ followers, have preached, financed building projects and worked in schools, churches, orphanages or homes for the severely deprived and marginalized. This appears to serve as proof that any future racial prejudice is deemed impossible.

As Majority World non-white believers and leaders, if and when our difficult experiences are believed, there is often much denial, ridicule, accusation of prejudice and isolation. Unmuting painful voices is one path towards creating a place for engaging with an ongoing problem that echoes through the ages. As the body of Christ, we must go beyond frequent acknowledgement, and act on the promises to do better for ourselves, the world around us and generations to come.

The narratives of previous generations of Western missionaries, who are set apart as heroes and as the standard for all missionaries, do not expose inevitable blind spots. Exemplary sacrificial service in mission does not serve as proof of racial equality. All missionaries are products of their time and carry within themselves world-views that are located within a fallen world. At the same time, like the apostle Peter, missionaries past and present carry within them the redemptive work of grace through the Holy Spirit in 'vessels of clay'.

Just like the apostle Peter, the good that is accomplished does not mean that there are not issues that may cause repercussions in the ever-changing cultures of the worlds we live in. However, this does not mean that racism and postcolonialism (notice the term is not hyphenated) cannot be addressed most especially within the space we call 'mission'. Before I discuss the term 'mission', allow me now to unpack the term 'postcolonialism'.

Postcolonialism

Racism and postcolonialism are inevitably, and I believe permanently historically linked. Postcolonialism does not define a historical moment when 'colonialism' ended. Americans would argue that their independence from the British Empire ended the rule and control of the British over the geographical location of the land mass known to us as North America. Native Americans, African Americans and First Nation indigenous people groups of the Global South would argue that colonization may have decreased but its influence has not ceased.

A case in point is the United States of America. The language is still primarily English. The culture is inextricably linked to British colonialism. Hence while Britain may not have political control over North America, in its postcolonial state, the influence of those whose political power was overthrown in 1776 is still very much apparent. Notably, even those Americans whose roots are in other European nations have for the most part lost their languages from their nations of origin and function in English only. For example, recent people movements from Latin America to North America maintain a stronger cultural and linguistic connection to their country of origin and the previous Spanish colonizers. This is one simple illustration of ongoing postcolonialism.

In the British context, the African Caribbean migrants of the Windrush generation arrived in Britain before the South Asians from India and East Africa. However, they were twice displaced in that their ancestors had originally been taken from the continent of Africa as slaves, but they came to Britain from the Caribbean as a labour migration. The African Caribbean migrants referred to their migration to Britain as going home to their motherland. They soon found that their sense of identity was irrelevant in Britain where they were perceived at best as cheap labour and at worst as less than human. I recall images on television of footballer Cyrille Regis having bananas thrown at him when he played for West Bromwich Albion football club as people of colour were commonly considered as less than human. Hence, we ought to be grateful for any kindnesses and condescension offered in the name of Christianity.

In defining postcolonialism, I hold to the idea that beyond the dismantling of the British and other empires, colonial practices are historical. They are imbedded within our world to such a degree that we are subconsciously and perhaps even at times consciously bound and subject to the historical template of the errors of colonialism at varying degrees. Perhaps it is part of history that, while overwritten with greater knowledge and understanding of a multitude of theological tomes, can never be erased from memory.

Inevitably postcolonialism in varying degrees is still a part of my past and present. My parents began their migration to Britain in the 1950s. They left India shortly after Indian independence just as the British Empire was unravelling. My father and paternal grandmother were part of the *Satyagraha* movement. The *Satyagraha* movement refers to the non-violent civil resistance against the British Empire. They practised Swaminarayan Hinduism, as an eighteenth-century sect within Hinduism that was influenced by British colonialism through connections between Swami Narayan, Bishop Heber and John Malcolm. The sacred writings of Swami Narayan include references to New Testament stories of Jesus. Hence many of the British South Asians expressions of Hinduism are inlaid with biblical and colonial history. Without these connections and my parents' migration, my own transition from Hinduism to Christianity would have been extremely unlikely. Evangelism in India beyond the poorest people groups has been largely unsuccessful as it is inextricably linked to colonialism. For many Hindu migrants, adapting their practices to include Christian festivals was part and parcel of the physical and ideological migratory movement. The colonial impact of the modern mission movement has continued to have postcolonial ramifications.

Postcolonialism thus makes way for greater influences to, from and through the former colonies. In more recent years, larger numbers of migrants from the African subcontinent are arriving with a form of evangelical mission that brings the gospel message they received in their countries of origin back to the land of the former colonizers. This is despite the fact that Christianity was in Africa prior to the arrival of the European colonizers.

Mission and Colonization

The term 'mission' must now be discussed. This chapter has limited scope, and so a debate of the wider variety of impacts of colonialism cannot be addressed. However, in terms of younger generations, second- and third-generation diaspora, the historical template of postcolonialism may not have the same hold. For them, it may be outdated and, in many cases, traps them into a world that did not have the benefit of growing up with a broader world-view since the Internet and accessibility to the world that continues to grow exponentially thanks to modern technology. Once again, I must own that this is located in my own past and ongoing life experiences. These include the cultures of a second-generation migrant and first-generation Christ follower. As a British-born convert from Hinduism, I cannot divorce myself from being located within the context of mission from a particular perspective within the English language and serving with European and American 'mission' institutions. Hence even my understanding of these terms is from perspectives that are atypical in comparison to those who are likely to engage with this chapter. Thus, I cannot lay claim to any objectivity. My understanding of mission is from my place within white, British, postcolonial privilege and yet some personal disadvantage due to my ethnicity.

First of all, in reference to the term 'mission', I begin with Matthew 28.19–20 (NIV):

> Therefore, go and make disciples of all nations, baptizing them in the name of the Father and of the Son and of the Holy Spirit, and teaching them to obey everything I have commanded you. And surely I am with you always, to the very end of the age.

Along with most evangelicals I have believed the following statement as a common and widely accepted interpretation of mission in ecumenical applications. Mission can be stated in a quote from the Lausanne Congress 1974 by the late Billy Graham as 'the whole church, taking the whole gospel to the whole world'.

John Stott references John 17, where Jesus prays for the disciples and all believers, as evidence of God's mission as opposed to the church's mission. The difference between what the church called mission and what might be God's mission was then under the term *Missio Dei*, as evidence of a perceived God's eye view rather than admitting that the church's perspective of 'mission' could not be considered biblical in its entirety as history, culture and language could not be separated from the work of the missionary (Stott, 1975).

So, for myself as a first generation convert from one religion to another, I have taken on the meaning of the term 'mission' from those who brought me to the knowledge of Christianity at my English Sunday School. I clearly remember being a ten-year-old gazing wide-eyed at the screen that showed the slides that accompanied the presentation by a missionary who served in East Asia. I also pinpointed this memory as the moment I 'felt the call to mission', even though I had yet to make a clear public confession of faith. The slides showed pictures of Asians standing up and teaching people. This was one of my very first recollections of seeing a positive image of Asians on a screen. My only other clear memory of a positive view of Indian people was a Coca-Cola advert from 1971 (Project Rebrief, 2012). This memory was so affirming that when it came on television, we would rush to our Indian neighbours' houses a few doors down and tell them to turn on their television. I grew up in the West Midlands in a poor working-class neighbourhood. In my world-view, no Asians could be as valued as any Europeans. Asians in Britain were employed in factories or at best in public transport. We were subject to frequent racial abuse and stereotyping in person and on television. But from my perspective, at least we were not as unfortunate as those who remained in India.

Looking back, I believe I saw the possibility of becoming a missionary as the opportunity to be able to teach others and with the added benefit of an improvement in my own social status. Arguably, one could also see evidence of my desire to escape the entrapment of a broadly held perspective of my family and myself and, perhaps more poignantly, my future within the Western world that was now my home.

Unpacking the translation of 'mission' outside of the evangelical context had not even occurred to me until I began my postgraduate studies just a decade or so ago. The word 'mission' does not appear in the biblical text. The subheading 'The Great Commission' in English translations is inserted just before Matthew 28.16. Michael Stroop (2020) argues that the use of the term in English is connected to a political, military and diplomatic application. The word may have an array of meanings in terms of assignment.

Stroop unpacks the term a little more by using the 'M scale'. The scale goes from M1 to M7; it attempts to give meaning to the term, using examples that range from M1 as meaning representation or personal assignment – for example, the mission of an individual or group to ensure all children have access to education is the representation. M2 could use 'mission' as a goal or aim for a corporate entity. M3 moves to a more personal sense of calling and might be applied in the sense of the priority of raising children according to a particular moral standard. M4 and M5 distinguish mission within a context that relates more closely to the evangelical practices. These include evangelism as proclamation in terms of persuading people to leave one religious tradition to join another and church planting.

Other forms of ministry emanating from the church might include issues of social justice. Finally, M6 and M7 become more focused on establishing structural systems that go beyond any necessarily clearly defined biblical basis or the confines of the church by holding to the idea that God's mission goes beyond church institutions. Stroop cites Mission San Juan Capistrano established in 1776 by Spanish Catholics of the Franciscan order (Stroop, 2020, pp. 5–8).

Arguably, no evangelicals would believe that current mission efforts bear any relationship with historical Catholic practices in the distant past. However, those from other faiths such as Islam and Hinduism are acutely aware of the impact of Christian mission on their nations, religions, cultures and languages. They do not separate Catholic, Protestant or modern mission history. Empire cannot be separated from the political impact of Christian mission. The origin of the structural mission systems is found within the 1452 Papal Bull of Nicholas V. This document evidences that mission is actually a military interpretation legalized and sanctified by the church. The propagation of the gospel was less relevant than to 'capture and subjugate any unbelievers to perpetual slavery and take their possessions and lands for profit and for personal gain'. The use of the term 'mission' in the English language is found in Francis Bacon's *An Advertisement Touching on Holy War* (1594): 'Just as the state has its forces for expansion, the church has its sword.' According to Michael Stroop, the connection with state/colonial expansion and mission were first connected by Francis Bacon (Stroop, 2020, p. 117).

While the Reformation can be seen as a separation from the colonizing history of the Catholic Church, the term mission still holds within it a colonizing history. The separation of colonial expansion and seizure of property along with perpetual slavery still echoes in modern mission especially in the minds of leaders in Muslim and Hindu governments. Protestant practices no longer required papal hierarchy or direction, but the influence of that era and the language cannot be erased. William Carey's 1792 *An Enquiry Into the Obligations of Christians to Use Means for the Conversion of the Heathens* uses the title chapter, 'A history of missionary efforts'.

In this chapter, the term 'missionary' and 'mission' are linked to the Gospel of Matthew and the book of Acts. Carey, known as 'the father of modern mission', was himself embedded within British colonial history. I find thus a connection in language from the Papal Bull of 1452 as military mission, Francis Bacon's use of the word 'mission' in English and the connection with state expansion and church expansion by the sword, to Carey's use of the term 'missionary' to describe the activities of early believers in the book of Acts.

Carey could not completely separate the idea of the propagation of the gospel from his own lens of the Empire and race. In many ways, this was a convenient short cut for many modern mission movements as the language of Empire, colonization and conversion overlapped. Gospel propagation still had the echo of mission as a revolutionary process, perhaps unknowingly carried along within the colonizing mindset of Catholic 'mission'.

Herein lies the root of postcolonial guilt in terms how we now process what is meant by antiracist mission in postcolonial Britain. Parts of the church in Britain today recognize the issues of extraction of traditional languages and culture when sharing the gospel message with people of other faith backgrounds. This revelation of the colonizing aspect of modern mission is a burden of guilt that paralyses so many who are attempting to share the message of the redemption message of the gospel.

Harvey Kwiyani from Malawi is a theologian serving as the executive director for *Missio Africanus* and director of Acts 11 Project: Centre for Global Witness and Human Migration at the Church Mission Society (CMS) in Oxford. His position suggests a definitive shift in terms of race, mission and postcolonialism in Britain. However, Kwiyani, in a recent lecture at Pittsburgh Theological Seminary, calls the church in the West to review their history and terminology along with theological training that has systematically removed the historical evidence of global Christian culture that began at Pentecost and resulted in the church, theologies and cultures in Africa and Asia prior to Catholic colonization.

In Kwiyani's regular podcast (Global Witness, Globally Reimagined, 5 September 2024), he interviewed Dr Zac Niringye, a Ugandan second-generation Christian convert who draws upon his own experiences in entering the works of 'mission'. Niringye recalls that within the Church Mission Society, it was impossible for a native to be a missionary. They were known as 'evangelists'. This may have been considered a more meaningful term. Furthermore, Niringye argues that language is not neutral. The word 'mission' has a set of meanings and practices rooted within essentially a European/American conception that goes back to the Roman Empire. There are linguistic power dynamics embedded within the term 'mission' itself. The word does not translate into other languages and is often inserted in English.

Niringye maintains that the term 'mission' doesn't really describe God's purpose in the world. He references Acts 1.8: '… be witnesses to Jerusalem, Judea and the uttermost parts of the earth.' Niringye claims that the Bible is used to prove the validity of, and thus endorse, our position, roles and authority among those to whom we believe we should do good works in the name of our God. It seems apparent that the terms 'mission' and 'missionary' apply selectively for the purposes of the understanding of mission from the contexts of gospel propagation, but that this does not come without our own culture, position and world-view. I had never considered the word 'missionary' as a term that cannot be translated into other languages and thus remains rooted within historic practices, some of which have strayed far from even the subtitle of 'The Great Commission', which precedes Matthew 28.16 (NIV). It is highly unlikely that most evangelical Christians worldwide have considered the idea.

Despite the number of reverse missionaries, or missionaries from the Majority World, planting migrant churches and evangelizing among the traditional white and non-white British population has its difficulties. Many of the churches in Britain find it a challenge to accept that those with deeply pigmented skin tones have either capacity or appropriate training or calling to claim divine direction to leave their home countries and relocate as missionaries. This may well be because the colonial and postcolonial perception of missions and missionaries remains firmly located in the West in a lighter-pigmented, white body.

It is hard to own that these ideas are deeply rooted within the European/American version of the expansion of Christianity and can further be replicated inadvertently perhaps even applying the same colonizing dominance.

Towards an Antiracist Mission

There are multiple perspectives at play in Britain. What are the implications in terms of evangelical mission, as it stands currently in Britain, located within and fulfilled from white and non-white perspectives to those that are white and non-white from other religious traditions such as Islam, Hinduism, Sikhism, Buddhism and secularism? How do those engaging in mission from the Majority World relate to the existing multigenerational diaspora in Britain?

There are aspects of colonial and postcolonial mission that perhaps inadvertently propagate racialized selectivity. I have on occasion been asked to fill a position in leadership because, 'We have never had a South Asian woman in such a leadership position.' I have no doubt I possess sufficient academic and practical experience in Christian leadership, but this type of reasoning may alienate me from potential colleagues. It can also create a hostility with those white British who are overlooked simply because they are white.

Racially discriminatory assumptions are not necessarily rooted solely in the ideology of the ethnically white Christian leaders. Many Majority World reverse missionaries have supplanted some of the inappropriate mission methods and measures that were applied to their ancestors and community. Other Majority World people in diaspora need to show evidence of their faith and leadership above and beyond white counterparts.

My own experience in Britain when I met South Indian Christian migrant churches who trace their Christian heritage to St Thomas, is a case in point. First, there is suspicion around my choice to identify as Christian. This is because there are very few first-generation Christ followers from a forward-caste Hindu background, even among the diaspora. The context in understanding forward-caste is that Christian conversion in India occurred almost exclusively among those who are referred to as Dalits or previously known as 'untouchables'. The benefits of conversion in terms of medicine, education and social mobility were understood and acceptable among the highly disadvantaged. However, those Indians who were not born in the disadvantaged Dalit social strata are referred to as 'forward-castes'. Second, the National Christian Council of Churches in India maintains that many Hindus choose to convert to Christianity for selfish motives such as education, medicine or to reject endogamy.

Clearly as a British Gujarati, I have access to education and medicine; hence, the assumption is that I became a Christ follower so that

I could disobey my parents by having inappropriate relationships with the opposite sex before marriage, as the local white British are assumed to do. The fact that I made a faith confession at the age of 11 does not allay their suspicions of the disingenuity of my choice of faith identity. I am often held at a distance, questioned and required to prove my commitment to Christianity among South Indian Christians. The fact that I married an American leaves a sense of ambiguity regarding my motives.

My roles in senior 'mission' leadership and academia are continuously being challenged in the way mission is explained and fulfilled. Recently, I was interviewed by an experienced, mature and respected leader in Christian mission as he conducted research for his master's dissertation. One of his questions to me began with, 'Now that God is using people from the Majority World in mission …' I stopped him for a moment and asked him to rethink his precursor to the question. He hurriedly apologized but moved on. His whole dissertation could have changed if he just pondered his own role in 'antiracist', 'postcolonial' 'mission'. He had a survey to complete and a degree to be awarded that would prove his ability to give evidence of his own enlightened position. This might further bolster his mission agency's proof and commitment to determine that they had self-corrected by showing how God is 'now' using Majority World people in mission.

I have thought often about his presumption and the unconscious positioning that he occupied. Within our structures and practices, there appears too little interest or opportunity to dig deeper, go further. It almost seems like an immunization against racism is sufficient. It was a condition from the past that new research is now better able to protect mission from the disease of racism.

Scratching just beneath the surface of the aforementioned Christian leader's comment perhaps is a subconscious underlying belief that God had previously used the Western world almost exclusively. The decline in European/American Christianity and attrition in mission leadership has made visible the growth of Majority World church to now have value in mission.

Not for a moment did my friend recognize that the structures created, sustained and propagated by him and other leaders with incredibly power-filled titles and roles, who looked, thought and spoke the same, had favoured this impressive man to serve in Christian ministry in a way that would limit others. These influential people are indeed the same ones that actually hinder, prevent, restrict, control, manipulate and, most often unknowingly, exclude Majority World people like me from mission. The only way for us to have any inclusion in the Great

Commission is through these structures (access to which is guarded by the dominating culture). The only way into the spaces of 'mission' is by those structures, which means not only accepting their version of us, but also recreating and perpetuating it for both the Western and Majority World.

Not for a moment did this brother, nor most of my fellow brothers and sisters in Christ nor in fact do I myself have any intention of positioning myself and Majority World leaders within the European/American hierarchy of race in mission. The perceptions of racial hierarchy and mission defined as God's will are so very deeply imbedded and inculcated. We all believe the ethnic, cultural, linguistic and location release of the gospel began at Pentecost and continues today. Perhaps more destructive are the subtle ways of those of us who believe ourselves to live and operate without any racial bias or beyond the influence of any colonial history.

My colleague and co-editor of this book, David Wise, articulates the history of Greenford Baptist Church, which he led to a multi-ethnic intercultural church culture that then carried through to impact the community. While the shifts in the church began in the 1980s, when the influence of the decolonized thinking was not as readily available, Wise included Majority World lay leaders to contribute to church practices in ways that were meaningful outside of the British church traditions. These shifts were not to exclude British Christian cultural habits but to broaden the many ways that tribes, tongues and nations are part of the culture of Christianity on earth as it is in heaven.

While Wise was one of the earlier practitioners of intercultural church, there is a growing definitive shift of postcolonial influence evident among the younger generations, as well as second- and third-generation diaspora. The historical template of postcolonialism may not have the same hold on younger generations of Western and Majority World Christ followers. For them, postcolonialism does not need to have the same relevance. Perhaps it is an outdated form of control and, in many cases, traps older generations into a world that did not have the benefit of growing up with a broader world-view since the Internet and wider accessibility to the world.

In this book there are several examples of Christian communities that are growing and choosing to engage in Christian witness beyond racial bias, mission and postcolonial hierarchies. Oscar Jiménez (Chapter 3) offers a shift from a colonial business approach to church growth by offering a perspective based upon Paul's letter to the Ephesians. Jiménez expertly demonstrates how the church is as a growing, international, intercultural family. Màiri MacPherson (Chapter 7) references the Centre for World Christianity research that found over 80 different global Christian groups in the city of Edinburgh alone. Nathaniel Jennings (Chapter 10) has skilfully researched the Northern Irish contexts in joint projects with the Evangelical Alliance, Global Connections and various churches and mission agencies, and together with a group of international intercultural Christian leaders established Intercultural Ministries Ireland.

Conclusion

I have provided various perspectives of the three terms ('antiracist', 'mission' and 'postcolonial'), and how, when combined, they relate individually and as collective points of discussion and practice.

Race as a construct has affected our reading of the Bible and thus changes our understanding of Scriptures. 'Postcolonialism' has not been adequately understood as a historical lens that impacts how Jesus is made known today. 'Mission' as a term has interpretations that directly impact those who come from the former colonies and affect the ways they hear, understand, receive and spread the gospel.

For some, the statements may be new, challenging or unacceptable, but hopefully thought-provoking. Often, current siloed approaches prevent us from being witnesses of the message of the gospel. This may be due to living within an echo chamber that resounds only with those voices, terminologies and languages that appeal to us. Fewer and fewer diverse voices are heard that might challenge long-held beliefs as a result of systematically extracting ourselves from those with whom we may disagree.

Antiracist mission in postcolonial Britain is not simply located within the church arena. The problems are part and parcel of the society in which we live. As followers of Christ, we should create places where discussions, ideas and hopes can be the locus of innovative thinking in ever-changing cultures that seeks to make sense of our world. The real challenges begin once followers of Christ walk out of the church building and into the communities beyond.

Undoubtably, in the twenty-first-century world of making Jesus known, there is no room for race, oppression or language that dehumanizes the other. Attitudes regarding race, postcolonialism and mission might be used as platform from which to look down on others. At other times, the terms are used to demonstrate personal superiority, tolerance or progress in comparison to other Christ followers in ways that are not helpful.

For many, the history of mission is a linear process that goes from a personal sense of calling, to Acts 2, to William Carey's mission efforts that were inadvertently located within colonialism and postcolonialism. While perhaps this served to stimulate many Europeans and Americans to become involved in the spread of the gospel, it may be time to consider alternative practices. Now must be the time to reflect on the relevance of the history of racial, cultural and religious backgrounds of the people who now call Britain their home. Antiracist mission in postcolonial Britain could be a place of ongoing repentance, redemption and reconciliation between us and God and also between us and the 'other'. This posture of hope and humility has the potential to bring us to ongoing renewed ways of listening, acting and being church. Race, mission and colonialism were all part of the lived experiences of the early church and indeed Jesus himself. However, the narrative does not end there.

The growth of intercultural churches and voices as expressed in this book, and a growing number of networks and publications, demonstrate that the entrapment of terminology and history need not bind or restrict the growth of the gospel in Britain. Instead, we come together as humble, forgiven and forgiving parts of the body of Christ holding together the past, present and future polyphonic voices of the growing variety of what it is to be church in Britain.

Bibliography

Carey, William, 1792, *An Enquiry Into the Obligations of Christians to Use Means for the Conversion of the Heathens*, Leicester: Baptist Mission.

Kwiyani, Harvey, 2024, 'How Problematic is the Language of Mission? with Dr Zac Niringiye', *Global Witness, Globally Reimagined*, https://harveykwiyani.substack.com/p/how-problematic-is-the-language-of-620?utm_source=podcast (accessed 3.3.25).

Pittsburgh Theological Seminary, 2024, 'Mission in the Margins: Lessons and Practices from the Global Church', *YouTube*, 18 November, https://www.youtube.com/watch?v=bvgETVMh4jE&t=3871s (accessed 3.3.2025).

Project Rebrief, 2012, 'Coca-cola 1971 – "Hilltop" | "I'd like to buy the world a Coke"', *YouTube*, 6 March, https://www.youtube.com/watch?v=1VM2eLhvsSM (accessed 3.3.2025).

Reifsnider, Usha, ed., 2024, *Unmuted: Speaking to be Heard*, London: Apollos.

Stott, John, 1975, 'Occasional Paper, The Lausanne Covenant: An Exposition and Commentary', *Lausanne Movement*, https://lausanne.org/occasional-paper/lop-3 (accessed 3.3.25).

Stroop Michael, 2020, *Transcending the Modern Mission Movement*, Oxford: Regnum.

Index of Bible References

OLD TESTAMENT

Genesis
1.26	199
1.27	255
12.1–3	86, 130, 138
12.3	74

Exodus
2.1–10	236
4.14–16	236
12.38	199
15.1	85
15.19–21	236
22.21	138
28.1	236

Leviticus
11.44	234
19.2	234
19.33–34	235
20.7	234
20.7–8	235
20.26	234

Numbers
24.4	82

Deuteronomy
9.18	82
28.25	98
30.4	98
32.4	243

2 Kings
5	130
25.1–26	130

2 Chronicles
20.18	82

Psalms
11.7	220
24.1	138, 244
86.9	74
89.14	243
95.5	82
96	74
136	85
150	73

Isaiah
1	220
1.11–17	221
1.17	202
6.1–8	82
19.23–25	74
42.1–4	243
49.6	98
53.3	241

53.4–5	242
58.6	253
61.1–2	244

Jeremiah

8.10–11	225
10.6–7	73
27	231
41.17	98

Amos

5.24	217, 253

Jonah

3.10—4.4	236

Micah

6.6–8	221
6.8	231, 253

NEW TESTAMENT

Matthew

2.11	82
5.10	215
5.44	253
6.10	250
7.3–5	218
22.39	254
24.7	235
26.39	82
28.16	273, 276
28.16–20	130
28.19	254
28.19–20	272

Mark

12.30	81

Luke

4.8	81
4.18–19	244, 253
22.20	86
23.34	242

John

1.14	74
4.18–19	253
4.21–24	79
10.7–10	141
13.31–32	84
13.34–35	139
16.13–14	84
17.21	230

Acts

1.8	74, 276
2	73, 236, 256
2.9–11	74
2.41–42	86
2.42–47	88
2.42	77
2.47	77
6	196, 208, 210
6.1	196
6.1–7	207, 247
8.1	98
8.1–3	130
8.26–39	130
10.34–35	236, 242
11	31, 256
11.19–26	247
11.19–30	100
13.1–3	100
15	256
15.5	247

Index of Bible References

17.26	185	4.6	87
21.28–30	248	6.2	216
22.21–22	248	6.16	86
28.28	248		

Ephesians

Romans

		1.3	53
1.19–20	39–40	1.4	250
8.15	87	1.4–5	52, 55, 62, 65
12.1	82	1.5	55, 66
12.2	48	1.5–6	62
12.15	204, 211, 226–7	1.10	54
14.1—15.6	99	1.17	52
		1.17–23	52

1 Corinthians

		1.20	51
1.23–24	242	1.20–21	54
3.6–9	65	1.22	54
8—10	99	1.23	50
10.17	86	2.1–3	50
11.25	86	2.3	55
12—14	87	2.3–4	52
12	40	2.4	55
12.3	87	2.4–5	52, 55
12.12–13	75	2.6	54
12.12–14	230	2.10	39
12.21–26	84	2.11	50
12.26	204	2.11—3.19	98
14.26	87	2.11–12	50
		2.11–16	238–9

2 Corinthians

		2.11–22	29, 74
3.17–18	241	2.13	50, 54, 62
3.18	81, 202–3	2.14	74, 180
5.21	240	2.14–15	254
7.11	211	2.16	58
12.9	185–6	2.18	55, 84
13.14	84	2.19	55, 62
		2.21–22	54

Galatians

		3.1	50
2.11–14	236, 242	3.4	54
3.26–28	267–70	3.6	50
3.26–29	86	3.8	50
3.28	74, 98, 222, 254	3.10	39, 51, 67

3.11	54
3.14–19	63
3.17	52, 55
3.18	55
3.18–19	52
3.20	51
4.2–3	64, 67, 84
4.12–13	63
4.13	64
4.15	52
4.15–16	63
4.16	64, 165
4.17	50
4.17–19	50
4.22–24	53
4.32	53
5.1–2	53
5.2	55
5.3–13	50
5.18–20	87
5.23	51
5.24	51
5.25	51, 53
5.27	51
5.29	51
5.32	51
6.10	54
6.23	53

Philippians

2.3–5	246
2.4–6	81
2.5–7	205
2.6–8	245
2.6–11	85
2.9–11	84
2.12	251
3.3	87
3.5	242

Colossians

2.2	39
3.5–14	44
3.11	74, 83
3.16	79, 83, 87

1 Thessalonians

2.8	183
4.3	240
4.7	240

2 Timothy

1.7	185

Philemon 58–9

Hebrews

4.12	85
9.15	86
10.10	249
10.24	87
12.2	186

James

1.1	98
2.1	230

1 Peter

	242
1.1	98
1.16	234
2.1–6	237
2.9–10	86
3.15	185

2 Peter

	242
1.3–4	241

1 John

4.7–21	138

Revelation

5.9–10	74	7.9–12	40
5.12–14	84	7.11	82
7.7–8	241	19.10	81
7.9	74, 136, 140, 199, 232	21.22–27	249–50
		21.24	250
7.9–10	90, 249	21.26	74, 250
		22.9	81

Index of Names and Subjects

Acosta, José de 42
Andrade, Neto and Michelle 180
antiracist mission 266–81
Ardener, Edwin and Shirley 32
Arikawe, Tayo 18–19, 30
assimilation 67, 148, 149

Bacon, Francis 274, 275
Barton, Mukti 225
Bavinck, Johan Herman 141–2
Beatitudes 225
Belfast 179–82
Belfast (film) 176
Bhabha, Homi 151, 152
birthdays 122
Bonhoeffer, Dietrich 216
Bosch, David 246
Britain
  ethnicity 28
  migration history 20–2
Britishness 20, 23–5
Brueggemann, Walter 224, 226, 227
Byrd, David 40

Callegarin, Myriam 203
Carey, William 275
Caribbean migration to Britain 21, 23
Cherry, Constance M. 80, 83, 84
Chinese culture 9, 153

Christianity, census data 95, 130–1
church
  as a business 60–1
  as family 50–68
  leadership 63–4
  as tapestry 38–48
church unity 140
  barriers to 143–4
City Church (Belfast) 180
Coleman, Kate 19
colourism 201
communion 86–7, 108
community cohesion 22–3
compassion 224
connection time 37, 119–22
covenant 86–7
Cross, Jesus' reconciling work 29
cross-cultural churches 17–19
cultural barriers 244–9
cultural diversity 22, 67, 73–5, 167–70, 184, 259
cultural identity 147–57, 184
cultural sin 268

dance, in worship 114–16
Darko, Dan 56
Derby 159–71
diaspora 136–7
diaspora churches 7, 94–108
diaspora Jews 196
differences 127–8

discipleship 63
  groups 165–7
  and racial justice 223–4
  and worship 81
discrimination 236–8
diversity 136, 140–1, 199–201, 222
  in leadership 257–8, 262–3
Douglas, Kelly Brown 220, 224
Dunn, James 44

Edinburgh City Mission 8, 131–5, 138
Elim church 2
emigration, from Ireland 175–6
empathy 204–6, 210–12
ethnocentrism 197
eucharist 86–7, 108
Every Nation Church Belfast 179–80

family metaphor 6, 50–68
fellowship, and racial justice 224–6
festivals 166, 246
flags 25–6, 124–5
Floyd, George 1–2, 191–2, 194–5, 228–9
food 123, 148–9, 161, 165, 255
forgiveness 241–3

generosity 139–40
Gibbons, Dave 152
Gibbs, Raymond 38
gift exchange 17
Gittens, Anthony 228
Givens, Terri E. 204
glossolalia 2
Good Friday Agreement 176
Greenford Baptist Church 6, 7–8, 37–48, 111–29

guilt/innocence culture 169

Hall, Stuart 152
healing 241–3
heaven 249–50, 253
Hellenists 196, 208, 210, 247
Hinduism 271, 277–8
holiness 11, 234–5
  of Christ 240–1
Holy Spirit 87, 145
home groups 166–7
homogeneous kingdoms 142
homogeneous units 98–9, 250
Hong Kong, migrants from 95–6
honour/shame culture 169
hospitality 165, 167, 169
household, in Roman culture 57–8
humility 245–9
Hylton, Owen 16

identity 147–57, 184
imago Dei 255
immigrants
  assimilation 22–3
  as gifts to the church 177–8
  in Northern Ireland 174–8
  suspicion of 96–7
  to be loved 235
incarnation 204–6
inclusivity 25–7, 113
  in worship 258
integration 22–3
inter-ethnic church 111
Intercultural Church Plants 164
intercultural churches 17–20
  biblical necessity 256
  conferences 2–3, 15, 18
  family model 66–7
  identity exploration in 155–7
  justice 211–32

Index of Names and Subjects

leadership 31, 170, 257–64
meaning 1, 18–20, 150–1
and racial justice 252–65
as 'third space' 9, 147–57
transition from mono-ethnic church 95, 263–4
unity in diversity 252–3, 264–5
see also worship
Intercultural Churches (charity) 164–5
intercultural justice 33–4
Intercultural Leadership Forum 3–4
Intercultural Ministries Ireland 178–9
intercultural mission 2–3, 28
International Community Church (Derby) 163–4

Jennings, Nathaniel 280
Jennings, Willie James 40–4, 47–8, 230
Jerusalem, Council of 247–8
Jesus
 brings justice 243
 brings reconciliation 183, 238–40, 254
 confronts inequality 253–4
 as the expected king 53–4
 as pioneer 142
 suffering 204–6
Jesus Generation Church (Newtownards) 180–1
Jews
 in Britain 21
 diverse people 199
 in the early church 196
Jiménez, Oscar 279
Jones, Ellen E. 197, 201
justice 10–11, 201–2, 206–7, 215–32, 243–4
see also racial justice

Kaba, Chris 195
kingdom of God 10, 210, 229–32, 254–6, 265
Korean diaspora church 7, 94–108
Kumbi, Hirpo 17
Kwiyani, Harvey 17, 94, 96, 108, 218–19, 275–6

language
 and power 30–1, 269
 in worship 30–1, 88, 113–14, 168
leadership 31, 170, 191–212
 diversifying 257–8, 263–4
Lee, Cindy S. 205
Lindsay, Ben 192
listening 78, 161, 166, 178, 211–12, 259
love, God's 52–3, 55–6, 138–9

M4 Intercultural 164
McDonald, Chine 149
McDonald, Kelly 194
McGavran, Donald 98, 99
McKenna, Megan 223
McPherson, Màiri 279–80
Man, Ron 79, 80, 82, 87
Marzouk, Safwat 150–1
Maynard-Reid, Pedrito 77–8, 86
Memory, Jim 192
metaphor 38, 56–7
Middleton, Julia 203
Milne, Bruce 16, 29
mission
 and colonial expansion 274–5
 meaning 273–6
 polycentric 32–3

and racial justice 226–8, 266–81
missions, and worship 88
Mosaic (Harrow) 148–9, 153
Mosaic South Church (Leeds) 73–4
multi-cultural churches, worship 116–17, 149–50
multi-ethnic churches 44
multicultural churches 1, 5–6, 16–17
  different models 25–7
music, in worship 79–80, 112–13, 116, 150
Muted Group Theory 32

Nasmith, David 133–4
Nations (ministry in Edinburgh) 135–45
Niringye, Zac 275–6
Northern Ireland 173–86

O'Brien, Peter 39, 40
Onesimus 58–9
Otaigbe, Osoba 3, 16
Ott, Craig 38

Padilla, C. René 98–9
Patten, Malcolm 16
Paul, his theology of the church 49–68, 165–6, 248
Piper, John 80
postcolonialism 266–81
power dynamics 18–19, 30–1, 78, 228, 268
prayer 61, 63
  multicultural 116–17
  sung 79
preaching 85
prejudice 236–8
  see also racial prejudice

prosperity gospel 61

Quilario, Danni and Benji 180–1

racial identity 153
racial justice 10–12, 33–4, 141–2, 193, 215–32, 247, 252–65
  biblical mandate for 253–5
racial prejudice 182, 254, 269–70
racism 40–4, 192–5, 196–9, 201, 242
  and 'British Christians' 1
  in churches 208–9, 219
  and the tapestry metaphor 46–7
reconciliation 58–9, 183, 254–5
  of Jews and Gentiles 238–9, 254
Reifsnider, Usha 32
repentance 211
righteousness 210, 215, 220, 229–32
Rohr, Richard 208
Root, John 17

salvation 62–3
sanctification 240
Scotland 130–1
  diversity in churches 8, 132–4
sin 209, 215, 230, 240
slavery 41, 195, 198
Smith, Christine A. 223
Snow, Martyn 17
solidarity 210–12
songs 83–4, 88, 112, 168
Songs2Serve UK 165
spiritual warfare 261–2
storytelling 223
Stroop, Michael 274
Sule, Ahmed Olayinka 194, 198

Index of Names and Subjects

tapestry metaphor 6, 37–48, 157
Third-Culture Kids 8, 15–17, 126–8, 152, 155–7
Third Space 151–2
transformational worship 81, 203
Trebilco, Paul 56
Trinity
 basis for racial harmony 29, 141, 199, 254–5
 worship 84
Turner, Max 58

Upbeat Communities (Derby) 162

Van Opstal, Sandra Maria 222
Vizagie, Johann and Andrea 179–80

Wambunya, Tim 2
Wang, Jenny 151
Warren, Rick 192–3
Welby, Justin 192
welcome 105–6, 117, 120–1, 127–8, 160, 163–4, 184
West, Cornel 218
white supremacy 42, 149
Windrush scandal 23
Wise, David 17, 278–9
Wolterstorff, Nicholas 209
worship 73–90, 111–12
 dance 114–16
 inclusive 258
 language 30–1, 88, 113–14, 168
 and missions 88
 and racial justice 221–3
 and transformation 81, 203

Zurara (chronicler) 41

www.ingramcontent.com/pod-product-compliance
Lightning Source LLC
Chambersburg PA
CBHW032335300426
44109CB00041B/900